The Student Sociologist's Handbook

Third Edition

Pauline Bart

Linda Frankel

Scott, Foresman and Company
Glenview, Illinois
Dallas, Tex.   Oakland, N.J.   Palo Alto, Cal.   Tucker, Ga.   London

Wendell Bell and James Mau. From THE SOCIOLOGY OF THE FUTURE edited by Wendell Bell and James Mau, © 1971 by The Russell Sage Foundation. Reprinted by permission.

Robert Bierstedt. From "A Design for Sociology: Scope, Objectives and Methods" edited by Robert Bierstedt, Monograph #9, April 1969, p. 152. Copyright © 1969 by The American Academy of Political and Social Science. Reprinted by permission.

The Dewey Decimal System. Reprinted from Edition 17 DEWEY Decimal Classification (1965) by permission of Forest Press Division, Lake Placid Education Foundation, owner of copyright.

Paul Goodman. From GROWING UP ABSURD by Paul Goodman. Copyright © 1956 by Paul Goodman. Reprinted by permission of Random House, Inc.

C. Wright Mills. From "Language, Logic and Culture" by C. Wright Mills from *American Sociological Review*. Reprinted by permission of The American Sociological Association.

C. Wright Mills. From THE SOCIOLOGICAL IMAGINATION by C. Wright Mills. Copyright © 1959 by Oxford University Press. Reprinted by permission.

William Butler Yeats. From "The Second Coming." Reprinted with permission of Macmillan Publishing Company, Inc., Michael and Anne Yeats and Macmillan London Limited from COLLECTED POEMS by William Butler Yeats. Copyright 1924 by Macmillan Publishing Company, Inc., renewed 1952 by Bertha Georgie Yeats.

Ralph Turner. From FAMILY INTERACTION, Ralph Turner, Copyright © 1970 by John Wiley & Sons, Inc. Reprinted by permission of John Wiley & Sons, Inc.

Preface

Sociology is a way of making sense out of the world. It is therefore important for students of sociology to learn how to view the world with a sociological perspective, to understand and evaluate sociological research, and to do such research themselves.

We like to think of *The Student Sociologist's Handbook* as a survival kit for sociology students. Included in the third edition is a brief overview of the field of sociology; a step-by-step guide for writing research or field work papers; expanded and updated chapters on periodicals, abstract and indexing services, bibliographies, bibliographic aids and other secondary sources which are invaluable aids when doing research; and a complete guide to governmental and nongovernmental sources of data, which provide statistics vital to sociological research. The sections on sex roles and women's studies journals have been revised and expanded to include current theories and information. A new section entitled Epilogue: Sociology at Work in the Community, addresses the problem of a shrinking job market for sociologists, and considers alternate career opportunities which would enable sociologists to utilize their sociological training.

It is our hope that *The Student Sociologist's Handbook* will prove to be a valuable resource tool for sociology students. With new and more extensive sources of data at their disposal, along with the guidance of their instructors, students will be able to explore the social problems of today more completely and thoroughly.

Our thanks go to the many publishers who permitted us to use material from the many sources quoted in Chapter 1, Perspectives in Sociology. These books and periodicals are cited in full at the conclusion of that chapter.

We would like to thank Mary Catherine Taylor, who participated in the initial planning of this handbook and also did preliminary research. Thanks also to Emily Potok, who assisted with some of the revisions for the second edition of the handbook.

Wendell Bell, who is in large part responsible for our involvement in this project, kindly read several of the chapters and made some helpful suggestions. He was also very considerate about arranging permission for us to use a selection from *The Sociology of the Future* (coedited with James Mau).

We are grateful to Mike Useem and Theodore Sarbin, whose suggestions for revision proved very helpful.

We are both indebted to the Women's Liberation Movement, particularly our respective small groups in Berkeley, Chicago, and Boston, as well as to the Berkeley Women's Caucus, whose loving support and encouragement were great survival insurance.

We thank Nancy Cygan for an excellent job of researching Chapters 4 and 5 to help us to bring them up to date for this edition, and Mary Gorney for the arduous task of typing and pasting up the revised manuscript with intelligence and accuracy.

Contents

Chapter 5
Guides to Research and Resource Materials   125

Chapter One

perspectives in sociology

SOCIAL CHANGE, SOCIAL ORDER, AND SOCIOLOGICAL THEORY

Turning and turning in the widening gyre
The falcon cannot hear the falconer;
Things fall apart; the center cannot hold;
Mere anarchy is loosed upon the world,
The blood-dimmed tide is loosed, and everywhere
The ceremony of innocence is drowned;
The best lack all conviction, while the worst
Are full of passionate intensity.

From "The Second Coming"
W. B. Yeats

Yeats is describing the world as we have come to know it. Indeed it sometimes seems to have gone askew. No longer do we have Browning's nineteenth-century certainty that "God's in his heaven, all's right with the world." Things *are* falling apart. The old myths no longer work. The governing elites no longer seem responsible.

Sociology develops in such an intellectual climate, because the distance one must maintain from one's culture as a sociologist— being *of* but not quite *in* society—is easier to establish in times of rapid and basic social change. Such basic changes occurred as a result of the industrial revolution. In the nineteenth century, the major social conditions (industrialization, rationalization, democratization), and the key intellectual traditions (dealing with the interpretation of the nature of reason and the relationship between the individual and society) which are reflected in the work of sociologists, were emerging. The roots and origins of contemporary social science are found in the writings of social philosophers and social thinkers who were either critics or apologists of the social order. The seminal sociologists of the nineteenth and twentieth centuries were concerned, like Yeats, with the problem of order: Émile Durkheim focused on social cohesion; Karl Marx focused on contradictions, change, and conflict; and Max Weber focused on types of authority. When Yeats speaks of anarchy being loosed upon the world, he is describing the normless state that Durkheim called *anomie.* Durkheim recognized the perils of this condition: he believed that individuals need constraints and limitations, that too much freedom leads to the societal instability of which suicide is an index. The individual/society and individualism/community dichotomies that are manifest in the thought of the nineteenth-century theorists retain great relevance today.

The eighteenth-century Enlightenment and its aftermath produced "rational man"—*homo economicus, homo politicus,* sagely measuring out life in coffee spoons, balancing pleasure and pain with a felicific calculus, and motivated by a rational view of self-interest. But the nineteenth-century Romantics responded to this rational construct by emphasizing the nonrational nature of people and institutions, and by exploring the importance of history, the values of community, and the moral variables of social life. For these thinkers, reason was not a universal precondition of social organization, but rather an emergent product of society which must be viewed in a problematic way.

Marx's concern with the nonrational nature of institutions was focused on the inherent contradictions of capitalism. Sociologists following the Marxist tradition use phrases such as "crackpot realism" (C. Wright Mills) to describe reality and rationality. In dialectical terms, the eighteenth-century thesis was rationality, the Romantic antithesis was nonrationality; Marx encompasses elements from both traditions, striving for a synthesis based on a rational perception of socioeconomic institutions and their relation to each other. His synthesis is directed towards effecting social change so as to create a new society based on the Romantic ideals of community and of the potential goodness of all men and women. Max Weber incorporates both rational principles and Romantic values, but he was never able to synthesize these dichotomous elements.

Durkheim, Marx, and Weber all focused on the problems of industrial society. Durkheim suggested a reorganization of society into occupational communities so that dependence on the division of labor would produce an organic solidarity, necessary to keep things from falling apart and to make the center hold. Marx criticized capitalist industrial society, although he considered it a necessary step in the dialectical progression towards the classless society. He described the alienation of industrial workers, their separation from the means of production, their dehumanization, their powerlessness, and their ultimate organization into a political force directed towards destroying the institutions of private property and bourgeois society. Weber, in his "dialogue with the ghost of Karl Marx" (Salomon: 1945), analyzed types of authority: *legitimate authority,* based on tradition; *bureaucratic authority,* based on formal organization; and *charismatic authority,* based on personal qualities. According to Weber, change occurs through charismatic leadership which ultimately becomes routinized into bureaucratic authority. Deeply pessimistic, he believed that the industrial revolution and the accompanying rationalization and dehumanization of existence were leading to the iron cage of bureaucracy. The terms *alienation* and *anomie* were used by all of these thinkers to describe the disenchantment brought about by industrialization. It is ironic that contemporary social scientists use these terms to describe people who do not *adjust* to this alienated society and who are therefore considered deviant (Horton: 1966).

Marx's sociology reflects the great importance of the theory of evolution to nineteenth-century thought. When applied to human history, evolutionary principles supplied the conceptual framework of progress. It was fashionable in the late nineteenth century to believe in a progression from cave dwellers to the upper-middle-class Victorian family, the apex of civilization. Marx did not believe that the millennium had already arrived, but he did believe humanity capable of evolutionary progress. He theorized that a society generates contradictions between the modes of production and the social relations of production, and that these contradictions lead to its destruction and to the establishment of a new order. The establishment of the new order does not take place automatically, but through political struggle among social classes. By this dialectic of social change, people had progressed from primitive times through feudalism to capitalism. The next stage would be the "Promised Land"—the classless society in which people could express their true natures through unalienated work. There they could "hunt in the morning and fish in the afternoon," rather than being subjected to the sterile specialization that characterizes industrial capitalist society. The distinction between the property owners and the propertyless proletariat would be abolished, placing power and control in the hands of the productive workers. Social class, Marx believed, is the crucial human grouping, and all history is a history of class conflict:

Insofar as millions of families live under economic conditions of existence that separate their modes of life, their interests, and their culture from those of other classes, and put them in a hostile opposition to the latter, they form a class.

(The Eighteenth Brumaire of Louis Bonaparte)

Thus class is a process, a position, and people thinking about a position. Marx distinguishes between a class *in itself*, when there are common situations and common interests; and a class *for itself*, when political action is taken in the defense of class interests. The concept of *false consciousness* is introduced to explain why people act against their class interests—why servants, for example, identify with their masters. For Marx, then, the key variable determining stratification in society is class position. All other criteria of ranking social positions—such as education, religion, ethnic or racial background, and life-style—are correlated to social class. Weber postulates three distinct, although somewhat interrelated, bases of social stratification: social class (economic); social honor or prestige (status); and political power and authority. These may not be directly correlated: for instance, high social honor may not always accrue to those in political power.

It is important to understand Marx and the Marxist perspective on society. Unfortunately, his teachings are often ignored in American society and even in some sociology books, where the reference may be simply to state that he was wrong. *Alienation, ideology,* and *class* are three Marxist concepts that are most useful to sociologists. Described briefly, the major Marxist contributions to sociology are:

1. The notion of inherent contradictions: that all societies prior to true communism contain inherent contradictions such as the existence of poverty along with productive surplus and great wealth; the ideology of increasing democratization and the persistence of unaccountable power concentrated in the hands of those who control the wealth; and the aggrandizement of social power and wealth paralleled by continued degradation of the worker.

2. The dynamics of alienation: the creation of social conditions by people being subjected to external forces, and the simultaneous alienation of those people from the objects of their creation.

3. The concept of social structure—not ideas or psychological states—as constituting society and social existence.

4. The notion of ideology: the "interested" use of ideas as tools of social interests rather than as free-floating entities. As we do not judge individuals by their opinions of themselves, Marx submits, we must not judge societies by their own consciousnesses. We must look behind the facade of social claims and beyond the limited visions of the time: theories of society are historically limited; they reflect social conditions, and their premises change in accordance with social changes.

5. The interactive nature of understanding and activity, theory, and politics: the necessity of proving the truth of ideas by bringing them to fruition in the world, testing theory against reality and subjecting reality to theory. Sometimes sociologists distinguish between Marx the theorist and Marx the polemicist. Marx himself does not make this distinction between thinking and acting: theory informs action, and action, in turn, brings true understanding.

In the sixties, with the rise of social activism in the universities, the works of Karl Marx were introduced into sociological theory and thus into sociology courses. The early humanistic writings of Marx had been translated and were easily available in *Marx's Concept of Man* (edited by Erich Fromm and published in 1961).

Until the 1960s, however, Durkheim and Weber were the European sociologists who most influenced American sociology. Durkheim's positivism, his emphasis on social control, and his functionalism were reflected in American sociological thinking. His dictum that social facts must explain social facts, that is, that one should explain social phenomena by using sociological, rather than other (e.g., psychological) variables, has been honored in the breach, yet has remained as a goal. His typology of *anomic, egoistic,* and *altruistic* suicides demonstrates his theory of social control: suicide is related to the extent and type of solidarity in a social system. In *Moral Education,* the behavioral rules for morality as applied to the reconstruction of a secular educational system emerge. According to Durkheim, social facts are *external* and *constraining.* In his study of the division of labor, a polemic against Herbert Spencer's individualistic contract theory of order, Durkheim studies the changing normal and pathological forms of social solidarity or control. He suggests that the former mechanical solidarity, characteristic of primitive societies held together by a strong *collective conscience,* will be replaced by organic solidarity in which people are interdependent because of the division of labor. Thus Durkheim considers the division of labor potentially good, while Marx considers it alienating. Both Durkheim and Weber, unlike Marx, believe in "value-free sociology"; that is, they believe that sociologists, both as sociologists and as scientists, should remain value-free in their work, and that science *can* be value-free. Durkheim sought to disentangle science and politics, giving authority to science as a useful means for solving social problems. Until society is understood quite well, he wrote, social and moral facts should be approached with humility and respect. In Weber's view, a necessary distinction must be maintained between fact and value, but each sphere is important within its own limitations; science, for Weber, cannot replace politics, just as for Durkheim politics cannot replace science.

Writing after Marx, Weber saw the rise of the managerial class and the growth of bureaucracy. Bridging the nineteenth and twentieth centuries in his lifetime, he returned to the theme of rationality, emphasizing rationalization as a major tendency in Western societies. Rationalization, in this sense, refers to the process whereby action becomes more systematic, coherent, and illusion-free. In his historical analysis of the unique characteristics of Western society which result in capitalism, Weber noted that rationalization, through disenchantment with magic and religion, also results in bureaucratization. The spirit of capitalism resides in the rational pursuit of wealth, a motive for rational behavior in a rationalized economic setting. The Protestant Ethic is also a form of rational social behavior which served as a motive for rational economic behavior. However, according to Weber, charismatic authority can break through rationalizing tendencies. Weber focused on social action, which he defined as behavior that is meaningfully oriented to others. The concept of *verstehen*, understanding or meaning, was crucial to his thinking. He thought that through this special method we could understand human history and social organization.

Weber's *Protestant Ethic and the Spirit of Capitalism* is often taken as an idealistic polemic against the materialistic determinism of Marx. But this view is oversimplified. Weber pointed out the significance of ideas as independent variables in shaping history, and he also stressed the character of political power and organization as important determinants. He was critical of Marx for what he interpreted as a failure to distinguish between what is strictly economic, what is economically determined, and what is merely economically relevant; that is, for reducing a number of causal factors to a single factor theorem. Although Marx stressed the conditions of social existence (the *substructure*) as primary, he nevertheless acknowledged the strength of the derivative political and ideological factors (the *superstructure*) and their relative influence on socioeconomic organization. However, a great deal of work needs to be done in order to work out these aspects of the theory in sufficient detail. (See the *Kapitalistate* journal described on page 111 of Chapter 4 for some interesting attempts to work out a Marxian theory of the State.)

In Marx's view, the modern economy is basically irrational, due to the contradiction between the rational technological advances of productive forces, and the nonrational obstacles of private property, profit, and unmanaged competition. For Weber, on the other hand, modern capitalism is the embodiment of rationality; bureaucracy promotes rational efficiency and compels man to become a specialized expert, qualified for accomplishment of a specific career through prescheduled channels. "Man is thus prepared for his absorption into the clattering process of bureaucratic machinery." (Weber: 1958; p. 49)

Weber has influenced American sociology with his concepts of *status, charisma, bureaucracy,* and the *Protestant Ethic,* with his distinction between the man of science and the man of politics, and with his nominalistic action theory, which makes no *a priori* definitions of the way someone will act. In other words, because people's orientations to their activities are different, they may act the same way for different reasons. Although Weber does not deny class struggles and their part in history, he does not consider them the central dynamic. He believes instead that socialism merely completes in the economic order what has already occurred in the political order. "For the time being the dictatorship of the official and not that of the worker is on the march." (Weber: 1958; p. 50) According to Weber, Marx's alienated laborer was merely one special example of a universal trend separating soldiers from the means of violence, scientists from the means of inquiry, and civil servants from the means of administration.

If you want to follow the Marx-Weber approaches in greater detail, see "Conflicting Interpretations of the Rise of Capitalism: Marx and Weber." (Birnbaum: 1953) Two additional useful sources are the introduction to *From Max Weber* (Weber: 1958), and *Consciousness and Society* (Hughes: 1961). We have dealt with the theories of Marx, Weber, and Durkheim in detail because they are prominent in modern sociology and because we consider them useful guides to the sociological perspective. (There are many useful biographies of Marx, Weber, and Durkheim, e.g., Henri Lefebre on Marx, Arthur Mitzman on Weber, and Robert Nisbet on Durkheim.) We can enlarge our own potentials for comprehension, creativity, and imagination by being exposed to alternative conceptualizations of the relationships between conflict and order, the individual and society, and action and understanding. These debates continue and are translated into modern terms in the sociological literature. An understanding of these differing theoretical frameworks is essential, for one's choice of concepts necessarily influences one's research methodology, one's interpretation of data, and one's conclusions.

THE SOCIOLOGICAL APPROACH

A standard joke about sociologists is that "A sociologist is a man who spends $100,000 to find a brothel, something any taxi driver will tell him for nothing." But it's not that simple. Not all of what we know through "common sense" or common knowledge is true. Another relevant joke tells of a British colonial administrator berating an Indian engineer for not using his "common sense." The engineer replies: "I have only an engineering education. Common sense is a rare gift of God." For example, it is only "common sense" that groups who are upwardly mobile (entering into a higher social status than that of their parents) would be happier with their status than groups who stayed in the same status. Yet sociologists studying the army in World War II (Stouffer et al.: 1949) found that air corps officers were the most dissatisfied with their status, while military policemen were the most satisfied: the air corps had the highest promotion rate and the military police the lowest. However, these people were comparing themselves not with other servicemen, as a group, but with other air corpsmen or other military policemen. Thus the social-psychological concept of *reference group,* that group to which you compare yourself, was conceptualized.

So sociology is not the same as common sense. But then what is a sociological level of analysis? Durkheim said that social facts must explain social facts, so psychological and psychoanalytical explanations are not sociological, even if the dependent variables they explain are social. For example, war is a social fact. But societies, not individuals, are at war. To explain war in terms of the death instinct (Thanatos) or of individual aggressive needs is "unsociological." Other examples of "unsociological" thinking are explaining student revolutionaries in terms of their psychological relationships with their families, or explaining the causes of pollution in terms of individual irresponsibility and prescribing individual solutions such as antilitter campaigns or recycling bottles. But now that we have some idea of what is not sociological thinking, let's turn to what sociologists define as their sphere of investigation.

Robert A. Nisbet names the following five concepts as constitutive elements of sociology: *community, authority, status, the sacred,* and *alienation.* Between 1830 and 1900, an increasing concern with these ideas and their interrelationships marked the emergence of sociology as a science distinct from moral philosophy, the precursor of all modern social sciences. The most important ideological disputes over the past 150 years have been between the values of the first four concepts and those of *"individualism, equality, moral release, and rationalist techniques or organization and power."* (Nisbet: 1966; p. ix) The present conflict between civil liberties and law and order exemplifies such a conflict. Sociology at its finest, according to Nisbet, takes these conflicts out of ideological controversy and converts and refines them "in a host of theoretical, empirical, and methodological ways—into the problems and concepts that today give sociology its unique position in the understanding of not only the development of modern Europe but of the new nations that are now undergoing some of the same kinds of social change that were still vivid in Europe and the United States two generations ago." (Nisbet: 1966; p. ix)

Community in Nisbet's vocabulary does not refer merely to a local community; Nisbet uses it in the same sense in which the communes which are now springing up again use it—as similar to "family." That is, it "encompasses all forms of relationship which are characterized by a high degree of personal intimacy, emotional depth, moral commitment, social cohesion, and continuity in time. . . . Community is a fusion of feeling and thought, of tradition and commitment, of membership and volition." (Nisbet: 1966; p. 47) Its archetype is the family and its opposite is the impersonal "society." Most communities use the nomenclature of the family; for example, the various liberation movements—black, gay, female—use the terms "sister" or "brother" with one another in their attempt to become communities. The quest for community is said to be present in many social movements today. Sociology is full of dichotomies referring to the distinction between community and society; in Ferdinand Toennies' *gemeinschaft* and *gesellschaft,* status and contract, folk and urban, sacred and secular, and so on. Durkheim's work in particular is marked by these distinctions.

According to Nisbet, *authority* "is the structure of the inner order of an association . . . and is given legitimacy by its roots in social function, tradition, or allegiance." (Nisbet: 1966; p. 6) The nature and types of authority have been described by Weber. One reason for the social upheavals we have been having is, in Nisbet's view, that former forms of authority are no longer considered legitimate by segments of the population.

Status is "the individual's position in the hierarchy of prestige and influence that characterizes every community or association." (Nisbet: 1966; p. 6) Most of American sociology's concern with social stratification has focused on comparative statuses (Warner's Index of Status Characteristics, for example) and on the numerous rankings of occupations.

The sacred encompasses all the nonrational religious or ritualistic behavior patterns "that are valued beyond whatever utility they may possess." (Nisbet: 1966; p. 6) Western society is characterized by a decline of the sacred, but if you think nothing is considered sacred anymore, try burning a flag, or teaching sex education to children at a school where it has not been specifically approved.

Alienation is the "perspective within which man is seen as estranged, anomic and rootless when cut off from the ties of community and moral purpose." (Nisbet: 1966; p. 6) Though Nisbet does not include *powerlessness* in the above definition, powerlessness is the central meaning in Marx's use of the term. See "The Dehumanization of Anomie and Alienation" (Horton: 1964) for an incisive discussion of the uses of alienation in American sociology.

The sociologists we have discussed have approached society mainly from a structuralist, social system, or macrolevel of sociological analysis, focusing on institutions, classes, social organization, systems of stratification, and social change. Such analyses are found in Marx and Durkheim, and more recently in functionalists such as Talcott Parsons or Neil Smelser.

Microanalysis—or social psychology—complements the macroanalysis of society. One sociologist who has been very influential in this micro area is Neil Smelser, a Berkeley sociologist who has written on a wide variety of topics—from historical and economic sociology to personality and social structure. Three of Smelser's five conceptual frameworks of sociology are actually "social psychological"; they are based on the belief that sociology interprets data "within a special type of conceptual framework" rather than delimiting a special class of empirical data (Smelser: 1969; pp. 1–29). In other words, it's not what we do but the way that we do it that defines us as sociologists. Smelser has found five distinctive conceptual frameworks for identifying and describing the subject matter of the field.

1. Demography and ecology: interpreting events as they relate to human organisms observed in their physical and biological environments, without taking psychological systems or social relations into consideration; this framework explains population variability and regularity, births, deaths, physical movements, and spatial arrangements.

2. Social psychology: interpreting behavior in terms of its "psychological significance to the individual considered as self or per-

son." (Smelser: 1969; p. 4) This conceptualization is also present in psychology.

3. Social groups: studying aggregates of individuals with some common orientation.

4. Social life: observing "from the vantage point of the relations between persons" (Smelser: 1969; p. 4) using the concepts of roles and person. This can also be considered social-psychological.

5. A framework concerned with phenomena such as norms and values that regulate, legitimize, and make meaningful social behavior.

Thus sociology lacks one specific conceptual framework, and there is widespread controversy in the field between commitment to conceptual frameworks stressing conflict and change (represented in the works of Lewis Coser and Ralf Dahrendorf) and those stressing integration and stability (represented in the works of Parsons). There are also those who stress class and power and those who dwell on the significance of norms and values. Other controversies have to do with the relative fruitfulness of various methodologies, most succinctly expressed as a quantitative versus qualitative orientation. Most sociologists, however, understand the appropriateness of various methodologies, which depend, to a considerable degree, on the nature of the problem to be studied.

A large number of American sociologists consider social psychology to be within the range of their interests. This is not surprising because the relationship between the individual and society has been a major concern of American sociological theory. An influential group of scholars at the University of Chicago—including G. H. Mead, John Dewey, W. I. Thomas, Robert E. Park, William James, Charles Horton Cooley, Florian Znaniecki, Robert Redfield, James Mark Baldwin, and Louis Wirth—used the symbolic interactionist approach or contributed to its intellectual foundations. This approach is a very important contribution to social psychology.

George Herbert Mead, the founder of the symbolic interactionist tradition in American society, analyzed the development of the social self. Like Marx, he was influenced by evolutionary thinking, and he is considered an *emergent evolutionist* since he believed that, because of language, man is qualitatively and quantitatively different from his animal ancestors. Rooted in the rationalist tradition, he believed that human beings could direct the evolutionary process and thus change institutions. Human beings can take themselves into account because their "selves" are reflexive. There is a dialectical relationship between the "me" part of the self, which represents society (the "generalized other"), the organized, relatively stable set of values which the self assumes, and the "I" (the source of impulses, drives, and spontaneity and creativity) which responds to the "me." Thus we can take ourselves into account when acting toward others. In addition to the generalized other, there are significant others—those persons whose opinions of us are particularly important in maintaining our self-esteem.

As this approach to social psychology is not generally well understood, it deserves further elaboration. In symbolic interactionist theory, each person possesses a "self." Through the agency of the "self," humans, as distinct from other animals, are able to make indications to themselves about the relevant objects of their environments and to construct their actions on the basis of the socially designated meanings of these objects. The self is not conceived of as an inherent psychological organization or structure (such as the *ego, superego,* and *id*); rather, the concept of self implies a process of self-interaction or reflexivity which is developed by the individual within a context of social interaction. One learns to objectify oneself by taking the role of others toward oneself. Through a continual process of internal communication, human actors are able to plan and organize their actions with regard to what they have designated and evaluated. Thus, human beings, as objects of their own actions, cannot be regarded as mere responding organisms. Conscious, rationally constructed action encompasses the existential meaning of the self. Human beings do not automatically respond to the play of internal or external factors on their psychological organization; rather they must interpret situations and manipulate meanings in order to construct relevant conduct.

In the view of the symbolic interactionist, meanings are socially created; objects are defined and given meaning through the activities of people as they interact. Group action consists of a continual fitting together of the lines of action of the participants. This is accomplished through the dual process of making indications to others and interpreting the indications made by others. The actors exist in a world of objects and are guided in their orientation and action by the meanings of these objects. The emergent joint action is connected to previous joint action by the world of objects, sets of meanings, and the schemes of interpretation which individuals already possess, and which they bring to their encounters. This ongoing process of social interaction provides the underlying basis for both the change and the reaffirmation of meanings. The functioning of social institutions and patterns of group life depend on how people define the situations in which they must act and what they are prepared to do.

We can see from this brief description what the emphases of symbolic interactionism are. Action is constructed by individuals in interaction with themselves and with others; the interpretive process is crucial in this regard. Action can be understood only from the point of view of a milieu which the actors designate as meaningful. (Howard Becker has given a clear exposition of the socially meaningful milieu of marijuana smokers in *The Outsiders.*) Acts have careers and are subject to redefinition and transformation. Symbolic interactionism stresses the human potential for change and the emergent, unpredictable quality of social interaction. Symbolic interactionism can account for transcendence of past experiences and for redefinition of the objects of one's world. According to this view, human beings are malleable and neutral; they create their own morality through participation in social interaction. This perspective, however, does not explain how differentials in power and access to experience and information prevent individuals either from conceiving of new alternatives or from acting to create new dominant social relations and sets of meanings. Nor does it explain how particular social conditions (such as class stratification, sexism, or racism) can give rise to conflicting sets of meaningful objects.

Further references to the symbolic interactionist approach can be found in *On Social Psychology; Selected Papers of G. H. Mead,* edited and introduced by Anselm Strauss, *Symbolic Interactionism: Perspective and Method* by Herbert Blumer, and Arnold Rose's *Human Behavior and Social Processes.*

Symbolic interactionists generally use observation rather than questionnaires to gather their data. To them, human life is a process and is continually in flux. The functionalists, on the other hand, see social life in equilibrium. Although socialization is one of the key interests of symbolic interactionists, they consider socialization a process which, instead of being confined to childhood, continues through life. Thus they are interested in careers—how one is socialized into a job or role or through the ranks of a profession (as in Howard Becker's and Blanche Geer's *Boys in White,* a study of how medical students become doctors). This is a useful perspective to take when studying changing or emerging roles, for symbolic interactionists speak of roles being negotiated while functionalists speak of adjustment to roles.

In addition to Mead, Charles Horton Cooley was an important early American sociologist working in this tradition. He coined the terms *looking-glass self* and *primary groups.* The latter describes groups derived from primary relations, which are characterized by a response to the whole person rather than to segments of his or her personality, and are marked by deep and extensive communication, with personal satisfactions having paramount value. Examples are the family, the neighborhood, and the school. These groups are called primary because they are fundamental to forming the nature and ideas of the individual. In primary relations, people supposedly are not used instrumentally; they are considered ends, not means. We no longer believe that primary relations have to be face-to-face encounters, though that was one of Cooley's criteria.

Some contemporary sociologists working in the symbolic interactionist tradition are Howard Becker (one of whose works on deviance has been mentioned previously—*The Outsiders*); Ralph Turner, who wrote about collective behavior and role theory (see his article on role in the *Encyclopedia of the Social Sciences* and his recent *Family Interaction;* Anselm Strauss and Rue Bucher, who have worked on the professions *(Psychiatric Ideologies and Institutions)*; and Norman K. Denzin, who has studied children ("Children and their Caretakers"; Denzin has also written *The Research Act,* which presents a symbolic interactionist view of sociological theory and methodology).

Hans Gerth and C. Wright Mills attempted to integrate Marxist and symbolic interactionist thought by using the concept of *role* as a link between the individual and the society *(Character and Social Structure).* This integration is not as far-fetched as it may seem at first glance. Marx's discussion of the social nature of the development of the self at the beginning of *The German Ideology* sounds very Meadian. It is possible to recognize a link between Marx and Mead through the relation of both to the thought of J. J. Rousseau. Mead's and Marx's ideas about human nature and the social psychology of Rousseau can be juxtaposed to the Freudian and behavioralistic traditions. While symbolic interactionism stresses the conscious construction of action, psychoanalysis searches for latent unconscious meanings, motives, drives, and forces. Freud explained behavior in terms of the conflicts and mediations between the parts of the mental apparatus—*id, ego,* and *superego.* He believed that individual behavior and action can be traced to instinctual sources which are innate and biologically predicated, and that the human organism possesses an inherent instinctual necessity or capacity to respond to stimuli in set ways. Human society and cultural adaptability necessitate transformation of one's basic sexual and aggressive instincts. According to Freud, the Oedipus complex plays a crucial role in socializing the human animal; an internalized sense of guilt, based on hatred for the father figure, is the foundation for suppression of the instincts and for transmutation of egoistic instincts into social instincts. However, the "primitive mind" is imperishable; the pressures of civilization induce a perpetual readiness of the inhibited to seek opportunities for gratification.

Several conclusions follow from these premises. Aggression is instinctually based and cannot be eliminated from people or society. Unhappiness is built into any civilization because its aims are diametrically opposed to the natural expression of instinctual needs. Revolution would be of little value in making people happy. The majority of people need an authority to which to submit. Consequently, new social conditions could never affect the essential human nature, which supports a system marked by war, domination, and repression. Whereas Freud stresses unconscious processes and nonsymbolic interaction, and posits a perpetual tension between primitive instincts and civilization, Marx, Mead, Rousseau, and those who follow the symbolic interactionist tradition stress the social nature of man; in their view people develop selves only by living in society and interacting with others.

A weakness of both symbolic interactionism and functionalism is the omission of the concept of *power* in their theoretical frameworks. Examples of how functionalists do not give power its due can be found in the works of Talcott Parsons, such as *The Social System* (1951), as well as in the writings of W. Lloyd Warner. Parsons takes values as givens and does not explain where they came from or in whose interest they are. In fact, the dominant values in a society are the values of the most powerful groups, or in the interest of those groups. Similarly, W. Lloyd Warner in his classic set of community studies of Yankee City (1941; 1942) does not address himself to the power relationships among the six social classes that he finds. In contrast, the Lynds, who are not functionalists, examine the effects of differential power relationships in their community studies (1929; 1937). While the amount of individual freedom posited by symbolic interactionists is reassuring to humanists and existentialists, it is also true that the nature of interaction depends in part on the relative power of the individuals involved. Durkheim said that social facts are external and constraining, but the ideas of constraints or limitations (such as class, sex, or race) are missing in the interactionist presentation.

As Marx said,

Men make their own history, but they do not make it just as they please; they do not make it under circumstances chosen by themselves, but under circumstances directly encountered, given and transmitted from the past. The tradition of all the dead generations weighs like a nightmare on the brain of the living.

(The Eighteenth Brumaire of Louis Bonaparte)

In the process of learning reciprocal roles, the less powerful person is more motivated to learn the other's role and to be sensitive to the more powerful participant. Thus children are more motivated to learn the teacher role, blacks more motivated to learn the white role, and women more able to put themselves in the man's place (this is why women are considered more "sensitive"). The less powerful, by definition, must achieve their ends by manipulation rather than through force; in order to manipulate successfully, they must be able to understand and empathize.

Symbolic interactionists state that interaction changes over time and modifies role behavior through the process of one individual taking the role of the other. This is particularly true when these roles are emergent and their components vague (noninstitutionalized roles). By adding power to the interactionist approach, we can see that those at the top of the power pyramid (e.g., young, healthy, upper- and upper-middle-class white males) do have more freedom in constructing their own realities, than those at the bottom of the pyramid (e.g., old, sick, poor, black females). Although we are all constrained to a certain extent in our outlook and activity by our social positions and roles, it is obvious that those at the bottom of a system of unequally distributed resources will be more constrained, alienated, and limited in their potential development and fulfillment.

Discussion of role conflict—how it arises and how it is resolved—has been a persistent theme in social psychology. The ability of individuals to compartmentalize their lives so as to reduce or handle the alleged role conflict (such as the army chaplain who preaches "Thou shalt not kill" and sends men off to war) has sometimes been underestimated. In addition, the relationship between role and adjustment has been frequently pointed out, as when the concept of role loss and the concomitant loss of self-esteem of women who have been over-adjusted to their role is used to explain the problems of middle-aged women who are experiencing the emptying of the nest (Bart: 1970).

Peter Berger is a microsociologist who in two of his popular works, *Invitation to Sociology* and *The Social Construction of Reality,* has dealt with the concepts of role, self, and ideology. According to Berger, sociology is an individual pastime for people who are intensely curious about human interaction, for "those who can think of nothing more entrancing than to watch men and to understand things human." (Berger: 1963; p. 24) To a sociologist, everything becomes data. As Berger says, the sociologist is a spy reporting as accurately as possible the terrain. "It is not a practice [like social work] but *an attempt to understand.*" (Berger: 1963; p. 4)

Sociologists consider themselves scientists, but differ as to what that means. Some think it means that sociology should be empirical like physics (or rather what sociologists think physics is), whereas others think of it as more like geology—descriptive and classificatory. The empirical sociologists sometimes consider the work of the classifiers mere journalism and atheoretical, while the latter sometimes consider the work of the former trivial and not making a contribution to a real understanding of the phenomena. However, in recent years this controversy has died down. Those sociologists who take a "hard science" position are more likely to be found in survey research centers which are attached to almost every major university. One such center is the Bureau of Applied Social Research at Columbia, where Paul Lazarsfeld and Samuel Stouffer made their important contributions, the former in voting behavior (*The People's Choice*: 1952). Sociology is officially a science: it has the official seal of approval from the National Science Foundation. Berger suggests that because of this commitment to science, sociological statements must be arrived at by following certain rules of evidence, and that this method must be made public so that others may replicate the work. To be considered true, the results of replicated studies should match the original finding. (See the discussion of reliability in the glossary of statistical terms.) Some sociologists have become so preoccupied with methodological problems that they tell us more and more about less and less; this might be called a "methodological cop-out."

Berger considers sociology "a peculiarly modern form of consciousness." (Berger: 1963; p. 25) In times of historical change people's self-conceptions are jolted; the official constructions of reality do not explain what is happening in the world. Sociology goes beyond common sense and, like foreign travel, can suddenly illuminate "new and unsuspected facets of human existence in society." (Berger: 1963; p. 23) The roots of sociology lie in France and Germany: they developed from the French attempt to come to grips with the Revolution and from the German attempt to solve social problems in the library rather than at the barricades.

The sociological consciousness has four motifs: debunking, unrespectability, relativizing, and cosmopolitanism. As we have mentioned, Berger views the key sociological concepts as role, self, and ideology. Ideology is a key concept for many sociological theories, particularly the sociology of knowledge. It is related to the debunking motif and its roots are methodological, not psychological.

The sociological frame of reference, with its built-in procedure of looking for levels of reality other than those given in the official interpretations of society, carries with it a logical imperative to unmask the pretensions and the propaganda by which men cloak their actions with each other. This unmasking imperative is one of the characteristics of sociology particularly at home in the temper of the modern era.

(Berger: 1963; p. 38)

Thus when you choose a problem to study, you should be aware that you are likely to find things that some people (who have a stake in the accepted version of the situation) won't want known. The implications of this are manifold. First of all, don't promise not to relate the finding without "their" permission. Second, be careful about studying a group that you think is "good" and doing an important job. Chances are that your findings may be used against the group. (For example, research on the social, political, and economic organization of peasant life in Southeast Asia has been used to develop military and political policies directed toward the disintegration of traditional peasant society, the destruction of the countryside, and the forced concentration of peasants in specified rural centers or urban areas.)

THE SOCIOLOGY OF KNOWLEDGE

This section deals with the sociology of knowledge, beginning with a discussion of C. Wright Mills's concept of a *vocabulary of motives* (Mills: 1963). This concept addresses the problem of diverse explanations for events, feelings, thoughts, and behavior. Which terms do we use? "Acceptable" reasons or motives change over time. In times past, religious vocabularies were invoked. People acted "crazy" because they were "possessed by the devil," people heard voices because the saints were speaking to them, and tragedies occurred because it was "God's will." Such explanations seem quaint and old-fashioned now. The vocabulary of sin and salvation has been replaced to some extent by the psychiatric vocabulary. People behave in certain ways because they are "sick," "have not resolved their Oedipal conflict," are "in rebellion against authority figures," are "castrating," etc. (Bart: 1968) Sociological vocabularies are currently being used, especially by the political Left. For example, our society is in bad shape because of the "dehumanizing effects of capitalism," and minority groups behave in certain ways because they are "oppressed." Problems are not individual but structural, and words such as "ethnic," "demographic," and "charisma" are invoked by commentators.

In "Language, Logic and Culture," Mills remarks that language can be thought of as a system of social control with vocabularies directing thought into socially desirable channels. He explains his concept of *vocabularies of motives* as follows:

What is the reason for one man is rationalization for another. The variable is the accepted vocabulary of motives, the ultimates of discourse of each man's dominant group, the group about whose opinion he cares. . . . When they appeal to others involved in one's act, motives are strategies of action. In many social actions, others must agree, tacitly or explicitly. Thus acts often will be abandoned if no results can be found that others will accept.

(Mills: 1963; pp. 448, 443)

Thus motivations are legitimized by social factors, by the groups to which one belongs or which have power over one's motives. The phrase, "Now what do you really mean?" suggests that the vocabulary of motives presented is unacceptable and another must be substituted. For example, if you are seeing a psychotherapist and he or she asks you why you take drugs and you say because you enjoy the feeling they give you, or because they are there, the therapist is not likely to accept these explanations. The therapist prefers a vocabulary of motives offering psychological facts such as the desire to escape, hostility to authority, or some similar explanation. In a comparison of women who were admitted to the psychiatric service of the Neuropsychiatric Institute at U.C.L.A. with those who were admitted to the neurology service but were discharged with psychiatric diagnoses ("hysterical" women), the latter were found to be more likely to have come from rural unsophisticated parts of the country and to have settled in small towns in California. In contrast, the patients admitted to the psychiatric service were more likely to be urban and to have more education. Thus, the neurology patients were more likely to come from less sophisticated subcultures where psychiatric explanations of illness were less prevalent. They could insist that their illnesses were organically caused and be supported by their dominant group in that explanation. On the other hand, in more sophisticated areas all illnesses are considered psychosomatic or psychogenic if organic causes are ruled out. Women can no longer be like Elizabeth Barrett Browning and other Victorian ladies who languished on a couch suffering from some unknown ailment. Now, rather than languishing on a couch the individual often is treated on a couch.

Our very language is a social product, as the burgeoning field of sociolinguists demonstrates. Psychiatric vocabularies of motives can be and are used to discredit people who in a previous generation would have been called "bad" or "sinful." Such explanations give the speaker an aura of modernity, of compassion, of being "with it." Thus, the Oakland, California, chief of police said that people who supported the "Peace and Freedom Party" (a radical political party in the 1968 elections) were "sick." In the urbane San Francisco Bay Area he would have seemed old-fashioned had he said that they were "atheistic communists," although in rural areas, particularly in the South, this might have been an appropriate label. Similarly, psychiatric vocabularies are used to discredit feminist leaders.

Rather than discussing the issues that are raised in women's liberation, many of its opponents have attacked the personalities of the leaders with such psychiatric labels as *castrating, sexually frustrated,* and *frigid.*

Other approaches to the sociology of language, knowledge, and culture are the German or Marxist approach, the French or structuralist tradition, and the American social-psychological analyses.

Marx and his followers emphasized the unmasking functions of ideological analysis in their attempt to lay bare the ideological roots of bourgeois thought and to use this knowledge as a weapon in the proletarian armory. In *The German Ideology* Marx ridiculed the pretensions of the German idealists, pointing out that they made "ideas out of hats," whereas the materialist conceptualizations turned things right side up and made hats out of ideas. Because the socioeconomic institutions, the relations of production, are the basic units of society, all other institutions are merely superstructure, reinforcing the beliefs, values, and power of those who control the productive forces of society. Therefore, the intellectual productions of society—the philosophies, theories, artistic creations—as well as the governmental, legal, and educational institutions, reflect the interests of the bourgeoisie, the controlling class. The basic question to be asked when confronted with a theory is, "In whose interest is this theory?" The causal chain in Marxist thought moves from the material to the ideational: the latter is a function of the former. As Marx said, "It is not the consciousness of men that determines their existence. Rather it is their existence that determines their consciousness." (*A Contribution to the Critique of Political Economy*)

Karl Mannheim, in *Ideology and Utopia,* has somewhat modified the Marxist approach. Mannheim was a Hungarian-born German sociologist who emigrated to London, England, when the National Socialists came to power. He combined Marxism and German historicism in an attempt to find an epistemological basis for a new consensus. According to him, it is not the proletariat who see things as they are, but rather it is the intellectuals, the rootless, marginal people whose perspective transcends class boundaries because they belong to no particular class. Mannheim distinguishes between ideologies, which characterize conservative thought and justify the status quo, and utopias, which postulate new forms of social organization.

The French structuralist approach has been less well known but is now gaining greater attention. For Durkheim and Marcel Mauss, the independent variable explaining intellectual products is the social structural arrangement. Durkheim suggests, for example, that the Australian aborigines believe that space is curved because they sit around the campfire in a semicircle. He and Mauss, in *Primitive Classification,* show the relationship between social structure and classificatory schemes. Claude Levi-Strauss is a contemporary social scientist who has expanded the structuralist mode of interpretation.

It is not surprising that the American approach to the sociology of knowledge has been social-psychological, since some of the major substantive contributions to American sociology have been in this area. Tamotsu Shibutani, a student of Herbert Blumer in the symbolic interactionist tradition, proposes the *reference group* as a setting for differing perspectives. He believes that we see the world through the prism of the group with which we compare ourselves or the group with which we identify.

Thus there is a reality$_1$, a reality$_2$, and so on, rather than a single Reality that we must confront. While we may not agree with some of the devotees of group dynamics when they suggest that all problems can be solved if only people would "really" communicate, it is a fact that many disputes stem from different perceptions and interpretations of the world and that these differences must be bridged for agreements to occur.

The contribution of C. Wright Mills to the sociology of knowledge through his concept of the vocabularies of motive has already been discussed. Robert Merton has written a useful summary and analysis of the sociology of knowledge in which he suggests that the American analyses of mass communication, particularly content analysis, are analogous to the European sociology of knowledge.

THE "SOCIOLOGICAL IMAGINATION"

The distinction between personal troubles, or private problems, and public issues is grist for the sociological mill. Troubles or personal problems pertain to the individual's self and his/her personal life. Thus, personal problems can presumably be solved individually. However, "issues have to do with matters that transcend these local environments of the individual and the range of his inner life. They have to do with the organization of many such milieux into the institutions of historical society as a whole, with the ways in which various milieux overlap and interpenetrate to form the *larger structure of social and historical life.*" (our italics) (Mills: 1961; p. 8) Public issues cannot be solved by individuals "getting down to business" or "straightening out" or using "will power." As the women's liberation movement acknowledges, "There are no individual solutions." This is true because any issue involves a "crisis in institutional arrangements." With the divorce rate as high as it is, particularly in certain age groups in certain sections of the country, the problem would seem to lie in the institution of the nuclear family or in the nature of poverty and the welfare system, rather than in men and women not "trying." A similar question of personal problem is the guilt for atrocities that are committed by troops in battle. Given the conditions of war, atrocities are structurally generated, independent of the particular personality configurations of particular soldiers.

Mills has further elaborated on the powerlessness of the individual to change structural configurations.

In so far as an economy is so arranged that slumps occur, the problem of unemployment becomes incapable of personal solution. Insofar as war is inherent in the nation-state system and in the uneven industrialization of the world, the ordinary individual in his restricted milieu will be powerless, with or without psychiatric aid—to solve the troubles this system or lack of system imposes upon him. In so far as the family as an institution turns women into darling little slaves and men into their chief providers and unweaned dependents, the problem of a satisfactory marriage remains incapable of purely private solution.

(Mills: 1961; p. 10)

As sociologists we must be aware of the idea of social structure and must trace the linkages sensitively. We must see where history and biography intersect. This is the function of the sociological imagination.

We will present some examples of the use of the sociological imagination and contrast it with other perspectives.

1. The small consciousness-raising groups of the women's liberation movement provide an excellent example of the intersection of history (and social structure) and biography. A group of about a dozen women assembles for a meeting. Each gives her biography.

As the stories are heard, common complaints emerge. The women all suffered the same embarrassments, experienced the same guilts and shames, had the same romantic disappointments; in short, had the negative experiences associated with being female in our society. However, each thought that she was the only one who was dissatisfied, and thus that it was "her fault." But clearly the women's problems were generated by the way the woman's role is structured in our society, the models they had when they were growing, and the ways in which our culture handles sexuality. What is learned from groups like these is that people often suffer not from private problems or inadequacies, but from structurally generated public issues.

2. Explanations of depression in middle-aged women furnish another example. Biologically oriented scientists have attributed the depression that sometimes accompanies middle age to the hormonal changes associated with menopause. Psychoanalysts such as Helene Deutsch have stated that "feminine, loving" women have an easier time during menopause than do "masculine, aggressive" ones. Bart (1970), however, found that depression in middle-aged women was caused by role loss, particularly loss of the mother role for women who had overprotective or overinvolved relationships with children who had left or were about to leave the "nest." Moreover, the "feminine" women who had bought the cultural definition of their role were more likely to have the problems. The cause of depression at menopause lies in our social structure, not in our ovaries.

3. Explanation of why women do not achieve as much as men in the occupational realm and are concentrated in the poorly paid, relatively unskilled occupations provides still another example of what constitutes a sociological perspective. Although we are using women as our example because it is one of our areas of expertise, needless to say the occupational problems of other oppressed minorities, races, classes, and ethnic groups are also structurally generated and are also public issues rather than private problems. Every black woman and man in this country could be psychoanalyzed, and the situation of blacks would not change. They would still be oppressed by institutional racism. Similarly, every couple living in poverty could be given marital counseling, and the marital problems that result from poverty would remain. It should be remembered that the women in these groups suffer the double burden of gender and class/race/ethnicity. For example, black women are the lowest paid group in the country because they are discriminated against on both counts. The "common sense" approach would hardly recognize these problems. "Women are distributed among the occupations differently from men because they *are* different from men. Everyone knows that. They don't want the cutthroat competition of the man's world. They work only to find a husband and then sit back and let him support them while they do the housekeeping, childrearing, and the tasks that are their part of the male-female bargain."

The biological approach is merely a restatement of the above in more intellectually respectable language. From this point of view, not only is anatomy destiny, as Freud said, but physiology is also destiny. Women are ruled by their hormones, which supposedly make them prisoners of their emotions and therefore unfit for responsible positions. Hubert Humphrey's physician exemplified this kind of thinking when he suggested that he wouldn't want a menopausal woman at the helm during the Bay of Pigs crisis. In addition, women are seen as slaves to their uterine needs and consequently either do not become trained for high-level positions or are irresponsible in such positions since they must leave each time they become pregnant. In this view women become pregnant to fulfill themselves. Various studies of animal behavior are invoked to support this position. So here the basic independent variables are anatomical and physiological. (See Lionel Tiger's first statement, *Men in Groups*, as well as his and Joseph Shepher's most recent statement, applying the theory of biological determinism to the kibbutz, for example.)

In the increasingly conservative late seventies such biological accounts of behavior have become increasingly popular, most dramatically in explanations of "mental illness." This popularity is probably caused by the *elective affinity*, to use Weber's term, between biological theories and conservative ideology. For if our troubles are rooted in our genes, then indeed little can be done to solve them. (See *Women Look at Biology Looking at Women*, ed. by Ruth Hubbard et al., published by G. K. Hall & Co., 1979 and *Biology as a Social Weapon*, ed. Ann Arbor Science for the People, Burgess Publishing Co., 1977, for critiques of such biological vocabularies of motives.)

Next, we can examine the psychoanalytical and psychological explanations for women's low level of occupational achievement. Freud, even though he transcended his Victorian milieu in some respects, accepted much of the Victorian view of women. He wrote that anatomy is destiny, but he did not mean this in a purely biological sense. According to Freud, women have inadequately developed superegos and they never quite recover from the discovery that they, unlike their brothers, have no penises. Those women who want to achieve in other than the traditional manner really are seeking a penis. Such women are pathological. The only acceptable solution to the woman's problem is for her to have a son and thereby have a penis. In this view, women and men are different psychologically and Freud celebrated the difference, as does Erik Erikson. Erikson believes that women are focused on their "inner space" which will in time be filled by a child or children. Women are naturally more nurturant and gentle than men, and since these traits are needed in the world, denials of such sexual differences are harmful and/or incorrect. As Phyllis Chesler points out, psychotherapy, based on these kinds of views, can be used to "cool women out" and make them content with their traditional role (Chesler: 1971).

David McClelland, in his comprehensive study of achievement needs, did not study women since their achievement needs were so much more complex than those of men. Matina Horner has studied this problem from another perspective. She found that high-achieving women are negatively perceived by others and this view is internalized so that women are ambivalent about achieving even when they possess the ability to succeed. Such ambivalence holds them back from fulfilling their intellectual potential. The ambivalence does not stem from their inner space needs or the primacy of the uterus. It stems from the societal response to their behavior, including the response of their families. While they were young they were rewarded (positively reinforced) for doing well in school but as they reached adolescence they were told that this was not really important. What was important was for them to be socially popular so they could catch an acceptable husband. Everyone knew that "smart girls don't show it."

Naomi Weisstein, in her classic methodological critique of psychologies of women (Weisstein: 1970), thinks it surprising that it takes until adolescence for girls to get the message that they are supposed to be stupid. Social psychologists, then, answer the question of women's low occupational achievement by pointing to female socialization with its double messages about achievement, to the nature of male and female roles which dictate that men are supposed to be equal to or superior to their wives intellectually and economically, and to the discrimination, subtle and not so subtle, against women out of their "place." They examine primary groups and reference groups. They examine who and what gets status in our society. The fact that the following story may appear to you as a paradox illustrates the nature of the problem:

A father and his son are driving on the highway and have a terrible accident. The father is killed and the son is seriously injured. He is rushed to the emergency room of a nearby hospital where he is prepared for emergency surgery. But when the surgeon enters the room the surgeon says, "I can't operate. He's my son."
How is this possible?

Few people are able to realize that the story is possible because the surgeon is the boy's *mother*.

However, subsequent researchers have not been able to replicate Horner's findings. Whether this failure is due simply to changes in rhetoric because of the diffusion of the ideas of sexual equality promulgated by the women's movement or to actual changes in *behavior* is still unclear. But women in increasing numbers have been applying to and attending medical and law schools, indicating that once the social climate became less punitive to women who wanted to enter traditional male professions, women's "motive to avoid success" seemed to wither away. We should not, however, be led to believe that there is no longer any gender based discrimination. The mean (average) income differential between full-time employed males and full-time employed females has increased as has occupational segregation. These facts have particular import since the number of female headed households is increasing. A sociological perspective takes such structural variables into consideration when analyzing society.

Rosabeth Kanter, in her prize-winning *Men and Women of the Corporation* (1977), has followed Durkheim's dictum and uses social facts to explain social facts in accounting for the failure of women to advance to the top of the corporate pyramid. Rather than attributing their overrepresentation in the lower echelons to the women's failure to "dress for success" or need for "assertiveness training," she presents a structural account focusing on the situation of token women (also applicable to tokens of any groups) in middle management.

1. When there is a small number of members of one category in a group that is mainly composed of members of another category, the former category, e.g., women, blacks, are more visible.

2. At the same time, the majority members tend to exaggerate the differences between them and the minority members "and this exaggeration leads to polarization resulting in the exclusion of minority members from activities."

3. Another process that occurs is assimilation which forces "minority members into playing limited and caricatured roles." Token women in the sales force Kanter studied were forced into one of the following four "role traps": (1) mother, (2) seductress, (3) pet, or (4) iron maiden. Kanter suggests that " 'fear of success' can be viewed as the fear of visibility of minority group members in token statuses. The prejudice of some women against others might be placed in the context of majority-culture loyalty tests. The unwillingness of some . . . women to take certain risks involving a change in relationships might be explained as a response to the time it takes a token to establish competence-based working relationships and to the threat of mistaken identity in new relationships." (Kanter: 1979; p. 7)

To paraphrase Marx, it is not the consciousness or lack of consciousness of these women that determines their existence. Rather it is their existence (structural position in the corporation) that determines their consciousness.

4. A striking example of a sociological perspective is the analysis of violence against women in terms of power. For years if rape, woman abuse, incest, sexual harassment in the workplace and violence in pornography and the media were recognized as social problems at all, they were considered to be in the domain of the mental health professionals. An examination of their literature suggests that traditionally they have been more likely to be part of the problem rather than part of the solution (Albin: 1978; Bart: 1979; Marolla and Scully: 1979). Battered women were considered masochistic, rape victims were provocative, unconsciously desiring the rape, and little girl incest victims were considered either seductive because they wanted the sexual activity, or had fantasies of having sexual relations with their father.

In contrast, sociologists R. Emerson and Russell Dobash have analyzed woman abuse in a number of papers, the title of one exemplifying their approach: "Wives: The 'Appropriate' Victims of Marital Violence" (1978). They note that both historical and contemporary documents "elucidate the legal, religious and cultural legacies which have supported a marital hierarchy, subordinated women in marriage, and legalized violence against them. Most of the ideologies and social arrangements which formed the underpinnings of violence against women still exist and are inextricably intertwined in our present legal, religious, political and economic practices." They present data from Scotland to support this institutional analysis. Similarly, Bart, when analyzing accounts of women who were raped (1975) said, "Psychoanalysts say a gun is a substitute phallus. In the case of rape the reverse is true; a phallus is a substitute gun."

Sociologists and social psychologists have recently been studying the male sex role, particularly focusing on its constraints. A review of this literature reveals that, for men as well as for women, the range of alternatives in socialization is too narrow. A collection of such works can be found in Joseph Pleck and Jack Sawyer's *Men and Masculinity* (1974). The ambiguities, the contradictions, the constraints in the man's role are more and more frequently being considered oppressive by some males. Men's roles are stereotyped in the books read by preschoolers and elementary school children. In these books, boys are active, playing outside, and having adventures—doing, not being. Boys don't cry and, in fact, the only emotion that is allowed, even encouraged, is aggression.

Sociologist Ralph Turner writes of the "strains of masculinity" and notes that the stereotyped, rigid definition of a male's role makes it difficult for him to be flexible, as he must be, in the marriage situation. Self-respect and masculine self-respect are considered equivalent, so conformity to the stereotype of masculinity is necessary for the man to have a positive self-image, to feel good about himself. "Parents and children use challenges to his masculinity as a technique to control disturbing evidences of childhood weakness and to protect themselves against the overdemanding requirements of sympathy." And threats of being considered a "sissy" or feminine are used as techniques of social control. In school, "the boy who chatters too much in class is threatened with being seated among the girls." (Turner: 1970)

And masculinity must be continually proven—either by occupational achievements or by behaving in a way that "embodies masculine traits." Thus the male can either be a successful businessman, craftsman, or professional, or he can perform heroically and courageously on the battlefield or the playing field.

The "privileges of manhood" may be obtained by "acting like a man," which means maintaining emotional control and impassivity "with resistance to human claims for sensitivity and tenderness . . . in all roles and situations," but there is discontinuity between boyhood and adulthood both in the opportunity and in the means to establish masculinity. What happens to the high-school hero? He becomes one of the many college athletes, and even the college star "is one of the team in professional athletics." Occupational validation doesn't come for one or two decades, so there is a hiatus between the high-school glory and the occupational ascendancy. And frequently, the latter never occurs. For example, in *Death of a Salesman*, Willie Loman's sons were high-school athletic heroes, but they were occupational failures as adults. Because of male insecurity, a pattern which Turner calls *exploitation-avoidance* emerges in which, because the man is sensitized to the dominance aspects of any interaction with women, "he is threatened by casual relationships in which there is no obvious dominance, and is on guard lest the relationship take a sudden turn to his disadvantage. The only way to escape this danger is to begin jockeying for control from the start. If the girl can be successfully exploited, there is a basis for reassurance regarding his masculinity.

"The general experience of the boy has been that in free interaction the girl is often likely to gain the upper hand. In many dealings there is less risk to the girl because her defeat or submission can be cast as an admirable indication of her femininity," so that she can use a number of interpersonal strategies. Therefore, frequently boys try to have little to do with girls "except when the situation is such that they have a good chance of successful exploitation.

"This exploitation-avoidance pattern makes any relationship of mutuality between sexes impossible." In a study of male heroes in short stories in men's magazines, Turner notes that "a much more important part was played by evidence of violence, dominance, and exploitation in dealings with women. Deliberately disregarding a woman's wishes, taking from her by coercion what she might willingly have given without force, treating her insultingly and insensitively appear frequently in these wish dreams for the would-be masculine man." This pattern was not found in the comparable group of women's magazines studied. If exploitation-avoidance attitudes toward women characterize premarital relationships between sexes, marital relationships are frequently characterized by what Turner calls "the *domination-abstinence* pattern in marriage, which is an expression of masculine strain." The husband asserts his domination whenever he is present and absents himself at times when he might not be able to maintain control. For example, by being late for dinner, by absenting himself physically or socially, he shows that he has no accepted obligations to conform to his wife's wishes. This places a severe strain on the task-functioning of the small family unit and results in impairment of the love sentiment. "In a relationship that is a constant potential threat to his male identity, it is hardly possible for the man to drop his guard fully and place his identity at the mercy of his wife . . . the masculine role strain is a major source of difficulty [in marriage]. These strains are accentuated because marriage takes place for most men at a time when masculinity is so precarious because the man is still not secure in his career, and occupation is the anchorage for the male role." In Turner's summary of male and female sex roles, he says that "the traditional personality differences between men and women are not conducive to a highly stable and mutually gratifying relationship and are no longer suited to any workable division of labor in marriage. *Their only clear utility would be to facilitate a relationship of inequality.*" (Turner: 1970; emphasis added)

We have tried to expose you to some of the possibilities and limitations of different sociological approaches. In conclusion we would like to quote from Bierstedt's summary of a conference on "A Design for Sociology: Scope, Objectives, and Methods" in which the following consequences may be attributed to what Nisbet describes as the triumph of the Toquevillian vision over the Marxist vision in much of contemporary sociology (Nisbet: 1966):

We have in sociology a discipline that can deal with an orderly society—there are canons and criteria, laws and norms, statuses and roles, customs and institutions, that explain the social order—but not with a shattered society, torn with dissension, rent by violence, and tending to a disorder that leads to anarchy and ultimately to anomy. . . . It may be that none of the social sciences, nor all together, have the capacity to solve the larger problems, the problems of race and poverty, of cities and war. We live in a time when racial tensions increase, when industrial wastes pollute the atmosphere, when populations reproduce themselves to the point of starvation, when poverty prevails even in prosperous societies, when wars continue to flourish, and when nuclear annihilation threatens us all. Problems like these neither individual talent, however superior, nor scientific method, however precise, has so far solved. It may be, as Coleman suggests, that it is not method we need, but vision. We need renewed respect for our objectives and an enlargement of our scope. The last especially could produce a new design for sociology.

(Bierstedt: 1969; p. 152)

In concluding this introduction to sociology we quote Croce:

"We no longer believe . . . like the Greeks, in happiness of life on earth; we no longer believe like the optimistic philosophers of the last century in a happy future for the human race. . . . We no longer believe in anything of that, and what we have alone retained is the consciousness of ourselves and the need to make that consciousness ever clearer and more evident, a need for whose satisfaction we turn to science and art."

We turn to sociological understanding and its implications for action.

(in Hughes: 1961; 428–429)

REFERENCES

Albin, R. S.
> 1977 "Psychological Studies of Rape." Signs, vol. 3, no. 2 (Winter).

Ann Arbor Science for the People
> 1977 ed., Biology as a Social Weapon. Minneapolis: Burgess Publishing Company.

Bart, Pauline
> 1968 "Social Structure and Vocabularies of Discomfort: What Happened to Female Hysteria?" Journal of Health and Social Behavior, vol. 9, no. 3 (September).
> 1970 "Portnoy's Mother's Complaint." Trans-Action, vol. 8, no. 1/2 (November/December): a special double issue on "The American Woman."
> 1975 "Rape Doesn't End With a Kiss." Viva, vol. 2, no. 9 (June).

1979 "Rape As a Paradigm of Sexism in Society." To appear in the International Journal of Women's Studies, forthcoming.

Becker, Howard
1963 The Outsiders. Glencoe, Ill.: The Free Press.
1964 ed., The Other Side. Glencoe, Ill.: The Free Press.

Becker, Howard, and Blanche Geer
1961 Boys in White. Dubuque, Iowa: Wm. C. Brown.

Berger, Peter L.
1963 Invitation to Sociology: A Humanistic Perspective. Garden City, N.Y.: Anchor.
1967 and Luckmann, T. The Social Construction of Reality: A Treatise in the Sociology of Knowledge. Garden City, N.Y.: Anchor.

Bierstedt, Robert A., ed.
1969 A Design for Sociology: Scope, Objectives, and Methods. Monograph 9 in a series sponsored by the American Academy of Political and Social Science, Philadelphia (April).

Birnbaum, Norman
1953 "Conflicting Interpretations of the Rise of Capitalism: Marx and Weber." British Journal of Sociology, vol. 4, no. 2 (June 1953):125-141.

Blumer, Herbert
1969 Symbolic Interactionism: Perspective and Method. New York: Prentice-Hall.

Chesler, Phyllis
1971 "Patient and Patriarch: Women in the Psychotherapeutic Relationship," in Gornick, Vivian, and Barbara K. Moran, Woman in Sexist Society. New York: Basic Books: 251-275.

Cooley, Charles Horton
1909 Social Organization. New York: Charles Scribner's Sons.
1922 Social Process. New York: Charles Scribner's Sons.

Denzin, Norman K.
1970 The Research Act. Chicago: Aldine.
1971 "Children and Their Caretakers." Trans-Action, vol. 8 (July/August).

Dobash, Rebecca E. and Russell P.
    1977-78 "Wives: The 'Appropriate' Victims of Marital Violence," Victimology, vol. 2, no. 3-4: 426-442.

Durkheim, Émile
    1961 Moral Education. Glencoe, Ill.: The Free Press.
    1968 Suicide. Glencoe, Ill.: The Free Press.
    1969 and Marcel Mauss, Primitive Classification. Chicago: University of Chicago Press.

Erikson, Erik
    1965 "Inner and Outer Space: Reflections on Womanhood," in Robert J. Lifton, ed., The Woman in America. Boston: Beacon Press.

Fromm, Erich
    1961 Marx's Concept of Man. New York: Frederick Unger Co.

Gerth, Hans, and C. Wright Mills
    1953 Character and Social Structure. New York: Harcourt Brace Jovanovich.

Horner, Matina S.
    1969 "Fail: Bright Women." Psychology Today, vol. 3, no. 6 (November).

Horton, John
    1964 "The Dehumanization of Anomie and Alienation." British Journal of Sociology, 15 (December): 283-300.
    1966 "Order and Conflict Theories of Social Problems as Competing Ideologies." American Journal of Sociology, vol. 71, no. 6 (May).

Hubbard, Ruth et al.
    1979 Women Look at Biology Looking at Women. Boston: G. K. Hall and Company.

Hughes, H. Stuart
    1961 Consciousness and Society. New York: Vintage Books.

Kanter, Rosabeth Moss
    1977 Men and Women of the Corporation. New York: Basic Books.
    1979 "Effects of Proportions on Group Life: Tokenism, Not Sex Discrimination." Sociological Inventory, sample issue: 5-9.

Lazarsfeld, Paul F., Bernard Berelson, and Hazel Gaudet
    1952 The People's Choice. New York: Columbia University Press.
Lynd, Robert S., and Helen M. Lynd
    1929 Middletown. New York: Harcourt Brace Jovanovich.
    1937 Middletown in Transition: A Study in Cultural Conflicts. New York: Harcourt Brace Jovanovich.
Mannheim, Karl
    1952 Ideology and Utopia. New York: A Harvest Book, Harcourt Brace Jovanovich.
Marolla, Joseph and Diana Scully
    1979 "Rape and the Psychiatric Vocabularies of Motive," in Edith Gomberg and Violet Franks, eds., Gender and Psychopathology. New York: Brunner/Mazel, Inc.
Marx, Karl
    1911 A Contribution to the Critique of Political Economy. Chicago: Kerr Publishing Co.
    1960 with Friedrich Engels. The German Ideology, Parts I and II. New York: International Publishers, New World Paperback edition, 1966.
    1963 The Eighteenth Brumaire of Louis Bonaparte. New York: International Publishers.
McClelland, David
    1961 The Achieving Society. Princeton, N.J.: D. Van Nostrand Co.
Mead, G. H.
    1964 On Social Psychology; Selected Papers of G. H. Mead, with an introduction by Anselm Strauss. Chicago: University of Chicago Press.
Mehring, Franz
    1962 Karl Marx, The Story of His Life. Ann Arbor: University of Michigan Press.
Merton, Robert K.
    1959 Social Theory and Social Structure, Part Three: The Sociology of Knowledge, 2nd ed. Glencoe, Ill.: The Free Press.

Mills, C. Wright
    1961 The Sociological Imagination. New York: Grove
        Press.
    1963 "Language, Logic and Culture," in Irving Louis
        Horowitz, ed., Power, Politics, and People. London:
        Oxford University Press.
    1963 "Situated Actions and Vocabularies of Motive," in
        Power, Politics, and People.
Mitzman, Arthur
    1971 The Iron Cage. New York: Grosset and Dunlap.
Nisbet, Robert A.
    1965 Émile Durkheim. Englewood Cliffs, N.J.: Prentice-
        Hall.
    1966 The Sociological Tradition. New York: Basic Books.
Parsons, Talcott
    1942 "Age and Sex in the Social Structure of the U.S."
        American Sociological Review. Vol. 7 (October).
        Bobbs-Merrill Reprint No. 217.
    1951 The Social System. Glencoe, Ill.: The Free Press.
Pleck, Joseph, and Jack Sawyer
    1974 Men and Masculinity. Englewood Cliffs, N.J.: Pren-
        tice-Hall.
Rose, Arnold
    1962 Human Behavior and Social Processes. New York:
        Houghton Mifflin Co.
Salomon, Albert
    1945 "German Sociology," in Georges Gurvitch and Wil-
        bert E. Moore, eds., Twentieth Century Sociology.
        New York: Books for Libraries.
Shibutani, Tamotsu
    1955 "Reference Groups as Perspectives," American
        Journal of Sociology. Vol. 60: 562-569.
Smelser, Neil J.
    1969 "The Optimum Scope of Sociology." In Robert A.
        Bierstedt, ed., A Design for Sociology (see citation
        above).
Stouffer, S., et al.
    1949 The American Soldier. Princeton: Princeton Univer-
        sity Press.

Strauss, Anselm, Rue Bucher et al.
    1964 Psychiatric Ideologies and Institutions. New York: Free Press.
Tiger, Lionel
    1969 Men in Groups. New York: Random House.
Tiger, Lionel, and Joseph Shepher
    1975 Women in the Kibbutz. New York: Harcourt Brace Jovanovich.
Turner, Ralph H.
    1970 Family Interaction. New York: Wiley.
Warner, W. Lloyd, and Paul S. Lunt
    1941 The Social Life of a Modern Community. New Haven: Yale University Press.
    1942 The Status System of a Modern Community. New Haven: Yale University Press.
Weber, Max
    1958 From Max Weber: Essays in Sociology. New York: Galaxy.
    1968 The Protestant Ethic and the Spirit of Capitalism. New York: Charles Scribner's Sons.
Weisstein, Naomi
    1970 "Kinder, Kirche, Kuchen: Psychology Constructs the Female," in Robin Morgan, ed., Sisterhood is Powerful. New York: Vintage.
Yeats, W. B.
    1952 The Collected Poems of W. B. Yeats. New York: Macmillan Co.

Chapter
Two

---

the sociology paper

Writing papers in sociology should be one of the more rewarding and least alienating aspects of college education; it can be a deeply involving experience which provides a real opportunity for creative and analytical expression on topics that you can relate to, topics that may even be explicitly relevant to your experience. But it is often difficult to appreciate this opportunity, and towards the end of the quarter or semester the campus abounds with glassy-eyed, dazed students experiencing end-of-quarter catatonia. The library is a vale of despair because none of the books that anyone needs seem to be there. Many are held by professors (and the library won't tell you which professors), or, more mysteriously, while they are not recorded as being checked out, the only proof of their existence is an entry in the card catalog. The aim of this chapter is to pass along the techniques and shortcuts gradually learned by those who have managed to survive this often frustrating situation. By following these suggestions, you can spend more of your time thinking and writing and less of your time waiting in library lines, recopying, typing, and frantically looking for missing pages. Moreover, many of these tactics can be used for papers in fields other than sociology.

Papers can vary both in subject matter and in the type of research they require, and there is, of course, some relationship between the two. They can be the result of field work experience, of library research, or of analytical thinking. Survey research, a common sociological procedure, cannot be successfully completed in a quarter or a semester because of the requirements such research entails (unless you are using a questionnaire devised by someone else or one that you know can validly be used with the group you want to study).

Since there is a great deal of freedom in the topics students are permitted to write on, there is no reason why you shouldn't be interested in the topic you have chosen. But interest is not enough; the topic should be appropriate to your capabilities and to the time available. You should delimit your subject so that you can complete the necessary work before the deadline date. (Research always takes longer than you thought it would.) Moreover, if your topic is not narrowed sufficiently, your report will be superficial. A study of poverty in the United States could not be researched thoroughly in one quarter, but poverty in a particular town (perhaps your home town or the town where the university is located, so that you can check out the information more easily) can usually be effectively researched. Similarly, studies of racism or sexism should be limited to a particular area or institution.

Even if you are interested in the topic and you have delimited it adequately, you must ascertain that the material you need is available. Chapters 5 through 8 give many data sources, but there are still important subjects for which accurate information may not be available, and all your time will be spent trying to get good data. For example, it is unlikely that you can write an accurate paper on the Mafia in your town, on the activities of the CIA in Vietnam, or on the sex life of your mayor. In addition, there are certain topics that are potentially dangerous in that the study may be misinterpreted by some group and therefore discredited. Although you should not necessarily stay away from controversy, it is important to use your imagination and empathetic ability when you plan your work in order to foresee trouble spots in your research design. Try to anticipate how you would feel if you were a member of a certain group and were asked the questions on your schedule, or if you noticed that someone was watching you and taking notes.

There has been growing concern within the discipline over the discrepancy in the large volume of research done on oppressed peoples as opposed to the limited amount of research done on oppressors. Martin Nicolaus has asked,

What if the machinery were reversed? What if the habits, problems, secrets and unconscious motivations of the wealthy and powerful were daily scrutinized by a thousand systematic researchers, were hourly pried into, analyzed and cross referenced, tabulated and published in a hundred inexpensive mass circulation journals and written so that even the fifteen-year-old high school drop-out could understand it and predict the actions of his landlord, manipulate and control him?

(Remarks at the American Sociological Association Convention, 1968)

In attempting to facilitate the redressing of this imbalance, the North American Congress on Latin America (NACLA) has prepared a research methodology guide for studying the American power structure. They present ten theses on conducting this type of inquiry which provide a valuable introduction and preparation for approaching sociological issues in terms of the power structure.

Once you have foreseen your research design, there are several more techniques that can help you to be more efficient.

1. Always make copies of everything. Head the different drafts "Draft I,""Draft II," etc. This technique will not only save you the anxiety of looking for missing pages, but it will also assure that you have a copy of the paper if the professor should keep it, or if you should lose it.

2. Color code whatever you can. You might, for example, make the copies yellow and use white paper for the original. If you have access to other colors, you can code your different drafts. If you are using IBM cards, use different colors for different important categories, which will result in more accurate analysis when using counter-sorting or other noncomputer data processing. Regular index cards can also be used for color coding research notes. This may seem petty, but color coding will help you to identify your material more easily and organize more efficiently.

3. Make an extra copy of your outline and attach it to the wall just above where you write or type. As you finish a section, cross it off on the outline. This may make your situation seem less dangerous, since it will show the progress you have made. If you get stuck in the writing process, try some of the techniques suggested in the book *Writing Without Teachers* by Peter Elbow.

These are general techniques for sociology papers. In addition, there are several suggestions to keep in mind when you are tackling a specific type of research, such as a field work study or an analytical paper.

WRITING A FIELD WORK PAPER

If you are assigned or choose to do a field work paper (that is, a paper where you are expected to observe certain behavior), you can find many useful techniques in *Field Projects for Sociology Students* by Wiseman and Aron. Field work assignments enable you to examine areas for which questionnaire surveys would not be appropriate. For example, if you want to study illegal behavior, such as drug use, you cannot expect cooperation from your subjects if you interview them. Or you might want to study children playing, or observe the interaction in the emergency ward of a hospital or on the streets of a particular neighborhood. Since the world is our field, and everything is grist for our sociological mill, such careful studies can provide us with new knowledge.

The field work experience is an essential aspect of sociological study. The origin of sociology in this country stems in great part from the "Chicago School" where students of Robert E. Park, Herbert Blumer, and others went out into the field and wrote about the ethnic and occupational subcultures in which they participated and observed. In this way they used their sociological imagination and battery of concepts to describe and understand the communities around them. For example, Louis Wirth wrote about the ghetto (at that time a term used to designate Jewish neighborhoods), and Horace Cayton and St. Claire Drake described black communities in their book *Black Metropolis.*

Many students find field observations more enjoyable than library papers, but you should not undertake field studies without knowing what is important to watch for, or at least having some fairly good hunches. You may begin with no specific hypothesis or you may choose to operate within a highly structured theoretical framework. For some purposes it may be more comfortable or desirable to take no notes at all while in the field (recording and organizing your observations afterward in as much detail as possible); in other situations note-taking may be prolific and even formalized. In any case, it is essential that you keep a notebook and record observations systematically from the outset of your study, carefully noting the times you were observing. Looking at some of the studies that have been done in this area may be helpful in giving you a hypothesis to test or variables to observe. For example, if you wanted to study mental hospitals, you would be wise to read *Psychiatric Ideologies and Institutions* by Anselm Strauss et al., or Erving Goffman's *Asylums.* On the other hand, you may prefer to read nothing in the area before you observe so that your preoccupation with phenomena that other scientists have mentioned will not prevent you from noticing a new and different phenomenon.

While such field work experiences have been essential to the development of sociology, Kai Ericson has also warned of the moral and sociological dangers involved in the participation method, particularly when one participates in a group for the sole purpose of sociological observation and analysis. There have been numerous debates concerning the ethicality and political ramifications of participant observation, one of the more recent revolving around Laud Humphrey's study of male homosexuals, *Tearoom Trade* (winner of the 1970 C. W. Mills award for a sociological work), in which he participated as a lookout for homosexuals engaging in sexual activities in rest rooms.

The oral tradition of preserving and passing from one generation to another family and communal history is much older than the written historical record. Contemporary oral history, the collection of eyewitness accounts and life histories, is a form of social investigation which has gained increasing popularity in recent years both among professional historians and the general public. More widespread access to portable cassette tape recorders has made it possible for people with varied backgrounds and experiences to create historical "documents." Many different groups—women, blacks, working people, union members, ethnic communities—have discovered the use of oral history as a valuable tool for uncovering and making known their hidden, unrecognized social and historical roles. Oral history can help to correct the biases of a top-down, elitist, male-centered history written from the perspective of dominant groups and cultures. It can be used to explore relatively uncharted and undocumented areas of social life—the changing patterns of personal and family life-style, the participation of women and minorities in labor, political, and social movements, the daily work lives of generations of men and women.

Since the technique is open to anyone who has the time and ability to listen and the imagination to ask questions, the creation of an oral history "document" is not restricted to experts. The method of oral history allows every woman (or man) to participate, as interviewer or interviewee, in the recovery, interpretation, and communication of her/his own past. A project based on this technique can provide an exciting way for a student to develop a vivid sense of identification, continuity, and shared heritage with family members, an ethnic culture or community, a political group, or others. At the same time, since oral history is created in an interactive process, the student will be helping interviewees to remember, reflect on, and feel pride in their personal and collective pasts.

There are three basic ways to structure an oral history interview or set of interviews (*Working Womenroots*, p. 2, see below).

1. The *biographical* or life history approach consists of recording a chronicle of the experiences of individuals over the course of a lifetime. *All God's Dangers*, "The Life of Nate Shaw," for example, is the life story of a southern black tenant farmer activist.

2. Another type of interview, based on an *event*, is illustrated by the film *With Babies and Banners*, in which a number of women tell about their participation in the Women's Emergency Brigade during the 1937 auto sit-down strike in Flint, Michigan.

3. One can also choose a broad topic such as "The Family During the Depression" around which to structure interviews. In practice, these three "ideal types" of interviewing tend to overlap. Those interviews which focus on a slice of an individual's life (whether in relation to a topic or event), rather than the whole life course, are methodologically closer to the open-ended sociological interview. However, there are differences: oral histories are generally more variable and personalized than the standard social science interview. Nevertheless, material generated through oral history can be framed in a social context, thus fulfilling C. Wright Mills' definition of sociology as the intersection of biography and history.

As we have pointed out, oral history is a very accessible form of research. However, it can be practiced with greater or lesser preparation, sophistication, and critical awareness. The skills involved in eliciting a richer, more valid interview and in interpreting the material can be sharpened by bringing to bear sociological and historical imagination and training. Many useful suggestions about conducting an interview, framing questions, and processing and evaluating the results can be found in these two excellent sources: *Working Womenroots: An Oral History Primer*, edited by Joyce L. Kornbluh and Brady Mikusko of the "Twentieth Century Trade Union Woman" oral history project, which can be ordered from the Institute of Labor and Industrial Relations, Oral History Project, 108 Museums Annex Building, University of Michigan, Ann Arbor, Michigan 48109; and *Frontiers*, volume 2, number 2, Summer 1977, special issue, "Women's Oral History," with guest editors Sherna Gluck and Joan Jensen, which can be obtained from the Women Studies Department of the University of Colorado, Boulder, Colorado 80309.

WRITING A LIBRARY RESEARCH PAPER

Probably the most common sociology assignment is a library research paper. Such a paper reviews the literature (that is, the studies done so far) on a particular problem. Your first task is therefore to define that particular problem. Let us say that you want to write a paper on the sociology of mental illness. You soon discover that the area is too vast to be covered in a term paper, but you are interested in the topic nevertheless. You then realize that you must focus on one sociological factor in mental illness. One such factor is status mobility; that is, are people with emotional problems more likely to be of a higher status than their parents, have approximately the same social status, or have a lower social status? You may want to know, in sociological terms, if patients are likely to be upwardly or downwardly mobile. Such considerations will narrow the subject down sufficiently for you to be able to write a meaningful paper.

Your first step should be to find a recent book or article in a scholarly journal dealing with this topic. Chapter 5 lists the journals and tells what types of articles they print. You will find an article more quickly by looking in a recent (probably unbound) issue of *Psychological Abstracts* or *Sociological Abstracts*. Once you locate the article you will find that it has a list of references at the end. By checking these references you can find more information on the problem and also gather other references. Then you can check through other indexes (see Chapter 5) to see if you have omitted any relevant articles. (Chapter 3 gives you a basic understanding of how to use the resources of the library; Chapters 5 and 6 list useful reference sources.)

Your next step should be to get some large index cards. When you find a reference, put the title, journal name, volume number, issue number, date, and page on the top of the card. The fastest (but most expensive) thing to do at this point is to photocopy all the articles you think you may use; a less expensive, but still time-saving, method is to copy only those parts of the articles that you think are relevant or will probably use in your paper. Staple or tape (use the tape you can write on) to the index cards the sections of the article that you think you will use, making sure that you don't cover up the necessary reference citation. Be certain that the page number is included since you will have to cite it for direct quotes. Do not make the common mistake of thinking that you will remember where you obtained the data, for you may discover at 3:00 A.M. of the morning the paper is due that you cannot write your bibliography because you do not have the information for correct annotation, or you need some more information from that article but don't know which volume it is in. Occasionally, if you have almost all the information and can contact a reference librarian by phone, she may help you by giving you the name of the publisher, the pagination, or the date; but don't count on this, especially not at 3:00 A.M.

While you are amassing cards, you begin to see what the important formulations are. The cards gradually become more than random empirical studies and seem to fall into a number of categories. If you were writing that paper on mobility and mental illness, you might discover that the information could be categorized under four headings: those studies that showed that upward mobility was associated with mental illness, those studies that showed that downward mobility was associated with mental illness, and the Durkheimian notion that any mobility was associated with mental illness. The last category, of course, would be for studies that showed no relationship between mental illness and social mobility. After sorting your cards into these four categories, you would be ready to begin the writing.

In a paper which reviews the literature, your contribution is making order out of chaos—explaining why different studies give different results, examining evidence that may be contradictory, or articulating the trends that emerge. By looking through the cards in the above categories, you will be able to find different methodologies, different assumptions, and different ideologies involved. Let us say that you find one study showing that downward mobility is associated with mental illness and one that finds no such relationship. The latter may have been done in a period of depression when a large part of the labor force was unemployed, while the former was done in more affluent times. Or one study may have used as its sample black men between the ages of 16 and 25 (a group with a high unemployment rate), while the other may have used a random sample of the population. The composition of the sample, the data-gathering techniques, the historical time period, all may affect the results so that contradictory outcomes are, in fact, not contradictory because the studies are not comparable. Sometimes, especially among clinicians, inferences are made about the entire population from a study of a clinical sample. When hospitalized patients are studied, you have to remember that only certain types of people with certain kinds of symptoms are in mental hospitals. If a mental health outpatient clinic provides the sample, you have to note what sort of people are using the clinics. Educated people, Jews, and women are generally more likely to turn to psychotherapy for help than other groups. Thus, the generalizations may be a result of the characteristics of the particular group rather than a function of the mobility pattern.

Similarly, studies of prisoners do not make up a random (representative) sample of those who have broken laws. Such studies describe those who were caught and whose lawyers were not able to keep them out of jail. People who are poor, and are therefore defended by the public defender, receive harsher punishment for similar crimes than those who have private attorneys. People who are arrested "on suspicion" are frequently ghetto residents. So if you have read three articles—one based on prisoners, one based on arrestees, and one based on actual lawbreakers—be sure to point out in your paper that contradictory or different findings are to be expected, and explain why.

Let us return now to the actual construction of the library research paper. When you have the cards stacked into piles that make sense, these groupings become the basis for the outline of the paper. The first part of the paper, the introduction, should tell why you are researching this topic and why it is important. You can include theoretical reasons (why this is important for sociology and social policy reasons, why this is an urgent problem for the nation to solve). If there is a personal reason for choosing a topic, which there often is, you can mention it here (e.g., "I became interested in alcoholism when my uncle joined Alcoholics Anonymous and stopped drinking"). In the last paragraph of the introduction you should indicate what you are going to do, giving the outline of the paper. In the last section, after summarizing your results, you can point out the types of information and research that would be necessary to answer whatever question you have raised in the paper. The phrase "Further research is needed" is a cliché, yet it would be useful for you to show what sort of research is needed and what questions it might answer.

When you have finished your outline and introduction, return to your groups of cards and order them within each group. One way is to organize your research chronologically, starting with the early studies and ending with the most recent. It may be more appropriate for you to order them in terms of the methods they use (such as field studies, interviews, surveys) or in terms of the population studied (students, faculty, administrators). You should, of course, choose the method that makes the most sense for the topic you have chosen.

Instead of retyping the photocopied pages from the journals and books, decide which sections of the works you are going to use, cut out those parts (with the bibliographical information), and staple or tape them to your paper when you want to quote from particular sources, working in your own analysis or summaries as it seems appropriate. A thesaurus such as *Roget's* or dictionary of synonyms such as *Soule's* is useful when writing papers of this type so that you don't keep repeating yourself when introducing quotes from relevant studies. When writing a sociology paper, you will need eighteen ways to say "he/she found that." Both the thesaurus and the dictionary of synonyms are in paperback so that you can have copies in school and at home—in all the places where you will be writing. You might also make a list of transitional phrases, such as *moreover, however, meanwhile, nevertheless,* and *on the other hand* and tack them to your wall. Using such words often makes your writing smoother, although you shouldn't depend on transitional words to make connections that are otherwise obliquely stated. It is a good idea to triple-space all your drafts so that you will have enough room to revise legibly; scrawled pencil corrections jammed between two lines are hard for you to read and impossible for a typist to read.

When you have finished this bulky middle section of your paper, you must move on to the summary and conclusions. In this last part you should attempt to make sense out of the disparate information that you have reported. An example of this type of summary, which works well with library research (review of literature), is the following excerpt from a study of middle-aged women:

We conclude this section fully aware that many questions about middle age have not been conclusively answered, but knowing that it is not necessarily a difficult life cycle stage for all women. . . .

The writers who focused on middle age as a crisis centered for the most part on what they thought was the individual's need to feel and be useful. If a woman's status was not maintained she might slip into hypochondriases or more serious mental illness. It was apparent from reading the nonproblem-oriented studies and the studies dealing with the post-parental role that middle age compared favorably with previous stages in the life cycle, especially if the women were "more wife than mother." Two studies emphasized the importance of flexible personalities that could cope with the changes taking place in middle age. Because of contradictory evidence, we could not conclude whether or not it was helpful for a woman to work at this stage. It appeared that low status jobs did not improve the woman's situation and we did not have enough information about women with high status jobs. Extrapunitive women had higher life satisfaction ratings than intrapunitive women did. Since the depressed middle-aged women we were studying were both intrapunitive and had rigid rather than flexible personalities, these data supported our hypothesis. Most of these studies were based on "normal" people rather than on clinical experience with people who had problems. However, when depressed hospitalized middle-aged women were studied, all the rhetoric of the "empty nest" was applicable. The methodologies of the various studies differed as did their samples, which may in part explain some of the divergent results. For example, it was only after being interviewed by social workers that hospitalized women whose conflict with their children was "latent" openly admitted their problems. Had these women been surveyed by questionnaire prior to their hospitalization, they probably would have been scored as having no problems caused by their children's departure.

Only when the same researcher using the same methods studies hospitalized and nonhospitalized middle-aged women from different social classes and different ethnic groups will some of the question raised be answered and the gap in our knowledge of middle age be closed.

If you write well, you may be able to type your final copy from the edited first draft, but two or three revisions may be necessary in some cases. Get a professional typist if you can possibly afford it; the copy will look better and you will be able to do other work. If you do give the work to a typist, be sure that he or she knows what your handwritten corrections say, and be especially careful about proofreading when you have had someone else do the typing. The best way to proofread is for one person to read aloud while the other follows the original copy, making sure that everything has been transcribed accurately.

WRITING AN ANALYTICAL PAPER

Writing an analytical paper takes a good deal of thought but requires much less time running around in libraries trying to find articles. The most fruitful way to write such papers is to use the tools of the sociology of knowledge and write an ideological analysis of the works you are reading. What are the assumptions, the givens, the taken-for-granteds? What was the intellectual climate at the time the book was written? What was the polemic context? In whose interest is the work? (This Marxist use of ideology does not imply a direct or conscious interest; for example, Moynihan certainly did not intend his work on the black family to be used as a weapon against blacks, but in fact it was.)

On pages 52 through 59 are two conceptual models that will be useful to the student writing an analytical paper in sociology. The first paradigm is Bell and Mau's (1971), which was devised to study the images of the future and their effect; it is used in our model to analyze schools of psychotherapy. A second useful paradigm, a paper on A. K. Cohen and Paul Goodman,[1] leans heavily on John

1. Written by Pauline Bart when she was a graduate student.

Horton's "Order and Conflict Models in American Sociology,"[2] an article which contains a paradigm into which you can plug the works you are analyzing.

FORM

Most sociologists would like you to use the ASA official form for your references. This style can be found on the inside cover of the *ASR (American Sociological Review)*, and it is reprinted on page 60.

Format of References in Text

All references to monographs, articles, and statistical sources are to be identified at an appropriate point in the text by last name of author, year of publication, and pagination where appropriate, all within parentheses. Footnotes are to be used only for substantive observations, and not for purpose of citation. There is no need for "Ibid.," "op. cit.," or "loc. cit."; specify subsequent citations of the same source in the same way as the first citation. Examples follow:

1. If author's name is in the text, follow it with year in parentheses. [". . . Duncan (1959) has proven that . . ."] If author's name is not in the text, insert at an appropriate point the last name and year, separated by a colon. [". . . some have claimed (cf. Gouldner: 1963) that . . ."]

2. Pagination (without "p." or "pp.") follows year of publication, separated by a colon. [". . . it has been noted (Lipset: 1964: 61-64) that . . ."] Incorporate within parentheses any brief phrase associated with reference. [". . . have claimed that this is so (but see Jones:1952:99 for a conflicting view.)"]

3. With dual authorship, give both last names; for more than two, use "et al." For institutional authorship, supply minimum identification from the beginning of the complete citation. [". . . occupational data (U.S. Bureau of the Census: 1963:117) reveal . . ."]

2. Horton, "Order and Conflict Theories of Social Problems as Competing Ideologies," *American Journal of Sociology*, Vol. 71, No. 6.

MODEL A

Application of the Bell & Mau Paradigm to Psychotherapy

Psychotherapeutic Orientations	Traditional Psychodynamic	Existential Self-Actualizing	Behavior Modification	Soviet Psychiatry
Major Theoretician(s)	Freud	Maslow, Carl Rogers	Skinner	Marx, Pavlov
Concept of Human Nature	*Hobbesian* existence of strong biological drives. Change in personality and behavior possible only through *insight* obtained in psychotherapy.	*Rousseauian.* Change possible through "real" communication, acceptance by others, development of non-cognitive, non-verbal skills and sense modalities.	*Tabula rasa.* Behavior change possible through changed patterns of reinforcement.	A function of the relations of production. Pavlov's view was a *tabula rasa*, Marx's view was Rousseauian.[1]
Time Focus (in psychotherapy)	Past	Present	Present	Present
Concept of Society	Relatively unchangeable, in equilibrium, although it is possible for the area of rationality to be increased through insight.	Progressing	Changeable through the application of reason (*Walden Two*)	Progressing through the dialectic of History to the classless society.
Concept of Cause	Generally deterministic	Anti-determinism	Deterministic	Deterministic
Values and Purposes of the Authors	Where id was, there shall be ego, i.e., increasing area of individual's conscious control of his behavior.	Self-actualization, humanistic values. High value placed on non-rational skills, body awareness, sensitivity to nature, aesthetic pleasures.	Elimination of symptoms thus increasing the patient's comfort. General value on rationality.	To make "good" Soviet citizens.

Images of the Future	No overt image. The implied assumption about the future is that it will consist of more of the same.	The future will consist of an economy of abundance, with the Protestant Ethic no longer appropriate. People will be able to actualize themselves (realize their potential), society will be more expressive in contrast to today's instrumental orientation.	The future will consist of a more rational society, resulting in less individual discomfort.	The classless society. There should be no social problems.
Consequences for the Future	If the focus continues to be on intra-psychic processes, then part of the "creative elite" will become "trained egoists" lacking concern for institutional problems. Such behavior would have deleterious consequences for the society.	If their world view gains more acceptance, the society will become more expressive. Should the Rousseauian image of man[2] function as a self-fulfilling prophecy, then in fact the good society may be upon us.	Increased technology of behavior modification, or mind control—to use a pejorative term—may lead to a greater use of these techniques. While on the one hand such a technology can lead to decreasing individual discomfort, in its worst form it can lead to a *Brave New World.*	Possible reduction of schizophrenia.

1. Soviet psychologists now posit a spontaneity in the human psyche, potentialities for certain aptitudes and abilities, and a predisposition towards certain types of temperament. These can account for the continuation of "social problems" in a socialist state.

2. It should be pointed out that a Rousseauian image of man, should it not function as a self-fulfiling prophecy, may have deleterious consequences for the future, since law makers may not build controls for individual liberty into their proposed legislation. In contrast, the framers of the Constitution, men with Hobbesian views of human nature, built checks and balances in which was preserved individual liberty.

MODEL B

A Comparison of A. K. Cohen's *Delinquent Boys* with Paul Goodman's *Growing Up Absurd*

Cohen   Goodman

What Is the Purpose of the Study?

To try to demonstrate that certain problems of adjustment tend, in consequence of the structure of American society, to occur most typically in those role-sectors where the delinquent subculture is endemic. Then we shall try to show how the delinquent subculture provides a solution appropriate to those particular problems and to its elaboration and perpetuation by social groups.

Cohen takes the evidence that delinquency is concentrated in the working class at its face value.

". . . the accumulation of the missed and compromised revolutions of modern times, with their consequent ambiguities and social imbalances have fallen, and must fall, most heavily on the young, making it hard *to grow up.*"

Goodman wants to show that "the structure of society that has become increasingly dominant in our country is disastrous to the growth of excellence and manliness . . ."

He is talking about *all* youth since the adjusted youth is sicker than the person who fights the system. He feels the statistics only reflect those delinquents who perform acts which guarantee getting caught. The statistics aren't accepted by him, as they are by Cohen.

What Is the Model of Society?

A structural functional model. Society is considered as an equilibrium. Action is conceived to be problem-solving to restore the disturbed equilibrium.

The sources of the problem are the actor's frame of reference and his situation; therefore, an effective solution must entail change in the frame of reference (p. 54).

(Note that the situation is given—Another solution could be to change the situation.)

Society is *not* considered as a given. It is shaped by the needs of human beings to grow and develop. It is a process and must change. Society is judged by Goodman in terms of its meeting human needs, not *vice-versa*.

Metaphysical Assumptions: Theory of Human Nature

A Transcendental Concept of Society

Youth must adjust to society or to a subculture. There are pressures toward conformity since the solutions must be acceptable to those whom they are dependent on for good will. This need for acceptance "imposes sharp limits" (p. 56) on the range of creativity and innovation.

Cohen therefore assumes that acceptance is a more important need than creativity for these boys.

Consensus validates the frame of reference which, in turn, motivates and justifies the conduct. People want and need status.

Cohen is a sort of neo-Freudian, feeling that child training patterns affect personality.

An Immanent Concept of Society

Goodman asks the question, "Socialization to what? Dominant society and available culture?"

Perhaps the organization to which the young are being inadequately socialized is against human nature, not worthy of human nature, and therefore there "is difficulty in growing up" . . . There must be changes in society to meet the potentialities of human nature which is not a *tabula rosa* upon which the culture is imprinted.

Social scientists are seen as part of the organized system.

"Man can no longer be defined as what suits the dominant system, when the dominant system apparently does not suit man."

Goodman does not have a relativistic concept of specialization. That is, he does not agree that the child can be socialized to want anything. "Growth, like any ongoing function, requires adequate objects in the environment to meet the needs and capacities of the growing child . . . until he can better choose and make his own environment." (p. 12)

Satisfaction comes from "bona fide activity and achievement."

His first chapter deals with "Jobs" showing the centrality of the concept of work to his theory. He agrees with Marx about the "imperative new essential" in human nature "man is a maker, he must use his productive nature or be miserable." (p. 7)

What Is the Polemic Context?

Cohen is against a psychological and psychoanalytical explanation of delinquency. He tries to stake out sociology's claim to it, though his position is not as extreme as Sutherland's. He is duly moderate in his claims as befits a good academic man.

Goodman is against the organized system which he sees as either a rat race or a squirrel cage. He is essentially an anarchist.

What Can We Do About the Problem Discussed?

Since Cohen assumes the continuance of our system, we can enable the working-class male to compete more effectively for status or change the norms so that the working class is not an inferior class. However, he is very cautious, since, if society is in equilibrium, any change will cause other changes and he is not sure we want this. Therefore, Cohen is "not prepared to make pronouncements."

Goodman focuses on change. He criticizes social scientists for not now being interested in fundamental social change and for thinking that to be a social animal means harmonious belonging.

". . . if something does not run smoothly, they say it has been improperly socialized." (p. 10)

He feels we can follow through on the missed and compromised revolutions of our time which he lists.

". . . if ten thousand people in all walks of life will stand up on their two feet and talk out and insist, we will get back our country."

"We should give youth meaningful manly work, a little money, self esteem, some space to hang around in that is not always somebody's property, better schools, more and better sex without fear or shame, and a share in the symbolic goods made so much of, e.g., cars. They should have a community and a country to be loyal to; they should claim attention and have a voice." These needs can't be met in our present system (pp. 50, 51).

What Are the Trends?

Cohen's analysis is static and ahistorical. He doesn't discuss trends.

Goodman feels the situation is getting worse, the class system more rigid. ". . . if fundamental social changes fail to take place at the appropriate time the following generations are embarrassed and confused by their lack."

Why Do We Have This Problem?

We have the problem because of the status-deprivation of the working class boy.

There is in American society a combination of personality and situation that produces problems of adjustment to which the delinquent subculture is an appropriate response.

The lower-class boy must to some extent have internalized middle class values, whether from his teachers who are middle class, from his parents, or from mass media, and he is evaluated by people having middle-class norms.

We have the problem because there isn't enough man's work. Boys find out that most jobs are rackets so that "Either society is a benevolently frivolous racket in which they'll manage to boondoggle; or society is serious . . . but they are useless and hopelessly out."

Some won't settle for this alternative. The organized system, furthermore, doesn't want men. They don't suit it (p. 14).

Goodman doesn't accept our society's definition of delinquency as a given. He feels some "delin-

Cohen lists the middle-class values, but these are the Protestant Ethic values that are, perhaps, not really salient today.

Margaret Mead, one of his sources, said recently that the middle class is becoming like the working class in its refusal to delay gratifications.

Cohen's child-training data are old. Middle-class children since World War II were allowed more permissive feeding and toilet training so that the differences between white middle and lower class instinctual gratification for children may not be as great as he assumes.

The gang is so effective, says Cohen, since the working class child is more dependent on his peers for approval, but the middle-class child, according to Riesman, must also get the approval of his peers in order to obtain the approval of his parents.

If the working class boy makes the delinquent response, he feels his status is higher than that of the college boys and the aggression against the manifest cause of frustration (the middle class) helps discharge the tension caused by his repeated frustrations.

Cohen feels part of the explanation of the irrational malicious hostility may be that it represents reaction-formation.

A Marxian would not feel that crimes against property are irrational. In a slum others with similar problems are easily accessible. Once the subculture is established

quent" acts would not be considered antisocial "if society had more sense."

He points out that property violation is not useless but is a way to feel grown up. He also sees delinquency as a masculinity testing pattern in a society where one's maleness is precarious.

Like Cohen he doesn't think females have many problems since they don't have to achieve. He and Cohen agree on this because they are both men. Females have to achieve and not achieve simultaneously so that while it is difficult for boys to grow up into men the way society presently defines men, it is impossible for girls to grow up to be women, because we don't know what women are or should be.

There is a similarity between the delinquent gang boy's values and the values of the organization man—both are hipsters engaged in role playing. Both groups believe society is a rat race.

then it can meet other needs, such as personality needs.

Delinquency confirms masculinity—"the delinquent is the rogue male." (p. 140)

What Is Their Attitude Toward the Delinquents?

While Cohen never makes this explicit, it is obvious from the adjectives he uses to describe them and their activities that he doesn't like them, e.g., they are deemed "malicious," "negativistic."

Goodman has a sort of grudging admiration for anyone bucking the organization. He refers to them as "getting the social message, not accepting it."

There has *not* been a failure of communication and the problem is *not* to provide better bait to socialize delinquents. Goodman says, "We are heartened by our crazy young allies," and, while Goodman admits that the level of creativity of some gag acts is not very high, delinquents are held to invent deviant objects themselves and "this is the beautiful shaping power of our human nature."

People are basically good; society is bad, says Goodman.

4. If there is more than one reference to the same author and year, distinguish them by use of letters (a,b) attached to year of publication, in text and in reference appendix. [". . . as was previously suggested (Levy: 1965a:331) . . ."]

5. Enclose a series of references within a single pair of parentheses and separate by colons. [". . . as many have noted (Johnson: 1942; Perry: 1947; Lindquist: 1948) . . ."]

Format of References in Appendix

List all items alphabetically by author and, within author, by year of publication, in an appendix, titled "REFERENCES." Use no italics and no abbreviations. For typing format, see the examples on page 62.

Davis, K.

    1963a   "The theory of change and response in modern demographic history." Population Index 29 (October):345-366.

    1963b   "Social demography." Pp. 204-221 in Bernard Berelson (ed.), The Behavioral Sciences Today. New York: Basic Books.

Goode, W. J.

    1967   "The protection of the inept." American Sociological Review 32 (February):5-19.

Moore, Wilbert E., and Arnold S. Feldman

    1960   Labor Commitment and Social Change in Developing Areas. New York: Social Science Research Council.

Sanford, Nevitt (ed.)

    1962   The American College. New York: Wiley.

Cohen's and Goodman's theories differ because the authors have different concepts of human nature, different feelings about the role of the social scientist, different intellectual antecedents, and I would guess different personalities.

Cohen is a Durkheimian. Goodman is a Marxist, but also an anarchist and a utopian, not a socialist. He experiences, therefore, the highest possible dissatisfaction with our system, the most urgent need for radical change to get his program into being, and the most favorable concept of human nature available in our intellectual tradition.

Their differences can be summarized in their answers to the question, "Who has to change?" For Cohen it is the individual and for Goodman the society.

My bias is apparent in the phrasing of the questions as well as the writing. While I am not a utopian and do not have a Rousseauian conception of human nature, I enjoy Goodman's iconoclasm much more than Cohen's report to the PTA.

Cohen is really not so conservative as I have made him out to be, since he feels the delinquent response is caused by the social structure rather than by innately wicked human nature, defective personality, etc. Were he compared with someone else he might come out a "bleeding heart liberal." But under no circumstances would he be a radical because he, given his functionalist orientation, takes society as it exists as a given. Goodman doesn't.

REFERENCES

Bell, Wendell, and James Mau, eds.
> 1971 Sociology and the Future. New York: Russell Sage Foundation.

Cohen, Albert K.
> 1955 Delinquent Boys: The Culture of the Gang. Glencoe, Ill.: The Free Press.

Elbow, Peter
> 1973 Writing Without Teachers. New York: Oxford University Press.

Frontiers. Vol. 2, no. 2 (Summer) 1977.

Goodman, Paul
> 1956 Growing Up Absurd. New York: Random House.

Humphreys, Laud
> 1975 Tearoom Trade: Impersonal Sex in Public Places. Chicago: AVC, Inc.

Moynihan, Daniel Patrick.
> 1965 The Negro Family: The Case for National Action. Washington, D.C.: U.S. Government Printing Office, U.S. Department of Labor, Office of Policy Planning and Research.

Wiseman, Jacqueline, and Marcia Aron
> 1970 Field Projects for Sociology Students. New York: Harper & Row, Inc.

Chapter
Three

the mechanics of library research

The major source of information for undergraduates writing research papers is the library. Rarely do students have either the time or the resources to gather data in the field or on their own; nor are they encouraged in this direction. Although this bias may be unfortunate, it is not entirely unfounded. While the student should be encouraged to approach research situations creatively and remain alert to the potentialities for sociological insight which flow from his or her experiences and milieu, he or she must also have a realistic awareness of the limitations imposed by the structure of the educational process and institution. Generally, students writing research reports must rely on data gathered by other researchers to test their hypotheses. Moreover, the majority of student papers are probably less frequently original papers than they are evaluations of research that has already been done on a specific topic.

It is in the library that the student must find the existent work on a topic. Even so, whether most of the student's research is in the library or in the field, he or she should start with a preliminary survey of the library to discover the kinds of approaches taken and the findings that have emerged in a particular area of interest. Library research itself should be viewed as the imaginative integration and evaluation of material gleaned from varied sources. Information and opinions gathered and expressed by others for their own purposes must be sifted, examined, weighed, evaluated, and reworked into a synthesis which reflects the purposes of your paper and your own analytical and evaluative framework.

Library research is appropriate to the examination of both historical and current sociological issues and social problems. Contemporary issues should be located within the continuum of dynamic historical and social processes; a sociological problem should be considered in a developmental context rather than abstracted in terms of an isolated, arbitrary social "moment." In addition to consulting the sociological literature, you will find it extremely useful and relevant to look at the publications of members of social groupings being studied. For example, if you were studying the unionization of teachers, you would want to read selected issues of teachers' unions periodicals, such as the American Federation of Teachers' publications; an analysis of the women's liberation movement would require an investigation of women's liberation books, journals, pamphlets, newspapers, etc.

The initial goal of library research is to locate material relevant to your research project. You must begin a process of clarifying and focusing on the key elements of a particular sociological problem. A basic understanding of the organizational techniques employed in the library will enable you to use its resources effectively in the exploration of your interests.

STRUCTURAL ORGANIZATION

Libraries are generally organized by department and/or topic areas. Large library systems are often subdivided along disciplinary lines (social science, education, business administration, etc.). These branches, as well as the main library may, in turn, be organized into a number of departments: reference, periodicals, government documents, books. Most university libraries prepare handbooks which describe the system and outline the location of the major collections of material in particular areas of interest, e.g., sociology. The librarians in the various specialized departments and branches are highly skilled, well-trained resource persons who should be consulted for information about the availability and location of material. It is important to realize that much information of sociological relevance may not be housed with the sociology collection in the library system; useful material may be found in the sections or branches devoted to economics, political science, business administration, psychology, anthropology, education, criminology, etc.

DEPARTMENTS

The Reference Department contains the library's collection of general and specialized encyclopedias, handbooks, dictionaries, abstracts, indexes, bibliographies, yearbooks, and other reference tools.

Current issues of periodicals may be shelved in a special periodical section or department alphabetically and/or by topic area; older copies are bound in hard covers and shelved in the stacks of the library. Cards are filed in the card catalog for each journal title, indicating which volumes are available and where they are located. Most libraries provide a separate serials catalog or metal flip index for periodicals. Libraries also subscribe to numerous newspapers: local, regional, national, and foreign. Older volumes are generally bound or placed on microfilm, for which the library provides reading facilities. Recent issues are often shelved with the current journals and serials.

Many larger libraries have documents divisions, which house government publications, and microcopy rooms, in which the library's microcopy collection of books, pamphlets, newspapers, magazines, documents, etc., is stored. Separate catalogs are often maintained in these departments.

Specialized research institutes or bureaus (such as Harvard University's Program for Technology and Society) often maintain collections of pamphlets, reports, working papers, duplicated document series, newspaper clippings, and similar materials.

INTERLIBRARY LOAN

Most university, college, and public libraries are linked into a network or system which allows them to share the resources of other local, regional, or more distant libraries. There is generally a special department in the library which can help you determine whether another library has a book or other reference you have been unable to find at your own library and can then order it for you from interlibrary loan. This can be very helpful if you only have access to a small, less well-endowed library.

CLASSIFICATION

Systematic classification of the library's books and materials by content and form allows for ease and convenience in locating and storing printed information. Materials are organized into classes by subject in order that the user may find books on related topics in the same location. Classification schemes divide knowledge into major categories uniting related facts in a logical arrangement proceeding from the general to the particular. Symbols (numerals, letters, or a combination of both) are assigned to each class and subdivision so that all books dealing with a particular subject can be identified and shelved together. These location symbols are the "call numbers," composed of the classification numbers and/or letters and the book number which is assigned to identify a specific book within a particular category. The call number appears on the binding of the book and on each index card for that book in the card catalog. One of two general schemes is used in nearly every library in the United States: the Dewey Decimal System, based on Arabic numerals, or the Library of Congress System, which uses letters. Both systems break down topics in a hierarchical manner proceeding from general to specific. The reference section of your library should have a set of Library of Congress Classification Schedules, which contain detailed listings for each class of materials (e.g., "H," social sciences). Abbreviated outlines may also be available in the library. These are also offered for sale by the card division, Library of Congress, Building 159, Navy Yard Annex, Washington, D.C. 20541.

The Dewey Decimal System divides knowledge into ten broad categories, numbered from 0 to 9; the material in each broad category is organized into classes and subclasses. Thus "the social sciences" (309-399) is comprised of ten classes:

300-309   The social sciences: general (especially sociology)
310-319   Statistics and demography
320-329   Political science
330-339   Economics
340-349   Law
350-359   Public administration
360-369   Welfare and association
370-379   Education
380-389   Commerce
390-399   Customs and folklore

These categories are further subdivided by the use of decimals:

301   Sociology
301.7   Kinds of societies
301.72   Nonliterate

A more complete breakdown of the classification scheme as it is applied to sociology and to related subjects may be found in the Appendix.

The Library of Congress Classification System uses a combination of letters and numbers which are organized around twenty-one main classes. Classes relevant to sociology are the following:

C   History: auxiliary science
D   History: general and old world
E-F   History: America and old world
G   Geography, anthropology, folklore, etc.
H   Social sciences (including sociology, economics)
J   Political science
K   Law
L   Education

Addition of a second letter denotes subdivisions within each class:

HM   Sociology. General works. Theory
HQ-HT   Social groups
HT   Communities, classes, races

Further subdivisions are made by adding combinations of numbers. Outlines of the relevant portions of the Library of Congress classification scheme can be found in the Appendix. Here is an example of how to use the information in the Appendix. If you were going to write a paper on the composition and stratification of the female labor force you would begin by checking the classification scheme for sociology. Relevant books might be classified in the following categories: Library of Congress—HQ 1381 "Woman and economics" and Dewey Decimal—DD-331.4. Useful subdivisions in related areas might be L of C—HD 6050-6220 "Economics: Women in Industry"; "Labor Economics: Women Workers"; DD-331.133 "Discrimination in employment."

Ideally, the classification system should be organized in such a way that material on any particular subject will be found in only one location in the library. However, due to the interrelatedness of knowledge and the interdisciplinary nature of many areas of study, classification schemes can never be totally successful. In reality, there is no assurance that all materials relevant to a sociological topic will be found exclusively in the class devoted to sociology in either the Dewey Decimal System or the Library of Congress System. Thus, material dealing with feminism may be found in as many as six different places in the library. Understanding the card catalog, cross-references, and subject headings will assist you in overcoming this problem and carrying out a more thorough search of the literature.

THE CARD CATALOG

The card catalog is an alphabetical, descriptive index to the books in the library; it generally takes the form of 3 × 5 cards shelved in alphabetically stacked trays or drawers. If a university has several libraries it will most likely have a general catalog (also called a dictionary, main, or public catalog) in the main library branches, noting in which branch or department a particular book may be found. In addition, the individual branch contains a card catalog which lists the material it possesses.

Each item in the library is represented in the catalog by three separate listings: author, title, and subject. Each card contains reference information about the item, along with the call number representing its location in the stacks. The information includes: author, title, date and place of publication, name of publisher, paging, notes of interest about the book, subject headings, and other technical notes.

The card catalog may be used to provide the student with three kinds of information: (1) reference to the existence and precise location of a particular book in the library (located by author or title); (2) information as to the availability of material on a particular topic (located by subject headings); and (3) access to standard descriptive information about a particular book (as listed by author, title, or subject).

Alphabetical listing follows the word-by-word rule, rather than the more common letter-by-letter arrangement found in dictionaries. This means that the spaces between the words of a phrase or term are acknowledged (power elite) rather than ignored (powerelite); the words in a phrase are considered separately. Thus, all titles beginning with the word "social" are filed before titles beginning with the word "socialism"; "social class," "social structure," and "social system" appear in the catalog before "socialism." Compare a list of words from the catalog and a dictionary to gain a better understanding of this important difference.

The rules cited above will assist you in using the card catalog. However, familiarity with your particular library's practices and peculiarities will ensure the greatest efficiency and comprehensiveness to your research efforts. Locating a reference to a specific publication is a straightforward procedure if one knows either the author or the title and is aware of the above-mentioned cataloging conventions. Authors may be individuals, organizations, research institutes, government agencies, and the like. In the case of private or public organizations that are representatives of larger organizations, the name of the responsible authoring agency follows that of its parent body. Thus a report issued by The Center for the Study of Law and Society is listed under California (State) University, Berkeley, Center for the Study of Law and Society. Similarly, documents issued by governmental agencies are cataloged under the name of the subsuming governmental structure, whether national, state, or local: U.S.—Bureau of the Census; California (State)—Coordinating Council on Urban Policy; San Francisco (City)—Board of Education. In the case of joint authorship, the main author card is filed under the name of the first author mentioned on the title page of the book; supplementary cards are filed separately in the catalog for each additional author.

Subject headings serve as guides to library material as it is organized by content. The student may use the subject catalog to survey the material available in the library on a particular topic. Subject headings are commonly subdivided according to form, subject, geographical, and chronological divisions.

Examples of *form*-denoting subject headings are:
Sociology—bibliography
Sociology—abstracts
Sociology—addresses, essays, lectures
Subject labels take a variety of forms besides single word entries, such as descriptive headings, phrases, compound, and composite headings. Examples of this type of subject heading are:
educational sociology (or sociology and/or education; sociology-educational)
social theory and social practice
sociology as a profession
sociology and anthropology of mental illness
automation—social aspects
Examples of *chronological* subject headings are:
Social history—20th century
Social conditions—U.S., 1918-1945
Social history—1600-1750
Examples of *geographical* subject headings are:
Revolution—China (Peoples' Republic of)
Social stratification—Peru
or, in the case of more general topics
U.S.—social conditions (location given first)

Arrangement of chronological subdivisions is in chronological sequence; the other forms are filed alphabetically. Geographical subdivisions may be interfiled with the subject and form subdivided cards, or they may precede them.

Initially, you may be confused by the form and arrangement of subject headings. The techniques of organization can be complicated and vary somewhat from library to library. It is best to carefully examine the catalog in your library in order to understand the particular principles of arrangement which are employed. In addition, you should consult any material or handbook which your library issues regarding its cataloging system. The reference librarian is a good resource person from whom to solicit aid and information.

For practical reasons, the catalog is limited in its ability to represent available material. Only a few cards can be filed for each book; classification of books can reflect only main themes rather than a thorough delineation of their content. It is important to remember that although books are classified according to their principal subjects, they may treat subsidiary concerns. In addition, the necessity of maintaining uniformity of subject headings limits the precision with which the contents of a book can be indicated. These difficulties often lead students searching for material by subject matter to hold two mistaken assumptions: first, that the library does not contain material on a topic because the subject heading is not listed; second, that they have located all of the books relating to a subject because they have checked all of the cards under a particular heading. Initiative, ingenuity, and flexibility are called for in conducting a comprehensive survey of the library's holdings in a specific area. The following subject-heading and cross-referencing aids may illuminate and facilitate your search:

1. "The Library of Congress Subject Headings" mentioned earlier (p. 68) is a useful guide to subject and "see also" headings; this volume can direct you to the various headings which may be appropriate to a given subject.

2. Many libraries provide shelf lists of subject classifications. These are listings of books in the classified order in which they stand on the library's shelves. Each portion forms a subject bibliography. The entries in the shelf list may be less complex and are often less accurate than those in the library's catalogs. However, shelf lists provide a useful supplement to the card catalogs. Catalogs of other library collections are often photocopied and bound. Material from libraries located within a reasonable distance from your university may be available through an interlibrary loan service. Check with a librarian for further information about your library's practices regarding interlibrary loans.

3. "See also" cards sometimes appear at the end of a group of cards indexed under a given subject heading. These list other subject headings under which the related material may be found: "Power (social sciences)"; see also "Law and Politics"; see also "Social Status"; see also "Elites (social sciences)." Another type of cross reference indicates the indexing term used in the catalog to refer to a specific topic, e.g., "Sociology of Knowledge," see "Knowledge, Sociology of."

4. Library "tracings" appear at the bottom of the catalog card. Listings preceded by Roman numerals represent other ways in which the book is listed (title, joint author, etc.). Arabic numerals are used to indicate the additional subject headings under which the book is indexed. These provide useful cross-referencing information and can direct you to relevant material indexed under related headings.

5. Two approaches are useful (independently and combined) when you are searching the card catalog by subject headings for material on a particular topic:

A. Break down the topic into related subject areas. For example, the topic "The alienating effects of bureaucracy on university students" suggests several related subject headings—"alienation," "bureaucracy," "the university," "students (college)."

B. Begin with specific headings and proceed toward more general ones until you have uncovered sufficient leads and sources. This procedure can be applied to the topic "Socialization in the middle-class family." First, look up the most specific subject heading—"socialization—the family—middle class." This might not produce any results but it is worth checking for the one or two sources which might be most pertinent. A more inclusive and fruitful category would be "socialization—family." This might be sufficient for your purposes. However, if you require further material you would check the headings "socialization" and "family" (first "family—middle-class" and then "family").

REPRODUCTION SERVICES

It is becoming increasingly common for libraries to provide reproduction services or coin-operated electrostatic copying machines for student use. Journal articles or other materials which may be especially relevant to your research topic are made readily accessible through electrostatic reproduction (e.g., xeroxing); this is quite useful if the periodical or source cannot be checked out and is restricted to library use. Also, it is generally more accurate and ultimately less expensive to make an electrostatic copy of a table of data rather than to copy the table by hand.

PARTS OF THE BOOK

Once you have located a potentially relevant book you will need to know how to approach it in an effective way. Aside from being able to evaluate the specific content of a book, an understanding of the general principles of organization (the conventional format) will make it easier for you to find what you want.

Preface

The preface generally consists of a brief statement of the author's purpose or justification for engaging in work on the problems he or she deals with in the book. The particular usefulness of the material covered, or the approach taken, may be pointed out in the preface. Either in the preface or the "acknowledgments," the author credits those who may have assisted her (him) and cites her (his) intellectual debts. These citations are important clues indicating in which sociological tradition the author might locate herself (himself).

Table of Contents

If this is especially detailed, it serves as a summary or analysis of the book. The importance of the table of contents stems from the information it conveys regarding the structure of the book, the connections of the parts of the book, and often the relationships among the ideas expressed in the body of the work.

Introduction

The introduction differs from the preface in that it deals specifically with the content of the book. Ideally a concise, cogent statement of the principal ideas, analytical framework, and direction of the book, the introduction functions as an interpretive guide and preparation for the material covered in the text.

Text

The main part of the book.

Notes

Explanatory material, information which is of interest in a some-what tangential way to the main thrust of the book, is included in the footnotes which accompany the text. Footnotes appear either at the bottom of each page, the end of a chapter, or the end of the book. Bibliographic references and citations are also accounted for in the footnotes.

Appendix

The appendix covers supplementary or additional material which cannot be easily incorporated in the text, e.g., tables, notes, bibliographies, graphs, etc. In sociological studies you often find methodological appendices which include interview schedules, explanation of methods used to code data, etc.

Bibliographies

A bibliography is a list of references and sources (books, journal articles, reports, etc.). A subject bibliography lists references which are pertinent to a specified area of interest. An author bibliography is a compilation of the works of a particular author. Bibliographies appear in a variety of contexts: at the end of a chapter; at the end of a book; following an article in a journal, encyclopedia, or other reference book. Bibliographies indicate where the author uncovered the information he has written about; bibliographic references appear in the text by number, name, or by footnote, as well as in the comprehensive listing located at the end of a chapter or book. Sometimes extensive bibliographies on a topic are collected and published in book form. Many such reference lists provide annotation, descriptive notes which assist the researcher in selecting the most valuable works. Access to good bibliographies for subjects that interest you will save you the time involved in working up your own reference list one source at a time from the card catalog or periodical indexes. Good sources of already compiled bibliographies include books, handbooks, journal articles, and dissertations. The catalog card of a relevant book will indicate if a bibliography is included, i.e., "Bibliographic footnotes," "Bibliography: p. 250-260," "Includes bibliography," etc. If a book seems especially pertinent to your topic and contains a bibliography, you will probably have uncovered a number of important reference sources. The publication date of the book will indicate the potential currency of the bibliographic material. Keep in mind that publication of a book takes approximately one year; articles appearing during that year will not be incorporated in the bibliography. Chapter 6 details other sources for bibliographies and lists a number of those available in various fields of interest. (See page 144 for information on bibliographic indexes.)

Glossary

This section lists and explains all technical terms or foreign words not explained in the body of the book.

Index

Usually found at the very end of the book, the index is an alphabetical list of subjects or names mentioned in the work. The index can be used to find page references for specific topics covered in the book. The most common type of index is the general index, which is a compilation of subjects, names, titles, and so on. In some books these various types of entries are listed in separate indexes. In the case of sets of books that group information under large subjects, a general index is the only guide to the subdivisions and less comprehensive subject headings. (See the *International Encyclopedia of the Social Sciences* for such an example.)

Editions and Reprints

All copies of a book printed at the same time constitute one edition. Additional copies printed at a later time are called reprints. However, if any changes are made in the book (bringing it up to date or adding material), it is called a new or revised edition, and is given a new copyright. This commonly occurs in the social sciences, especially in the case of textbooks. It is important to use the latest edition of a book unless you are specifically referring to an older edition that contains classic material.

Chapter
Four

---

periodical literature

Knowing what others have written on a particular issue is often a stimulus for formulating your own hypothesis for research. Periodical literature is an excellent source of familiarity with current sociological information and opinion. Journal articles often supply good bibliographies and background material for getting into a subject more extensively. In this chapter we hope to give you an idea of the variety and scope of the most important and/or the most interesting journals in several categories: the professional and official journals; foreign or international English language publications; journals dealing with a specific area of interest; generalized or interdisciplinary periodicals; social policy- and social problem-oriented journals; student-edited journals; radical or Marxist publications; and those periodicals of other disciplines or of general social interest which are relevant to the well-rounded student of sociology.

For ease in utilizing journals, many of the periodicals provide brief abstracts summarizing the content of the articles; these enable readers to skim through a large number of articles for the ones most pertinent to their interest. The various indexing and abstracting services described in Chapter 6 are indispensable tools for gaining access to relevant articles from among the large volume of selections. Additionally, the large number of book reviews found in many of the journals may be productively scanned for information concerning the current books available on your topic.

THE PROFESSIONAL AND OFFICIAL JOURNALS (AMERICAN)

The American Sociological Association publishes six major professional journals.

American Sociological Review

This is the prestigious bimonthly journal of the ASA. Its orientation is generally empirical and statistical, and it is a forum for new trends in sociological theory and research. The sociology of knowledge, religion, deviance, stratification, social interaction, and sociological methodology and theory are all represented in this journal. Typical articles are: "Religion and Occupational Achievement," "Ideal Types and Idealization Strategy," "Sociometric Location and Innovativeness," "Interorganizational Networks in Urban Society," "Premarital Sex as Deviant Behavior," "Marxist Dialectic and Pragmatism: Power as Knowledge." The *ASR*'s articles are listed in the *Social Science and Humanities Index, Public Affairs Information Service* (PAIS), *Psychological Abstracts, Sociological Abstracts, Ayers' Guide, University Microfilms,* and *Abstracts for Social Workers.* A cumulative index of articles is published every three years. A new section will convey research notes and reports.

American Sociologist

The official reports and news of the ASA are included in this quarterly professional magazine. Letters, employment information, and a calendar of annual meetings are regular features. In addition, several interesting articles about the discipline, teaching, and methodological problems are included, such as: "Sociology Today," "Lacunae, Emphases, and Surfeits," "Notes on a Forgotten Black Sociologist: W. E. B. DuBois," "Status of Women in Graduate Departments of Sociology, 1968-69," "Changing Styles of Presentation of Sociological Research," "Theorizing and Statistics," "Ideological Currents in American Stratification Literature," "Social Origins of American Sociologists," and "The Role of the Sociologist on Public Issues." This is a good source for information dealing with the sociology of sociology and for learning how professional sociologists regard the status, progress, and pitfalls of their field.

Contemporary Sociology

The ASA is now publishing book reviews in a separate journal appearing bimonthly. Reviews cover recent publications in the following areas: social theory, methods and statistics, social psychology, change and development, complex organizations, economy and society, politics, age and sex roles, race and ethnic relations, deviance and crime, population, urban and rural communities, occupations and professions, marriage and the family, education, knowledge and culture, stratification and mobility, medical sociology, and mass communications. The reviews, written by sociologists specializing in these areas, provide an excellent source of information on current trends in the discipline. Each issue features a number of symposia, survey essays and review essays, in addition to the bulk of shorter book reviews. The symposia provide a forum for contrasting evaluations of significant and controversial new books. The survey and review essays offer in-depth comments on either one or a number of books in a particular area. All articles, reviews, and letters are indexed annually in the November issue. A cumulative index for volumes 1-3 can be found in the November 1974 issue. Contents of this journal are indexed in the *Book Review Index.*

Journal of Health and Social Behavior

This journal, which appears quarterly, presents a sociological approach to the delineation and analysis of problems bearing on physical and mental health. Recently, articles have appeared dealing with the following topics: "Social Status and Stress," "Bureaucracy and Autonomy," "Social Worker Professionalism," "Marijuana and

Reality," "The Ideology of Physicians," "Attitudes on Mental Illness," "Low-Income Problem Patients," and "Spouseless Motherhood." Occasionally special issues are devoted to a particular problem in medical sociology, such as recreational drug use (June 1968) or patients and illness (December 1968).

Social Psychology Quarterly
(formerly Sociometry)

The editorial policy of this quarterly "journal of research in social psychology" is to select articles dealing with the development of empirical and theoretical concepts in the study of processes and products of social interaction. The focus of this journal, which covers the broad range of methodological interests and problems in social psychology, has become increasingly experimental. The articles are generally highly technical, mathematical, and limited in scope to the testing of theoretical propositions. Most of the articles contain reviews of past research on the problem being studied. Good bibliographies, sometimes very extensive, accompany the selections. Principal concerns are such concepts as social influence, innovation, pressure, conformity, motivation, game theory, roles, personality, the self, decision-making, labeling, small groups, the experimental situation, and socialization. The symbolic interactionist approach is represented occasionally in the content of this journal.

Sociology of Education
(formerly Journal of Educational Sociology)

This is a quarterly journal which expresses the following editorial policy: "Our primary responsibility is to publish papers that advance sociological knowledge about education. The journal also serves as a significant medium for the application of this knowledge to major issues of education policy and practice." This journal serves as a forum both for educators and social scientists devoted to international studies of education. In its articles, the theoretical perspectives of anthropology, economics, history, political science, psychology, and sociology are utilized to analyze educational institutions. Research notes are also featured. The journal is indexed in *Educational Index, Public Affairs Information Service* (PAIS), *Sociological Abstracts,* and *Psychological Abstracts.*

Other professional journals in the broad area of sociology include:

American Behavioral Scientist

Published every other month by Sage Publications, this journal has an interdisciplinary editorial advisory board composed of faculty members from American and foreign universities. An excellent feature of this periodical is "New Studies," a guide to recent publications in the social and behavioral sciences. Items for "New Studies" are selected and annotated by the staff of *ABS* in a periodic search of 360 journals and reviews, including nearly 100 publications outside the United States; books and pamphlets are selected from the total output of American commercial, governmental, and nonprofit publications, as well as from leading English and Continental publishing houses. The content of past issues has been devoted to topics such as the coming American welfare state, and law and social change. Editors rotate so that each issue is edited by a different scholar. The journal is indexed in *Public Affairs Information Service* (PAIS), *Mental Health Book Review,* and *Psychological Abstracts.*

American Journal of Sociology

This bimonthly publication and the *American Sociological Review* are the two most influential and prestigious journals in the field. The *AJS* is published by the University of Chicago Press, and the editorial board is composed of members of the department of sociology at the University of Chicago. The articles featured in the past often were concerned with fieldwork and case studies, and they were not as quantitatively oriented as those in the *ASR,* which was a reflection of the interests of the "Chicago school." Recently, however, the differences between the two journals have diminished, and the following selection of articles reflects the current scope of the publication: "Marital Status and Suicide in the U.S.A.: Test of Status Integration Theory," "Index of Riot Security and Some Correlates," "Mobility and Associational Membership," "Suburban-Urban Religious Membership and Participation," "Political Attitudes of Youth," "Sociolinguistic Census," "Sleep Deprivation and Psychotic Disorganization," "Education Aspirations and Marriage," "Stratification in Czechoslovakia," and "Encountering the Male Establishment: Sex Status Limits on Women's Careers in the Professions." A large selection of book reviews and a section of commentary and debate are included in the journal. Articles are indexed in the *Social Science and Humanities Index* and in *Sociological Abstracts;* book reviews are indexed in the *Book Review Index.*

Pacific Sociological Review

This quarterly publication is the official journal of the Pacific Sociological Association. It is abstracted in *Sociological Abstracts* and indexed in the *International Bibliography of Sociology.* Articles focusing on both theoretical and empirical interests are included, as well as methodological notes and papers about the discipline (the sociology of sociology). Attitude studies, survey research, experimentation reports, and case studies are included, with good bibliographies accompanying the articles. Some representative titles are: "Stability of Power Structures in Small Groups," "Women's Attitudes Toward Family Life and U.S. Population Growth," "Self-Images, Anxiety, and Neurosis," "Use of Alcohol Among High-School Students in an Abstinence Setting," "Marx and Sociology," and "Some Behavioral Aspects of Systems Analysis."

Social Forces

Subtitled "An International Journal of Social Research," this journal is edited and published at the University of North Carolina at Chapel Hill. Its format includes articles (with abstracts), book reviews, and research notes. The journal is indexed in a variety of sources, including *Psychological Abstracts, Public Affairs Information Service* (PAIS), and *Social Science and Humanities Index.* The articles deal with a wide variety of sociological interests. Empirical papers seem to predominate, although not to the exclusion of theory or methodology. The following titles are representative of the content of this journal: "The Declining Status of Women," "Apathy, Truancy, and Delinquency," "Correlation and Original Data," "Organizational Responses to Occupational Injury and Disease," "Governmental Legitimacy and Political Stability," and "Community as a Social Field." Deviance, political sociology, stratification, occupational sociology, behavioral and systems research, demography, and the social interactionist perspective are all represented in the content of the journal. The December 1978 issue featured articles on the theme "Social Change in Socialist Societies."

Social Research

The Graduate Faculty of Political and Social Science of the New School for Social Research publishes this international quarterly. The editorial policy seeks an interdisciplinary treatment of issues in the social sciences, and broadness characterizes the contributions. Special issues focus on selected problems which are examined by social scientists from different fields. General problem-oriented, polemical, or theoretical articles are included, as well as a few selections dealing with methodological concerns. Representative titles are: "Rationality and Irrationality in a Pluralistic Society," "Social Reality and Social Change," "Two Models of the Pattern Variables Paradigm," "Locke's Doctrine of Property," and "Psychology: A Human Science." The journal also aims to maintain the humanistic tradition by integrating the approaches of philosophy and history with that of the social sciences.

Social Science Quarterly
(formerly Southwestern Social Science Quarterly)

This journal is published jointly by the Southwestern Social Science Association and the University of Texas at Austin. It contains articles and research notes, an annual index, forum and book review sections, and news, notes, and reports of the Association. Contributions are drawn from the fields of history, sociology, political science, economics, and accounting, with an interdisciplinary approach that also extends itself to geography, business law and business communication, and management science. Symposia issues have been devoted to "Social Science and Social Policy," "Planned Social Intervention," "Oligopoly," "Current Research on Migration and Employment in the South," "Youth and Society," and "Black America." Treatment is variously historical, theoretical, experimental, or survey research. Traditional areas of strength have been race and ethnicity, law and law enforcement, and American politics. Cross-cultural material is also included.

Sociological Focus

This is a general sociological journal published quarterly by the North Central Sociological Association, which is affiliated with the American Sociological Association. The editors and publishers are located at the University of Akron in Ohio. Policy studies, social problems, sex roles, education and occupation, and social psychology are represented in the contents.

Sociological Inquiry

This is the semiannual journal of the National Sociology Honor Society (united chapters of Alpha Kappa Delta). Topics represented are interesting and varied: radical perspectives in sociology, Parsonsian theory, stratification, analysis of nonviolence in theory and fact, studies in adult socialization, and exploration in sociolinguistics. Individual articles treat these themes from empirical and theoretical perspectives, and each article is preceded by a brief abstract. Recent book length double issues focused on "The Sociology of Science," (vol. 48, no. 3-4, 1978) and "Religious Change and Continuity," (vol. 49, no. 2-3, 1979).

Sociological Quarterly
(formerly Midwest Sociologist)

This is the official publication of the Midwest Sociological Society. The selection of articles represents a broad spectrum of interests in the field, with a fair balance between theoretical and empirical material. The symbolic interactionist approach also has been given more representation here than in other journals. Recent articles have been: "Political Systems and the Role of the Military"; "Social Action, Behavior, and *Verstehen*"; "Urban Life and Differential Fertility"; "The Value of Value Judgments in Sociology"; "Social Values and Preschool-Aged Children"; and "Mannheim, Cooley, and Mead: Toward a Theory of Mentality." The journal is indexed in the *Social Science and Humanities Index* and in the *Book Review Index*.

Sociological Symposium

Four times per year this multiperspective journal of behavioral science publishes an issue with articles on a designated theme. Topics have included deviant occupations, stages of the life cycle, youth and politics, and violence. The journal is published and edited at the Department of Sociology of the Virginia Polytechnic Institute and State University.

Sociology and Social Research

This international journal is published quarterly at the University of Southern California. The general approach is interdisciplinary, and the editorial content is broad in scope. Contributions are generally drawn from social scientists, but some articles by business management specialists are included. Special sections of the journal are devoted to book reviews and notes on comments. Titles of articles are indexed in the *International Index to Periodicals* and abstracted in *Sociological Abstracts* and *Psychological Abstracts.*

FOREIGN AND INTERNATIONAL JOURNALS

The following journals are either published outside the United States or contain contributions mainly from foreign scholars. Familiarity with these works will prevent you from becoming a provincial American social scientist who knows nothing of work done outside this country, unfortunately an all too familiar type. Furthermore, articles critical of American sociology, often by American sociologists, occasionally appear in these forums.

Acta Sociologica
(Scandinavian Review of Sociology)

This quarterly journal is the official publication of the Scandinavian Sociological Association. A typical selection of articles is "Search for Predictors of Residential Mobility," "Community Context and Politicization of Individuals," "Performance Expectations and Behavior in Small Groups," "A Critique of the Pluralist Model," "Evolutionary, Structural, and Institutional Characteristics of Societies." An issue published in 1973 focused on the sociology of education in cross-cultural settings.

British Journal of Sociology

This journal is published quarterly for the London School of Economics and Political Science. The articles cover the wide spectrum of empirical, theoretical, and methodological interests in the field.

The content is generally more historical and theoretical than that found in the *American Sociological Review*. A selection of typical titles will demonstrate the nature and variety of concerns represented: "The Working Class Vote in Chile," "Marxism as a General Sociological Orientation," "Censorship, Social Control, and Socialization," "Divination and Face Work," and "What is Structuralism?" In addition, some articles of anthropological interest are included. Contributions are drawn from international sources, and polemical pieces by American sociologists appear occasionally. A special issue in December 1978, "Contemporary Britain: Aspects and Approaches," focused on current crises in British economy, politics, and society. This journal prepares an annual index, which includes book reviews, and a ten-year cumulative index.

Canadian Review of Sociology and Anthropology

This is a quarterly publication of the Canadian Sociological and Anthropological Association. The combined treatment of the two disciplines adds special interest to the journal. Written in French and English, the review is indexed in the *Canadian Periodical Index*. Its issues include case studies, methodological articles, research notes, and comments, as well as topics of theoretical interest. Empirical material and survey research seems to be favored, although there are some theoretical papers on key concepts, such as one on "Social Networks as Subjective Constructs." Special issues are occasionally devoted to single areas of study such as the sociology of education (February 1970). Useful bibliographies accompany many of the articles. Most of the material relates to Canadian society, although not exclusively so.

Coexistence

This periodical has as its subtitle "A Journal for the Comparative Study of Economics, Sociology and Politics in a Changing World." The principal focus is on social science in the context of international conflict or cooperation. It is published in England, and the editorial board is composed of social scientists from Europe. Socialism, colonialism, and welfare theories are primary interests. The nature of the journal may be gauged from the following selection of recent articles: "The Nature of Colonialism and the State of Nationalism It Produced in Africa," "Development Strategy and Welfare Economics," "Why Socialism Requires Democracy: Czechoslovakia," "Political-Economic Problems of Peaceful Coexistence," and "Marxist-Christian Dialogue."

Current Sociology/La Sociologie Contemporaine

This journal is sponsored by the Association for International Sociology of the International Committee for Social Sciences Documentation and published with the aid of UNESCO. Each issue treats a particular theme, such as "The Sociology of Mental Illness (1950-67)" or "The Sociology of Leisure (1945-65)." A long article in French discusses trends and developments in research and theory relating to the chosen theme, and a summary in English follows the French essay. The rest of the issue is devoted to a classified, annotated bibliography of the subject matter, drawing on international sources. The bibliography covers a relatively long period of time, which varies according to each theme. An author index is also featured. (See Chapter 5 for further information.)

Ethnic and Racial Studies

This is a new journal (vol. 1, no. 1, January 1978) which features five major articles in each issue on the relations between ethnic and racial groups in Western, Socialist, and Third World countries. History and social science material is included. The contributors are drawn from an international arena. The journal also publishes English translations of major articles on race and ethnicity which originally appeared in other languages.

European Journal of Sociology (Archives Européenes de Sociologie)

This journal, founded in 1960 and published twice yearly in Paris, contains articles in French, English, and German. Critical comments are also featured. This is a good source for theoretical material. Special issues have been devoted to the following themes: "Industrial Society and Representative Government"; "The Welfare State"; "In Quest of Political Participation"; "De Tocqueville, Marx, and Weber"; and "Paradoxes of Transitional Societies."

International Journal of Comparative Sociology

This quarterly is sponsored by the Department of Sociology, York University (Toronto) and is published in The Netherlands. It aims primarily at furthering pure research and encouraging inquiry into those areas of research which are in the interest of man and society. The journal describes its content as follows: "[It] presents a detailed and scholarly account of studies made in different cultures on a comparative basis with a view to reaching a common level of abstraction, and thereby showing areas where culture bias might be involved." A special issue has been recently devoted to the internationalism of the blue-collar worker. Other topics have been "The Dynamic of Stratification Systems," "Realignment of Class Attitudes in the Military and Bourgeoisie in Developing Countries," and "Ethnicity and Mobility."

International Journal of Sociology

This quarterly journal publishes translations of material from scholarly books and journals throughout the world. Guest editors bring together articles on such themes as "Marxian Theory and History," "The Southern Question in Italian Sociology," and "Changes in Polish Social Structure."

International Labour Review

The International Labour Organization publishes this monthly review in Geneva. The journal contains articles, current information, bibliographies, review essays on publications of the International Labour Organization and the United Nations, and reviews of other books dealing with labor topics. This publication is frequently cited in the field of industrial sociology, and it provides information on all aspects of industrial organization and labor on an international scale. The review is also a good source for comparative studies. The following topics are some of the many represented in this periodical: education, employment, planning, law, structure of the labor force, rights and opportunities, manpower utilization, collective labor relations, job training, rural community development, economic growth, and social justice.

International Social Science Journal

This quarterly journal, which reflects concern with social research of international significance, particularly in relation to the issues of development and world peace, is published in France by UNESCO. Specific issues of this periodical have been devoted to: "Social Science in the Third World," "Approaches to Rural Problems," "Social Research Policy and Organization," "Inequalities of Development and World Tensions," "Futurology," and "The Sociology of Science." A review of documents and books on these topics comprises a large section of this journal, and there are short descriptive annotations on publications of the United Nations agencies dealing with such topics as health, housing, social structures, social services, economics, legal and political questions, human rights, and science. This journal is indexed in *Public Affairs Information Service* (PAIS), *Psychological Abstracts,* and *Social Science and Humanities Index.* (See Chapter 5 for further information.)

International Studies in Sociology and Social Anthropology

This journal is published by Toronto's York University, and its editors rotate with each issue. The following diversity of articles represents the content of recent issues: "Sociology of the Blue-Collar Worker," "Passing of Tribal Man," "Studies in Multilingualism," "Case Studies in Social Power," "Traditional and Modern Legal Institutions in Asia and Africa," "Politics and Social Change," "Family and Marriage," "Urbanism and Urbanization," and "Kinship and Geographical Mobility."

Journal of Asian and African Studies

Published by Brill in Leiden, The Netherlands, this internationally edited quarterly specializes in Third World studies. The journal presents a scholarly account of man and society in the developing nations, and the contributions unite anthropology, sociology, history, religion, and social science in a concerted effort to stress the building up of systematic knowledge for the reconstruction of societies entering a phase of advanced technology. Some representative articles are: "U.S. and Socialism in Africa," "Ambitions and Risks of Cooperative Socialism in East Africa," "Matrilineal Descent and Marital Stability: Tanzanian Case," "The Nature and Extent of Urbanization in Zambia," "Asian Drama: Prospects for Development," and a special issue on "The Sociology of Japanese Religion."

Journal of Southern African Studies

Articles by African, British, and other scholars are published in this multidisciplinary journal edited biannually in Great Britain. Underdevelopment, research on peasants, and the history of protest are some of the issues which are treated in the Southern African context.

Race and Class

This journal was formerly published under the title *Race:* "A Journal of Race and Group Relations." The Institute for Race Relations in London remains as the publisher, joined by a new sponsor, the Transnational Institute. The new title *Race and Class:* "A Journal for Black and Third World Liberation," reflects the political shift in the focus of the journal. Representative articles include: "Multinational Banks in Chile," "Asian Women in Britain," "Class, Ideology and Literature in Northern Ireland," "The Dialectics of Class and Tribe," and "The U.S. Media and Vietnam." Publication is quarterly.

Sociological Review

The University of Keele in Staffordshire, England, publishes this interdisciplinary journal four times a year. Contributions from sociologists and political scientists associated with universities in the British Commonwealth are presented. Representative selections have dealt with the following topics: "Sociology and the Study of Psychiatric Disorder," "What's Wrong with the New Criminology?" "Careers, Work, and Leisure Among the New Professionals," and "Functionalism and Explanation in the Social Sciences." This journal is indexed in the *British Humanities Index, Psychological Abstracts,* and the *Social Science and Humanities Index.*

Sociology

This journal of the British Sociological Association is an influential, scholarly publication of sociologists and political scientists from British universities. Articles, research notes, and a large section of book reviews deal with theoretical and methodological concerns. Class, social stratification, occupations and organizations, and educational socialization receive a great deal of attention. Representative titles of articles are: "Status Consistency, Relative Deprivation, and Attitudes to Immigrants," "Social Change and Opportunity in Technical Workers' Education," "Measurement, Structure, and Social Theory," and "Social Class Differences in the Relevance of Language to Socialization."

Translation Journals

The International Arts and Sciences Press puts out a series of translation journals from Soviet, Eastern European, Asian, and other international sources. The articles are selected to reflect developments in sociological research from these areas which may be of interest to English-speaking sociologists.

SPECIALIZED JOURNALS

Administrative Science Quarterly

"Dedicated to advancing the understanding of administration through empirical investigation and theoretical analysis," this journal is a good source for material on institutional structure and functionings of formal organizations. Prominent sociologists, as well as scholars from other disciplines, contribute articles.

American Journal of Economics and Sociology

This journal is published quarterly "in the interest of constructive synthesis in the social sciences." It is indexed in the *Social Science and Humanities Index* and the *Public Affairs Information Service* (PAIS), the *Social Science Reporter*, and the *Book Review Index*. A typical issue might include articles on the following topics: land reform in developing countries, community power and public welfare, disjunction of political science and political philosophy, conduct of public corporations.

Annals of the American Academy of Political and Social Science
(found in most libraries under American Academy of Political and Social Science—Annals)

Published bimonthly in Philadelphia, this journal covers topics in all fields of the social sciences, with international affairs, government, and socioeconomics predominating. Each issue since 1902 has been a symposium devoted to a specific theme, containing ten or twelve articles, each by an authority in the field, on various aspects of the topic. Examples of topics covered are "Society and Its Physical Environment"; "Protagonists, Power and the Third World"; "Evaluating the War on Poverty"; "The Sixties: Radical Change in American Religion." Since 1961 each issue has also carried an article or two summarizing developments within one of the social science areas. These surveys are useful for the nontechnical and professional manner in which they are presented and for their extensive bibliographies. The extensive book department surveys four to five hundred new titles a year in all fields of the political and social sciences, emphasizing American writing and affairs. There is an index in each issue, and the journal itself is indexed in *Readers' Guide to Periodical Literature* and *Public Affairs Information Service* (PAIS).

The Black Scholar
(A Journal of Black Studies and Research)

This important monthly publication, subtitled "A Journal of Black Studies and Research," features the work of black writers on topics relevant to the black situation. Typically, each issue carries a theme or combination of themes. Examples are Black Studies, The Psychology of Blackness, Black Culture, Black Revolution, Black Labor, The Black Soldier, and The Black Woman. Themes of Pan-Africanism also are explored.

Economic Development and Cultural Change

The editorial board of this journal includes scholars in the fields of sociology, economics, geography, social relations, and anthropology. This quarterly publication is edited at the Research Center for Economic Development and Cultural Change of the University of Chicago. The primary emphasis is economics, with political, social, and cultural implications of economic growth being considered, especially as related to the developing nations. The following titles represent typical selections: "The Plantation Economy and Industrial Development in Latin America," "Measurements of Urbanization," "Theory of Peasant Economy," "High Growth, Unemployment and Planning in Venezuela," and "Foreign Investment and Export Dependency."

Ethnicity

The editors of this "interdisciplinary journal of the study of ethnic relations" are connected with the Center for the Study of American Pluralism of the National Opinion Research Center in Chicago, Illinois. In this quarterly journal they promote an interest in ethnic diversity and integration around the world. Both theoretical and empirical articles are included in the format.

Human Organization

This "scientific quarterly for the study of developmental change" is published by the Society for Applied Anthropology, whose primary objective is "scientific investigation of the principles controlling the relations of human beings to one another . . . and the wide application of these principles to practical problems." Past special issues have been symposia on the following themes: "Poverty and Social Disorder," "Dimensions in Cultural Change in the Middle East," "American Indians and Their Economic Development," "Social Science in Action in Sub-Saharan Africa," "Mental Health and Preventative Medicine." The journal is indexed in *Current Contents*.

Industrial and Labor Relations Review

The New York State School of Industrial and Labor Relations at Cornell University publishes this journal.

Industrial Relations

This is a "journal of economy and society," published by the Institute of Industrial Relations at the University of California, Berkeley.

Jewish Journal of Sociology

Published twice a year for the World Jewish Congress, this journal addresses itself to sociological research and theory concerning the Jewish people. Typical of the content are recent articles on "Factors in Jewish Identity, Mixed Marriage in an Israeli Town," "The New Left and Anti-Zionism," and "The Political Struggle Within the Elite of Poland."

Journal of Applied Behavioral Science

This quarterly is published by the National Institute for Applied Behavioral Science (associated with the National Educational Association). The journal "seeks to improve communication between research workers in the social sciences and leaders in groups, organizations, and communities. It focuses on the processes by which individuals and institutions are changed. The objective of the journal is to improve research done in the behavioral sciences and to facilitate its application by influential practitioners." Organizational research and experimental methods are prevalent in its articles, which include the following topics: "Analysis of Encounter Group Behavior Changes," "Head Start Parents in Participant Groups," "Learning Theory and Social Systems Perspective," and "Initiating Planned Change in Health Care Systems."

Journal of Homosexuality

This quarterly journal, dealing with a topic that has been underresearched and misunderstood in the past, started in 1974 to correct that state of affairs. It presents empirical research on lesbianism, male homosexuality, and gender identity from the behavioral sciences, including sociology, medicine, and law, as well as editorials and book reviews.

Journal of Marriage and the Family
(formerly Marriage and Family Living)

The National Council on Family Relations also sponsors this quarterly journal. Special issues have been devoted to areas such as cross-cultural family research, family planning and fertility control, adolescence, government programs, and the family. In general, articles deal with such topics as family role structure, marital satisfaction or dissatisfaction, premarital sex, family planning, and theory of the family. Abstracts precede each article. Statistical and empirical studies are prevalent, although some theoretical articles are included; notes on methodology appear frequently. A section of international articles is part of the regular content of this journal, as are book reviews.

The Journal of Mathematical Sociology

The concern of this journal is to "present a selection of advanced work on a variety of topics characteristic of contemporary social network research." Twice a year the journal appears with articles on the application of math and statistics to significant sociological problems. The logic of measurement, math models, and computer methodology are covered by this journal.

Journal of Southern African Affairs

With the aid of an international editorial board this journal is published quarterly by the Southern Africa Research Association and the Afro-American Studies Department of the University of Maryland, College Park. The scope of the journal is interdisciplinary with research and writing on the economics, politics, history, law, international affairs, sociology, anthropology, geography, technology, and cultures of Southern Africa. The objective of the journal is to present an Afro-centric approach to the study of this region. Recent issues (1978) featured guides and bibliographies to contemporary resources and reference materials on Southern Africa.

Law and Society Review

The Law and Society Association in Denver, Colorado, publishes this quarterly review. It serves as a source of information on the relation of legal issues to social life and organization.

The New Scholar

This journal is a multidisciplinary forum for research on the Americas. "New Directions in Chicano Research" was the special theme of the 1977, vol. 6 issue. Other topics have included native American cultures, contemporary Mexican culture and politics, and Brazilian culture and history. Publication is biannual from the University of California, San Diego (La Jolla).

Public Opinion Quarterly

This quarterly, an organ of the American Association for Public Opinion Research, is editorially sponsored by the Advisory Committee on Communication at Columbia University. The material is selected to illuminate problems of communication and public opinion. Sociological interests are represented on the Advisory Committee on Communication by Robert Merton and Paul Lazarsfeld. Book notes, book reviews, and a report on recent polls are regular features. A section entitled "Current Research" is reserved for brief reports of research in progress and discussions of unsolved problems. Methodological studies and public opinion data are not extensively analyzed or interpreted. This journal is a source for material relating to the media, census data, the press, elections, ideology, public opinion and public policy, and other topics in the field of political sociology. Most of the content is empirical in nature, in the form of survey research and polling of opinions and attitudes (e.g., towards war, political protest, racial questions). Some experimental studies are included, as well as articles discussing a particular issue, such as the effects of lowering the voting age or the fluoridation controversy.

Qualitative Sociology

This journal is "dedicated to the qualitative interpretation of social life." Some representative articles are "Dogcatchers: A Descriptive Study," "The Myth of Modernity in Popular African Art," "At Home on the Rails: Ethics Is a Photographic Research Project," "New Places-New Identities: Settings in the Lives of the Old" and "Class in America: Qualitative Distinctions and Quantitative Data." The journal appears three times a year and also includes book reviews and notices.

Review: "A Journal of the Fernand Braudel Center for the Study of Economies, Historical Systems and Civilizations"

This new (1977) quarterly journal is edited at S.U.N.Y., Binghamton by Immanuel Wallerstein. It is a forum for those scholars who use a world-systems approach to analyze historical development. Articles cover a vast historical and geographic range.

Rural Sociology

Published four times a year by the Rural Sociological Society and "devoted to scientific study of rural and small town life," this journal contains brief articles, book reviews, and news of the society. The selections are primarily empirical and deal with topics and interests in the field of rural sociology, such as "Structure of Support for the Environmental Movement," "Urban Poverty and Rural to Urban Migration," and "School Desegregation and the Educational Projections of Rural Black Youth." A brief descriptive abstract precedes each article.

Sex Roles: A Journal of Research

This journal is conceived as a "cross-disciplinary" forum publishing research and theoretical articles "concerned with the basic processes underlying gender-role socialization in children and its consequences." It covers such topics as the effects of sex role attitudes in work and social relationships, gender-role socialization and sexual behavior, and factors maintaining sex role attitudes. There is a book review section. Some recent articles are "Masculinity-Femininity: Current and Alternate Paradigms," "Women in the Draft Resistance Movement: A Case Study of Sex Roles and Social Movements," and "Sex Differences in the Self-Concept in Adolescence."

Social Science Research

This is "a quarterly journal of social science methodology and quantitative research" which publishes empirical articles using a variety of methodologies, from content analysis to models to multivariate analysis.

Sociological Analysis
(formerly American Catholic Sociological Review)

This journal of the sociology of religion is published quarterly. The articles, which are both empirical and theoretical, deal with such topics as the church as a social institution (particularly as it responds to social issues), the religious beliefs of specific groups (e.g., mental health professionals), and correlations between such factors as religious attitudes, church attendance, or sexual permissiveness. Sometimes extensive bibliographies, related to the specific study but broader in scope, will accompany an article. The journal is indexed in *Sociological Abstracts*.

Sociology of Work and Occupations

This quarterly "international" journal contains a book review section and an index, and provides an international forum for research and theory in the substantive areas of work and occupations. It welcomes a range of contributions on such topics as the meaning of work, studies of work and leisure, interaction within work settings, the structure and process of occupations and professions, occupational socialization, and occupational structures in relationship to other social structures. *Sociology of Work and Occupations* encourages interest in delineating the relationships between occupations and other social systems. The editors are particularly interested in cross-national studies and the development of comparative methodologies in work and occupations. A broad spectrum of theoretical and methodological approaches to the subject are represented. Some typical articles are "Judgment and Decision-Making in a Medical Specialty," and "Honor in Dirty Work: The Case of American Meat Cutters."

Sociology: Review of New Books

This bimonthly review magazine consists entirely of short, non-polemical summaries of recently published books in sociology organized by subfields such as complex organizations, socialization, and medical sociology. *Sociology* usually reviews more of the newest books than *Contemporary Sociology,* and its reviews are more descriptive than evaluative. An annual index is provided in the November-December issue.

Technology and Culture

The Society for the History of Technology publishes this quarterly journal which deals with the relation of technology to science, politics, social change, economics, and the arts and humanities. Articles relevant to sociologists have included "Household Technology and Social Status: Rising Living Standards, Status, and Residence Differences in Housework" and "Swords Into Ploughshares: Agricultural Technology and Society in Early China."

Urban Affairs Quarterly

This journal, sponsored by the City University of New York, examines urban issues from an interdisciplinary viewpoint. Contributors work in the area of sociology, anthropology, political science, public health, economics, and social welfare. A special issue in June 1974 dealing with "The City in Comparative Perspective" demonstrated the journal's intent to include articles discussing cities outside the United States. Typical articles deal with such topics as urban planning, urban violence, urban poverty, community action programs, juvenile delinquency, and urban school segregation.

Urban Life
(formerly Urban Life and Culture)

Published quarterly since 1972, this journal carries the descriptive subtitle, "A Journal of Ethnographic Research." It is indexed in *Sage Urban Studies Abstracts, Sociological Abstracts*, SSCI, PAIS, CIJE and *Current Contents*.

Urban Studies

Since 1964 this journal has appeared three times a year from Edinburgh, Scotland.

HISTORY AND SOCIETY

Comparative Studies in Society and History

This international quarterly, represented by a very well-known group of editors, provides a "forum for the presentation and discussion of new research into problems of change and stability that recur in human societies through time or in the contemporary world." It sets up a working alliance between specialists in all branches of the social sciences and humanities. Debates and review articles bring the reader in touch with current findings and issues. "Contributions are descriptive, analytical, and theoretical." A recent special issue dealt with the area of cultural innovation. Other areas covered are ideology, modernization, political development, culture contact, revolution, political emigration, bureaucracy, urbanism, peasantry, societies, and cultures. The journal is published by the Cambridge University Press and is generally a source for many interesting articles.

Journal of Family History

The National Council of Family Relations (assisted by Clark University) is the sponsor of this new quarterly journal which publishes "studies in family economy and demography." The editor, Tamara Hareven, has drawn together a group of international scholars to serve on the editorial board. Articles present research on family structure across times and cultures. A recent special issue concentrated on the family in Latin America. A cumulative author and title index for volumes 1–3 appeared in the Winter 1978 (vol. 3, no. 4) issue.

Journal of Interdisciplinary History

This journal is published four times a year by the Massachusetts Institute of Technology. Many of the articles are relevant to sociologists with cross-national and comparative historical interests. One issue was devoted to the family in history. Other typical titles are "French Sexual Attitudes" and "Suburbanization and the American Family."

Journal of Social History

This journal is a quarterly publication of the Trans-Action Periodicals Consortium based at Rutgers University. (The Consortium also publishes *Society,* discussed on p. 106.) It is a good source for background material in terms of historical examples, contexts, comparisons, and development in social configurations. Case studies of a historical and international nature are featured, as well as some theoretical articles. The following titles are representative of the scope of review articles: "New Approaches to the Study of Women in American History," "Social Origins of Radical Intellectuals in Nineteenth-Century Russia," "Listening to the Inarticulate," "Urbanization of Negroes in the United States," and "Sociological History: The Industrial Revolution and the British Working Class."

Labor History

This is the major journal of American labor history published quarterly by the Tamiment Institute. The editors solicit articles on specific unions, labor problems of ethnic and minority groups, the theory of labor history, comparative studies of foreign labor movements, and radical groups and history in relation to American labor history. Also included are book reviews and archives, library, and conference news.

Social History

Since 1974 this journal is published three times a year in Great Britain. It is a major showcase for empirical and theoretical work in social history. Articles have dealt with class struggle in eighteenth-century English society, worker culture and politics in an Italian town, and theoretical and methodological problems on the study of the crowd in history.

Social Science History

This is the official journal of the Social Science Historical Association which publishes it quarterly from the University Center for International Studies at the University of Pittsburgh. The journal encourages more rigorous theoretical history and longitudinal social science analyses. A goal is to foster familiarity with other disciplines on the part of social scientists. Articles on comparative social history, politics, and economy are published here.

SOCIAL PSYCHIATRY, PSYCHIATRIC SOCIOLOGY, AND MENTAL HEALTH

American Journal of Orthopsychiatry

This is the official publication of the American Orthopsychiatric Association, an interdisciplinary organization dedicated to "better understanding of human behavior and to the more effective treatment of behavior disorders." The journal has an interdisciplinary flavor, combining social work, psychiatry and sociology, education, medicine, and psychology. Articles dealing with mental health which stress the societal (in contrast to the biological or the individual family constellation) aspects can be found here. Some typical articles are: "Conformity, Rebellion, Learning"; "Patterns of Response Among Victims of Rape"; "Children in Poor Families"; "Research and the Black Backlash"; "Community Psychiatry and Ethics; The Congress and the Social Sciences." The journal appears five times yearly, with one issue devoted entirely to the proceedings and papers of the annual convention.

Community Mental Health Journal

Published bimonthly, this journal is "devoted to emergent approaches in mental health research, theory, and practice as they relate to community, broadly defined. Mental health is seen as more or less congruent with the general concept of social well-being." Topics of typical articles include: "A Research Project in Teaching in a Women's Prison," "The Day Care Neighbor Service: An Interventive Experiment," "Community Mental Health Ideology," "Dogmatism and Political Conservatism," "Social Class and Participation in Outpatient Care by Schizophrenics." Brief descriptive abstracts precede the selections. Book reviews and film reviews appear in each issue.

International Journal of Social Psychiatry

This quarterly journal, published in England, is edited by behavioral scientists and psychiatrists from the United States, England, and Europe. The articles discuss sociocultural factors in mental illness, practical aspects, halfway houses, and mental health training. Articles dealing with suicide, conjoint and group therapy, and cross-cultural studies are common.

Psychiatry

"A journal for the study of interpersonal processes," *Psychiatry* is published quarterly by the William Alanson White Psychological Foundation, Inc., through the work of psychiatrists associated with the Harry Stack Sullivan school of psychiatry. Articles are accepted from branches of the social sciences which deal with the individual and collective problems of human life. Clinical and field observations, original research reports, surveys, and critiques of scientific literature in the fields of methodology, epistemology, and philosophy are included. This is a useful journal for those interested in the interrelationship of sociology and psychiatry. Many important articles appear here, such as David Reisman's articles on Freud.

SOCIAL PROBLEMS AND SOCIAL POLICIES

Sociology in this country was originally problem-oriented. (See C. Wright Mills, "The Professional Ideology of Social Pathologists," for the implications of this orientation.) When sociologists attempted to differentiate their discipline from social work and make it more "scientific," problem- and policy-oriented research came to be considered unimportant; thus the individuals conducting such research came to have lower status than methodologists and theorists. However, in recent years sociologists have again emphasized the need for sociological information on areas of current concern such as race and poverty. This concern is evidenced in several new journals discussed in this section.

Contemporary Crises

"Crime, Law, and Social Policy," as the subtitle indicates, are the concerns of this quarterly international journal. The journal features critical, radical, Marxist, and conflictual analyses of social problems. Publication is by Elsevier in Amsterdam, The Netherlands.

Crime and Social Justice

The former title of this journal, *Issues in Criminology*, now serves as the subtitle. Eight biannual issues had been published under the new title as of Winter 1978. The journal is still edited in Berkeley, California, although the former association of the editors with the School of Criminology at the University of California was broken when the University administration abolished the school. The concerns of the journal remain focused on issues in radical criminology. Titles suggestive of the topics covered include "Prospects for a

Radical Criminology in the United States," "Delinquency and Collective Varieties of Youth," "Labor Market and Imprisonment," and "Chile: Crime, Class Consciousness, and the Bourgeoisie." Other features of the journal are course outlines and book reviews. Two criminologists we respect consider this the best and most stimulating journal available in its field. For further information, the address is P.O. Box 4373, Berkeley, California 94704.

Criminology

This interdisciplinary journal (formerly *Criminologia*) is the official publication of the American Society of Criminologists. In the words of the journal, it is "devoted to crime and deviant behavior, as found in sociology, psychology, psychiatry, law, and social work as well as in newer disciplines such as urban design, systems analysis, and decision theory as applied to crime and criminal justice." The major emphasis of the articles is on empirical research and scientific methodology.

Journal of Human Resources

Published quarterly by the University of Wisconsin Press under the joint auspices of the International Relations Research Institute, the Center for Studies in Vocational and Technical Education, and the Institute for Research on Poverty, this journal contains research and review articles, book reviews, and communications dealing with "education, manpower, and welfare policies." Its articles deal with areas such as vocational education, health and wealth policies, and general manpower problems as they relate to the labor market, economics, and social development. This journal is of special interest to scholars, teachers, and students in economics, education, sociology, psychology, commerce and industrial relations, and to research personnel in government, business, and labor unions. Most of the articles are empirical.

Journal of Social Issues

The Society for the Psychological Study of Social Issues, a division of the American Psychological Association, publishes this journal quarterly. The Society, which is composed of psychologists and allied social scientists, seeks to bring theory and practice into focus on human problems of the group, community, and nation, as well as those of international scope. The stated goal of this quarterly is to communicate scientific findings and interpretations in a nontechnical manner without sacrificing professional standards: the journal, in short, is problem-oriented. Problem areas covered include education, race, sex, social movements, ideology, urban life, and communities. This journal has also published a special comprehensive "Free Clinic Handbook" (vol. 30, no. 1, 1974).

Law and Contemporary Problems

This journal, published quarterly by the Duke University School of Law, offers an interdisciplinary approach to legal and social problems, largely based on research in the fields of law, economics, political science, sociology, and international relations. Themes of typical issues have included a two-issue symposium on "Communications" (Spring and Summer 1969; the latter issue dealt with media) and "Transatlantic Investment and the Balance of Payments."

New Society

This is a London weekly magazine dealing with issues and problems in the social sciences and society. Some selected typical articles are: "The Future of Higher Education," "Parents Under Strain," "Economists and the Environment," "Computer Psychiatry," and "Black and White in Prison." To some extent, this is a British analogue of *Trans-Action* in that it attempts to put social science into laymen's English in order that the people who are subjects of discussion may understand the articles.

The Public Interest

This interdisciplinary quarterly deals with policy issues of interest to the public as well as to social scientists. A selection of typical topics includes: "Reexamining the Military Budget," "Urban Transportation," "The Housing Crisis," "Economics of the Sixties," "Academic Confrontations," "Welfare Reform," "Urban Growth," "Rich, Poor, and Taxes," and a "Focus on New York Schools." The editors are primarily and predominantly New Deal liberals, and for that reason *Social Policy* was originated as a more radical response to these same issues.

Social Policy

This bimonthly periodical, which first appeared in May/June 1970, is "a magazine of debate, analysis, and theory devoted to today's major movements for social change." The focus is on particular issues in the human service areas of health, education, welfare, and community development. Its editorial concern is with the dialectical, polemical, and policy aspects of major social issues, and unorthodox and explorative material is encouraged. The journal seeks to secure basic structural changes in American society; the editorial board views the publication as a participatory process that joins thinkers and activists as both readers and writers. Book reviews, editorial comments, reviews of films of special interest to sociologists, and a section called "Notes on the Service Society" are regularly featured. This periodical was founded in response to the more conservative *The Public Interest.*

Social Problems

This journal is put out five times a year by the Society for the Study of Social Problems, a group of problem- and policy-oriented sociologists that came out of a social movement to make sociology more humane as well as scientific. Considering itself "the overseer, the critic, and gadfly, the auditor and the conscience of the sociological profession," this journal contains articles on racial and sexual inequality, social movements, social class, policy and power, poverty, delinquency, and mental illness. The editors plan to increase the international scope of the journal to counter the ethnocentrism of an "American" social science. Also planned is an intensified critical focus on national and international problems of political economy.

Society (formerly Trans-Action)

This magazine of "social science and modern society" is published bimonthly by a group of behavioral scientists who purchased it from its original subsidizer, Washington University in St. Louis, so that it could be controlled by people in the social science professions. Although its huge board of advisory editors is interdisciplinary, sociologists contribute most of the articles and predominate in the regularly featured comments, book and film reviews, and photo essays. The articles treat issues in the social sciences and problems of general public concern, with an approach that is more popularized than in other professional journals. Some recent articles show *Society's* diversity: "Young Intelligentsia in Revolt," "Living with Eskimos," "White Institutions and Black Rage," "How Community Mental Health Stamped Out the Riot (1968-70)," and "The Moral Career of a Bum." Occasionally issues are devoted to a single theme, such as "The American Empire at Bay," "State Politics and Public Interests," "The Ethnic Factor," and "Cities, Families, and Schools."

Victimology

In 1976 a new quarterly international journal was organized to serve as a forum for research on such victims as battered women, rape victims, abused children, and political prisoners. The journal publishes material in a variety of forms: articles, research and project notes, book reviews, newsline, comments and replies, legal reports, and interviews. Two items which reflect the concerns of the journal are an article entitled "Battered Women Are Still in Need," and a critique of research on "battered husbands."

Working Papers for a New Society

A concern with contemporary policy issues and alternatives for social change pervade this magazine. The style and format are similar to *Social Policy* and *Society*. Publication is quarterly by the Cambridge Policy Studies Institute in Cambridge, Massachusetts. Urban communes, workers' control, day care, and the Left's dilemma are some of the topics which have been examined. The articles are generally better written, more lucid, and more readable than those in some of the more scholarly journals.

Yale Review of Law and Social Action

This new publication of the Yale Law School is "devoted to exploring methods for effecting social change." Articles on juvenile justice, political trials, consumer protection, and the Federal Trade Commission, and exclusionary zoning are representative of the content.

STUDENT JOURNALS

Some of the most innovative articles, especially in radical or critical sociology, are found in the journals edited by sociology students.

Berkeley Journal of Sociology

Generally the best student-edited journal, this is an annual publication of the Graduate Sociology Club of the Department of Sociology, University of California at Berkeley (410 Barrows Hall, University of California, Berkeley, California 94720). The journal is conceived as "a publication offering critical review essays on recent literature in sociology and related disciplines which challenges the social sciences to confront the crises of the world with intellect, curiosity, historical awareness, and theoretical competence." Many excellent, thought-provoking articles by students and established scholars are included in this forum. The content is predominantly analytical, critical, and polemical. The following selections indicate the content of the journal: "Recent Developments in Critical Theory," "Why Men Don't Rear Children," "Medicine and Socialism in Chile," and exchange of comments on black culture and liberal sociology and sociology-building, and "Women in Revolution." The articles are abstracted in the *Sociological Abstracts*. A cumulative index is available for volumes I-XI.

Catalyst

This publication appears quarterly from Trent University in Ontario, Canada. Articles and book reviews are included. A recent special issue was devoted to symbolic interactionism.

Cornell Journal of Social Relations

This journal is published twice a year (spring and fall) at Cornell University in Ithaca, New York. It is under the sponsorship of six departments and administrative units within the university: anthropology, psychology and sociology, rural sociology, the School of Child Development and Family Relationships, and the School of

Industrial and Labor Relations. The editorial board is composed of a graduate student editor in each of the sponsoring units and departments, each student under the direction of faculty advisors. The work of undergraduates and graduates in these fields is solicited. The journal was established in 1966 "to provide a publication outlet for works of young scholars in the various subject matter fields of social relations and general behavioral science."

Harvard Educational Review

This "journal of opinion and research in the field of education" is edited on a quarterly basis by graduate students at Harvard University. Review essays and articles deal with a broad range of problems and policy issues related to children and schooling, such as sex role culture and educational practice, children's television, and pluralism and education. Special issues have dealt with "The Rights of Children" and "Equal Educational Opportunity."

Heuristics

This innovative graduate journal of sociology presents works of midwestern university graduate students. It is published twice a year (in December and May) by Northern Illinois University.

The Human Factor

Three times a year the graduate Sociology Student Union at Columbia University publishes this journal. It is about "criticism, relevance, and dialogue. It is dedicated to the development of new forms of sociology relevant to understanding our society and our relation to it . . . its pages are open to articles critical of dominant trends, as well as articles that add to the genuinely scientific understanding of man and society." The journal is open to all kinds of imaginative, critical, and relevant work in the field of sociology. Representative articles are: "Radical Medical Sociology," "Critique of Modernization Theory," "A Liberal Critique of Radical Sociology," "Internal Colonization in the British Isles." This journal has a national distribution.

Humboldt Journal of Social Relations

Two times a year the faculty and students at California State University, Humboldt in Arcata, California, put together original papers dealing with current social issues from contributors in all the social sciences. The emphasis is on nontraditional approaches. The journal is abstracted in *Sociological Abstracts* and *Psychological Abstracts*.

RADICAL AND MARXIST JOURNALS

Familiarity with another set of periodicals, radical or Marxist journals, is a valuable source of perspective, criticism, and theoretical analysis for the student sociologist. These sources contain viewpoints not generally represented in professional journals, and they are important forums for radical scholars.

Antipode

Although this journal is subtitled "A Journal of Radical Geography," it is of interest to sociology students because it conceives of geography in a socially rooted sense and, therefore, treats issues of social significance. For example, topic headings have included energy and the environment, poverty, access to social services, racism, native Americans, Appalachia, and planning. The journal appears three times a year from Clark University in Worcester, Massachusetts. A bibliographic index for the years 1969–1978 was included in a 1979 issue.

Concerned Demography

This journal, which seeks to relate the study of population to the larger social and political context, comes from the Department of Sociology at Ithaca College in New York. It is published sporadically; thirteen issues have appeared since 1969.

The Insurgent Sociologist

The Insurgent Sociologist is published four times a year by an editorial collective in the Department of Sociology at the University of Oregon in Eugene. The associate editors represent a national constituency of radical sociologists. The journal covers news and research from the radical movement in sociology. Articles reflect current debates in sociology within the Marxist framework (on work, sex, race and class, the state, and imperialism). A special issue in the Fall of 1978 (vol. 3, no. 2-3) was devoted to "Essays on the Social Relations of Work and Labor." Power structure research is another featured topic. A very useful article on research resources appeared in the Winter 1978 issue (vol. 8, no. 1): Hill and Shapiro, "Training the Radical Researcher: A Course on Bibliographic Methods for Document Research." This periodical is indexed in the *Alternative Press Index* and abstracted in *Sociological Abstracts.*

Kapitalistate (vol. 1, 1973)

This journal coordinates the work of internationally based groups of people (England, Germany, Italy, Japan, Sweden, France, Scandinavia, The Netherlands, Spain, and the United States) who use Marxist political economy to study the modern capitalist and imperialist state. The San Francisco work group sees *Kapitalistate* "as a gathering point for activist-oriented people/intellectuals doing work around the State. We want to develop a social and political network which will better enable us to develop theory and practice and help build the left internationally." The format of the journal includes analyses of current events, reports on ongoing projects, cooperative communications, theoretical notes, working materials, bibliographic information, book reviews, and surveys of journals. Recent articles have been: "Corporate Regionalism in the United States," "Nation States and Multinational Corporations," "The Abolition of Market Control and the Problem of Legitimacy," and "Japanese Monopoly Capitalism and the State." For further information write: *Kapitalistate,* P.O. Box 1292, Palo Alto, California 94302.

Latin American Perspectives

This "journal on capitalism and socialism" seeks to bridge the gap between Latin America and the United States. The first issue was published in 1974, and the journal includes participating editors from the entire American continent. Three issues per year are published with articles and book reviews relating to special themes such as "A Reassessment of Dependency Theory" or particular countries such as Chile and Argentina. This is an important new forum for theory and research on Latin America from a radical perspective.

Marxist Perspectives

This is a new quarterly journal of history, ideas, political economy, and cultural criticism. A goal of the editors is to ". . . revitalize Marxist thought and to replace dogmatism with respect for evidence and a healthy dose of skepticism." An international perspective is provided in a section called "From the Other Shore" and in many of the feature articles. The journal hopes to serve as an arena for Marxist debate and consideration of the problems inherent in the development of a class interpretation of society.

Monthly Review

This "independent socialist magazine" is a leading Marxist political economy journal edited by Leo Huberman (1949–1968), Paul Sweezy, and Harry Magdoff (since 1968). Articles that it has published include Margaret Benston's article on "The Political Economy of Women's Liberation," "Anthropology: Child of Imperialism," by Kathleen Gough, and "The Nuclear Family," by Bobbye Ortiz, associate editor. Themes of articles include struggles in the Third World, world economic crises, and socialist development. Book reviews and editorial essays are included in the format. Monthly Review Press publishes many important books which analyze the contemporary and historical development of capitalism and socialism.

New Left Review

Published bimonthly in England, sections of this journal include book reviews, debates, and analyses of recent political and economic developments in the world, and scholarly articles. This review is a very important forum for the work of major theorists and Marxist scholars in the United States, Europe, Asia, and Latin America. The following titles will give you an idea of the contents of the journal: "Frankfurt Marxism: A Critique," "Analysing the

Bourgeois State," "Politics and Culture in Bengal," and "Myths of Underdevelopment." *New Left Review* also has a publishing arm, New Left Press, which offers a number of important theoretical and historical works (distributed in the U.S. by Schocken Books).

Politics and Society (vol. 1, 1970)

This quarterly journal was founded and continues to be edited by a group of scholars and activists that encourages work that is concerned with the roots of society and social change. The journal is open to a variety of methodological approaches on significant problems; it particularly seeks to promote traditionally unsupported areas of research which oppose the dominant ideological trends of the social sciences. A scanning of the content of the journal shows the following articles: "On the Study of Power," "The Vocation of Radical Intellectuals," "The Political Economy of Health Care," "Political Education and Sexual Liberation," "Property, Politics and Local Housing Policy," and "Advanced Capitalism and the Welfare State."

Radical America

This journal published bimonthly in Cambridge, Massachusetts, originated as an outgrowth of the dissolved *Studies on the Left*. Although the editors are historians, the magazine is more generalized with primary emphasis on social and political theory and praxis. The journal has published a number of interesting articles on women, blacks, labor and the working class, professional workers, youth, and culture.

Radical History Review

The Mid-Atlantic Radical Historians Organization (MARHO), founded in 1973, publishes this journal which is edited by collectives in Boston, New York, and Providence, Rhode Island. The scholars, students, and teachers who participate in this forum seek to develop a critical Marxist history which incorporates social and political concerns. Perspectives on the Great Depression of the 1930's, a symposium on the black family, and class struggles in the Third Reich are representative themes. Interviews and book reviews are also featured. One entire issue, Spring 1978, was devoted to "Labor and Community Militance in Rhode Island." The journal, formerly quarterly, is now slated to appear three times a year in the spring, autumn, and winter. The offices of MARHO are located at John Jay College, CUNY, 445 West 59th Street, New York, New York 10019. The British counterpart of *Radical History Review* is *History Workshop*, "a journal of socialist historians," published twice a year by Pluto Press. The address of the journal is P.O. Box 69, Oxford, OX2 7XA, England.

The Review of Radical Political Economics

This is the forum for the Union of Radical Political Economists which has groups all over the United States. The review comes out at least four times a year with articles on advanced capitalism, imperialism, underdevelopment and dependency, socialism, and the State. Special issues are also devoted to topics such as "The Political Economy of Women" or "The New Economic Policy." The review publishes other resource materials such as reading lists in radical political economics and a bibliography for investigating and promoting socialist alternatives for America.

Science and Society

Founded in 1936, this is an established independent quarterly journal of Marxist scholarship in philosophy, the social sciences, and the humanities. Theoretical analysis is a featured priority of this journal, as the theme of a special issue (Fall 1978) indicates: "Women and Contemporary Capitalism: Some Theoretical Questions."

Socialist Review
(formerly Socialist Revolution (vol. 1, no. 1, January-February 1970))

This quarterly publication is prepared by collectives working out of San Francisco, California, and Boston, Massachusetts. In some ways it may be considered a successor to *Studies on the Left;* several of the original editors were previously associated with the former publication. Issues have included articles on politics and social movements, the fiscal crisis of the state, ideology and social theory, Eurocommunism, socialist-feminism, and capitalism and the family. Significant debates have been published on "The Prospects for the Socialist Left in the United States." The journal now includes book and film reviews edited by the Boston group.

Southern Exposure

This lively, critical, and penetrating publication is put out quarterly by the Institute for Southern Studies in Chapel Hill, North Carolina. It is the most interesting and comprehensive, nonacademic forum for Southern studies. Material on labor history, contemporary Southern politics and economics, and Southern life and culture is presented in a large magazine format which includes photo essays, art, and poetry. The articles are well researched and written in a clear and readable style. General issues are interspersed with single theme issues. Among the many themes explored in depth have been: "Still Life: Inside Southern Prisons," "Just Schools: A Special Report Commemorating the Twenty-Fifth Anniversary of the Brown Decision," "Generations: Women in the South," and "No More Moanin': Voices of Southern Struggle."

State and Mind
(formerly RT: A Journal of Radical Therapy, Rough Times, and The Radical Therapist)

In contrast to the standard mental health journals, this publication takes an explicit political orientation to social psychological issues and institutions. Since 1970 the journal has featured articles on the personal/political aspects of everyday life, alternative mental health approaches, and women's, prisoners', and gay issues. Publication is quarterly.

Studies on the Left (Fall 1959 to Summer 1967)

For a good discussion of the content, goals, and history of this very interesting journal, see *For a New American, Essays in History and Politics from "Studies on the Left 1959-1967"*, edited by James Weinstein and David Eakins (two of the former editors of the magazine). This publication contained, at various times, scholarly research, essays in criticism, analyses of historical and contemporary subjects, considerations of traditional methods and theories in the social and natural sciences, material on literature and the arts, book reviews, and analysis and commentary on contemporary movements for social change. Contributions by sociologist Hans Gerth, historian William Appleman Williams, philosopher Jean-Paul Sartre, biographer Isaac Deutscher, literary critic George Lukács, historian Staughton Lynd, and Irish literary and political figure Connor Cruise O'Brien appeared in this forum.

Telos

For those interested in the philosophy of social science and social theory, this "journal of radical theory" is a good source of interesting analysis and debate. *Telos* publishes translations of the writings of prominent European theorists such as Sartre, Adorno, Habermas, Lukács, and Gorz. Articles treat such themes as the domains of phenomenology, existentialism, neo-Marxism, critical theory, and psychoanalytic theory and all the cross-currents between them. The journal is edited and published in the Department of Sociology at Western University, St. Louis, Missouri.

Theory and Society

Subtitled "Renewal and Critique in Social Theory," this journal has described itself as "a forum for an emerging worldwide community of social theorists." This serious commitment to internationalism is reflected in the impressive list of corresponding editors from all over the United States, Canada, and Europe. The editors see social theory emerging from the dialectic between philosophical perspectives and empirical commitment and hope to encourage those theorists working in the advancing edges of social theory: critical theory; phenomenological sociology; the neo-Marxisms; comparative, historical, and macroscopic sociology; structuralism; and linguistically sensitive sociology. In practice this has meant the publication of the following articles: "Marxism and Social Theory," "Epistemology and the Sociology of Knowledge," "Towards a Sociology of Social Anthropology," "A Critique of Political Sociology," and "Ethnomethodology, Positive Thinking, and the Power of Words."

SPECIALIZED RADICAL JOURNALS, NEWSLETTERS, AND BULLETINS

These publications are very useful for keeping up-to-date on current events and social issues. Most of these publications are indexed in *Alternatives Index Press.*

Africa News

Extensive coverage of contemporary news pertaining to Africa is published weekly by Africa News Service, Inc., Box 3851, Durham, North Carolina 27702.

Bulletin of Concerned Asian Scholars

Published quarterly by the Committee of Concerned Asian Scholars, Box W, Charlemont, Massachusetts 01339, this bulletin includes critical articles on the history, politics, and culture of Asian and Asian-American societies.

Cuba Review

Published quarterly by the Cuba Resource Center, Box 206, Cathedral Station, New York, New York 10025, each issue explores in depth one aspect of Cuban society, such as education, labor, women, or United States–Cuban relations.

Dollars and Sense

This monthly economic bulletin, which analyzes and explains economic trends and developments in business, labor, government policy, and the international economy, is published by the Economic Affairs Bureau, Inc., 304 Somerville Avenue, Somerville, Massachusetts 02143.

Health/Pac Bulletin

This bulletin prints bimonthly news, reviews, articles, and debate on the United States health system. Issues addressed include national health insurance, profits in medicine, occupational and environmental health, health worker issues, women and minority health, and strategies for change. The address is 17 Murray Street, New York, New York 10007.

MERIP Reports

These monthly reports cover political and economic developments in the Middle East with particular regard to the role of the United States in this region. Important issues such as the energy crisis, Israeli settlements, and the Algerian revolution are documented and analyzed, along with other topics in the areas of labor, women, and industrialization. Box 3122, Columbia Heights Station, Washington, D.C. 20010 is the address.

NACLA's Report on the Americas

This publication of the North American Congress on Latin America examines the relationship between the U.S. and Latin American countries with regard to such issues as immigration, "runaway" shops, labor, and agribusiness. The report appears bimonthly and the address is Box 57, Cathedral Station, New York, New York 10025.

Pacific Research and World Empire Telegrams

Twice a month the Pacific Studies Center, 867 W. Dana Street, No. 204, Mountain View, California 94041 reports news and research focused on the Pacific and Asian areas.

Southern Africa Newsletter

Available monthly from the Southern Africa Committee, 17 West 17th Street, New York, New York 10010, this magazine includes interviews, news, book reviews, and articles on Southern Africa with a focus on a particular country in each issue.

Union W.A.G.E. Newsletter

This is the bimonthly newsletter of the Union Women's Alliance to Gain Equality. It covers news of women's labor struggles as well as information on resources of interest to working women on such issues as occupational health and safety and reproductive rights. Coverage is mainly oriented to the western part of the country; the newsletter is published in San Francisco, California, P.O. Box 40904 (zip: 94110).

(Note: *A Catalogue of Political Magazines* was consulted in preparing this list. It is available from Political Publications Group, #13D, 320 Riverside Drive, New York, New York 10025.)

GENERAL PERIODICALS

Publications of general interest frequently contain articles of sociological import. *Daedalus, The New York Review of Books, Commonweal,* and *The New York Times Magazine* are only a few of the periodicals that might be investigated. *Daedalus* is the official journal of the American Academy of Arts and Sciences, and each of its issues treats a particular theme in the social sciences from a variety of perspectives. Polemical or critical selections of interest to social scientists are frequently published in *The New York Review of Books.* Articles written by social scientists to express their views on curent social issues appear occasionally in *The New York Times Magazine. Mother Jones,* a radical magazine, and *Commonweal,* a liberal Catholic publication, often presents articles on vital social issues. *Ms.* frequently has articles of interest on female and male sex roles, some written by well-known behavioral scientists. These magazines are good sources for keeping abreast of current controversy and debate on public and social science issues and for synthesizing ideas about some trend or problem in which you are interested.

For contemporary news and commentary, two interesting publications are *The Nation,* a weekly magazine, and *In These Times,* a weekly independent socialist newspaper with predominantly national, and some international, coverage (P.O. Box 228, Westchester, Illinois 60153). For more extensive coverage of world affairs and U.S. foreign policy, two good sources are the bimonthly *Internews International Bulletin* (Box 4400, Berkeley, California 94704) and the monthly *Newsfront International* (Peoples' Translation Service, 4228 Telegraph Avenue, Oakland, California 94609).

WOMEN'S STUDIES JOURNALS

Chrysalis

This is a "magazine of women's culture" which appears quarterly. It publishes feminist theory, poetry, art and book reviews oriented toward the reexamination and redefinition of concepts of reality and the building of alternative culture and institutions. Topics of interest have been a critique of Freud's treatment of incest, transsexual surgery, redesigning the domestic workplace, and women and sports.

Feminist Studies

In 1969 this journal was "founded for the purpose of encouraging analytic responses to feminist issues and to open new areas of feminist research and critique." The first issue appeared in 1971 and the journal continued to appear throughout the early 1970's. After a publishing hiatus of a few years, the journal reappeared in 1978 with support from the Women's Studies Program at the University of Maryland, College Park. The editors and consultants are women drawn from a broad spectrum of fields in the social sciences and humanities. The editorial policy expresses a desire ". . . not just to interpret women's experiences but to change women's condition." Women's studies, abortion, motherhood, the history of women, women and culture, women and the family, and women and religion have been some of the areas explored in this forum for feminist analysis, exchange, and debate. The journal appears three times a year and is indexed in *America: History and Life, Sociological Abstracts,* and *Women's Studies Abstracts.*

This "journal of women studies" is published by an editorial collective in association with the Women Studies Program at the University of Colorado, Boulder. Since its origin in 1975, the journal has sought to bridge the gap between university and community women by presenting interesting and accessible interdisciplinary contributions on diverse topics. Some themes which have been explored include the politics of reproduction, feminist psychotherapy, mothers and daughters, and women's workplace problems. A very useful special issue (vol. 2, no. 2, Summer 1977) was devoted to "Women's Oral History" (see section on oral history in Chapter 2 of this handbook).

International Journal of Women's Studies

This bimonthly journal first appeared in 1978. The editorial policy seeks to encourage quality research and writing from all perspectives in order to function as a major medium for serious studies on the roles of women in society. A goal of the journal is the "cool and critical discussion" of sex role issues. "Sex Role Stereotypes in the Mass Media and the Schools," "The Social Role of Japanese Women," and "Rape as a Paradigm of Sexism in Society" illustrate the topics of some articles which might be useful to sociology students. The journal is published by Eden Press Women's Publications (Montreal, Quebec, Canada and St. Albans, Vermont). The press also publishes a number of monographs in women's studies.

Isis

Isis, a resource and documentation center of the International Women's Liberation Movement, was set up in 1974. It publishes a quarterly journal with theoretical and practical information from women's groups around the world. It includes resource listings, reports, and notices to increase communication among women in various countries. Special issues on such topics as women's health and socialism and feminism have been prepared. You can contact them by writing to Isis, Case Postale 301, 1227 Carouge, Geneva.

Papers in Women's Studies

This is a quarterly interdisciplinary feminist journal published by the students and faculty of the Women's Studies Program in Ann Arbor, Michigan. A sampling of articles shows the following interesting titles: "Women's Alienation in the Workplace," "Femininity and Mental Health," "Two Careers and One Family," and "Change and Women's Status in Andean Social Structure."

Psychology of Women Quarterly

This journal is sponsored by Division 35, The Psychology of Women, of the American Psychological Association. It limits itself to articles dealing with women's psychology such as women's socialization, women's personality, and women's sexuality.

Signs

Beginning in September 1975, this "journal of women in culture and society" published quarterly by The University of Chicago Press provides a showcase for intellectual work on women, culture, and society from the United States and abroad. The journal is both interdisciplinary and international in scope. It has published work in sociology, history, economics, biology and medicine, political science and law, criticism, aesthetics, literature, psychology, and theology from a variety of ideological and theoretical perspectives. The format includes original research articles, essays, reports, commentaries, book reviews, historical documents of contemporary interest, and review essays on the state of the art of research about women in particular disciplines or areas of life. Special issues have treated such themes as "The Women of China," "Women and Education," "Family History," "Women and National Development," and "Women in the Workplace."

Women's Studies

Women's Studies is another interdisciplinary journal which presents scholarship and criticism about women from a variety of viewpoints: sociological, legal, historical, and so on. The three issues per annual volume also include book and film reviews.

Women and Health

This quarterly journal is the scholarly arm of the Women's Health Movement. It had been published quarterly since 1976, sponsored by SUNY Old Wesbury; in 1979 Hayworth Press became the publisher. Articles relevant to women's health on such topics as childbirth, including alternative methods, especially midwives and home births, abortion, gynecology, and self-help have been published. This journal also includes film and book reviews, a section on health and public policy, as well as a News and Notes section. A recent issue had articles on medical risks and late childbearing, women and health statistics and female illness and illness behavior.

CULTURE AND IDEAS

A number of journals and periodicals deal with topics in the areas of popular culture, mass media, and ideology. Two standard journals associated with the Popular Culture Association are the *Jour-*

nal of American Culture and the *Journal of Popular Culture.* A more critical source is the journal *Social Text:* "Theory, Culture, and Ideology" (vol. 1, 1979). Since film can also be seen as an important medium for learning about society and social images, two magazines of film criticism may be useful. Both of these publications critically analyze the political, economic, and social content of current cinema; they are *Cineaste,* published in New York, and *Jump-Cut,* published in Berkeley, California. They review documentary as well as feature films and include articles on the history and literature of filmmaking.

Chapter
Five

---

guides to research and
resource materials

This chapter deals with those tools of research which will help you glean relevant material from the large body of published literature. These aids are abstract and indexing services, bibliographic aids, bibliographies, and secondary sources. The secondary sources include handbooks, resource guides to the literature, encyclopedias, and dictionaries, and are excellent means for reviewing the issues and research in a particular area of interest. Familiarity with and ability to use all of these tools will enable you to locate important material quickly without duplication of research. In addition, by browsing through these materials, you may discover new ways in which to organize material, possible strategies for research, or new aspects of a particular topic. Be creative and open-minded in your approach; let references from one source suggest leads to additional sources and to different approaches to a particular problem.

PERIODICAL ABSTRACTING JOURNALS
AND INDEXING SERVICES

As indicated in Chapter 4, the quantity of periodical literature of interest to sociologists is quite extensive. It would be impossible to keep up with all of this material on a current basis, and therefore several indexing and abstracting services have been developed to aid social science researchers in gaining access to relevant information. Next to the card catalog, these services are the most important key to the library's materials.

Indexes and abstracts vary with respect to form, comprehensiveness, and specificity. In addition, the currency of each index varies and it is wise to browse through the most current issues of relevant journals to find material which has not yet been indexed or abstracted. Use the descriptions of journals in Chapter 4 as a guide to those periodicals which might contain articles pertinent to your particular interests. The following annotated list is a brief introduction to the nature and functions of many of the relevant guides to periodical literature. In order to maximize efficiency and effectiveness in using a specific guide, a few general guidelines might be helpful.

To begin with, learn the entry form, organizational basis, and general orientation of each guide; note the particular abbreviations indicating bibliographies, tables, and reference information; determine which journals and areas of sociology are covered. Secondly, when noting a reference to a specific article in which you are interested, carefully copy all of the necessary information, including the author and the page numbers. Next, learn how your library records and catalogs its periodical holdings. This may take the form of cards in the card catalog, visible index files, catalog books, or microfiche. Another point to remember when using these guides is to follow cross-references carefully. The number of subject headings in an abstract or index is necessarily limited, and therefore, the most productive use of this type of reference tool requires checking of related topics and subheadings. Many larger libraries now offer computerized searches of major abstracts, indexes, and unprinted data bases. This can save time, provide more recent information, and coordinate more detailed topic headings. However, a fee is charged for this service.

ABSTRACTS

Abstracting journals serve a dual purpose: the indexing of current literature in a specified field and the digesting of important articles and books. Good abstracts provide objective, descriptive summaries of content, indicating the scope of an article, the thesis or point of view of the author, sources used, and any new interpretations of facts or other contributions to scholarship. As a result, abstracts are useful guides to pertinent material. When you have a topic in mind, look in the table of contents or the subject index of a suitable abstracting journal. There you will find page listings for all the relevant articles included in that issue. If there is a cumulative index for the year or for several years, this will aid you in quickly locating references for a longer time span. Copy all the listings under your specific topic and any related subject headings. Remember, there may be several cross-listings that could apply to your topic. Author indexes can also be useful. If you find a particularly suitable article, note the name of the author and use the author index to locate other articles by the same author in your area of interest. Next, look up each reference and read the brief abstract which describes the article or paper. If the article seems important and useful, copy all the reference data (title of journal, volume, year, page, etc.) that will help you locate the original article. When employing the abstract as a researching tool, always refer to the original article for substantive information. Do not use the abstract as a substitution for reading relevant studies as this may lead to misinterpretation and misrepresentation of the material. Sometimes reprints of articles are available from the abstracting service or directly from the journal. However, if your library has the journal on hand it is easier to xerox it yourself.

Abstracts in Anthropology

This abstracting journal has been published four times per year since 1970. It provides 300-word abstracts of books, monographs, articles from major anthropological journals, and papers from professional meetings. The section on cultural anthropology might provide some useful references for a cross-cultural perspective on sociological issues. Author and subject indexes and a list of journal sources for abstracted articles will help you locate useful citations.

America: History and Life

This abstracting journal has been issued quarterly since 1964 and covers articles on the history of the United States and Canada. It also incorporates articles dealing with current American life and times. Since this service covers twenty-two hundred serial publications from throughout the world, it can prove to be quite useful. Beginning in 1974, there have been four parts to this journal: (a) article abstracts and citations, (b) book reviews, (c) American history bibliography and (d) annual index. A five-year index has appeared in 1964/1965 and 1968/1969.

Crime and Delinquency Abstracts

Formerly *International Bibliography on Crime and Delinquency* prior to 1966, this abstract is published by the National Clearinghouse for Mental Health Information of the National Institute of Mental Health, Bethesda, Maryland, and prepared by the Information Center on Crime and Delinquency of the National Council on Crime and Delinquency. This source consists of abstracts of current publications of scientific and professional literature and of current ongoing research projects in the areas of crime and delinquency. Subject and author indexes are provided.

ERIC

ERIC stands for Educational Resources Information Center. The main body of this monthly journal is comprised of résumés (which highlight the significance of each research report and provide good descriptions) and subject/author indexes. Coverage includes all material relevant to education under very broad subject headings. Subject headings reading "women professors" and "working women" would include reports on dual careers; the labor market experience of women; the importance of the diversity of choice in women's roles; and a study of attitudes of married women toward married women's employment. The *ERIC* maintains a staff in

Washington, D.C., as well as twenty clearinghouses located in universities and professional organizations throughout the country. All of the data cited in the Documents Résumé Section is available from the *ERIC*, and reproduction service is provided except where noted.

Historical Abstracts

This publication has appeared quarterly since 1955 and summarizes articles on political, diplomatic, economic, social, cultural, and intellectual history for the period 1775-1945. Listings are drawn from periodicals, including yearbooks, published in all parts of the world. Cumulative indexes exist for the periods 1955-59, 1960-64, 1965-69. This can be useful if you are searching for historical trends and analogies. Since 1971, this publication has been divided into two parts: (a) *Modern History Abstracts* and (b) *Twentieth Century Abstracts*. After 1964, the United States and Canada were excluded and incorporated into a new abstract—*America: History and Life*.

Human Resources Abstracts

This extremely useful abstracting service (prior to 1975 known as *Poverty and Human Resources Abstracts*) is now being published quarterly by the Institute of Labor and Industrial Relations at the University of Michigan and Wayne State University and is edited by an interdisciplinary board of psychologists, social workers, economists, research administrators, sociologists, and public health personnel. Information on poverty and human resources, in terms of manpower and labor force participation, programs and services, policies and perspectives, legal rights and assistance, is given with data on population, class, income, education, integration, blacks, social mobility, and employment. Each issue includes approximately two thousand abstracts drawn from publications of government agencies, private foundations, major journals, periodicals, books, unpublished papers and conference reports, and literature referred to by specialists on problems of manpower, poverty, and human resources. A subject index and a classification listed under broad subject categories facilitate access to material on particular issues. Annual subject and author indexes are provided.

Psychological Abstracts

This abstract, published monthly since 1927 by the American Psychological Association, Inc., contains nonevaluative summaries (approximately 100–150 words) of all published articles in most of the domestic and foreign journals relevant to psychology. The broad class of social psychology is subdivided into more detailed groupings: cultural and social processes (including sociocultural structure and social role, the family, social change and programs, ethnology, religion, cross-cultural comparison); sexual behavior; attitudes and opinions; group and interpersonal processes (influence and communication, social perception and motivation); communication; esthetics; and tobacco, drug, and alcohol use. Complete bibliographic reference is given so that the article may be located, and the abstracts are arranged in useful classes, some of which are especially pertinent to sociologists.

Sage Race Relations Abstracts

These abstracts are published by the Institute of Race Relations, London, England, and were limited at first to the British situation. However, as the service developed, it included wider references to race relations in the United States and Europe. Appearing quarterly during 1968 and thereafter three times a year, the topical coverage includes: urbanization, social change, institutions, social control, employment, population and groupings, culture, and crime (all classified under sociology and social psychology), as well as topics relating to politics, economics, education, psychology, and public health. Bibliographies and reviews of literature are occasionally included, e.g., The Black Family.

Resources in Education

This publication (formerly known as *Research in Education*) prepared by the U.S. Department of Health, Education, and Welfare, Office of Education, National Center for Educational Communication, and the Education Research Information Center provides a nationwide network which acquires, stores, retrieves, and disseminates the most significant and timely educational research.

Sociological Abstracts

Perhaps the best procedure in researching a sociological topic is to begin by looking in the index of the recent issues and volumes of the *Abstracts* for relevant material. When using this source, copy the identifying numbers of the abstracts and look them up in the main section of the issue. Reading the abstracts should give you an idea of which original studies might be pertinent to examine, and most likely you will find a few years of *Abstracts* to be sufficient. The reference lists in each of the articles should lead you to abundant source material. Each issue of the *Abstracts* usually includes items published during the current year and for about four years previously. You should be aware that abstracts are often slow in appearing, and as a result a brief check of the most recent issues of relevant journals will keep you up to date on a particular area of interest.

Sociological Abstracts is cosponsored by four major sociological associations since 1952, including the American Sociological Association, and now appears six times per year. The last issue of the year is the cumulative index issue for that year, and is published within nine months of the appearance of the previous issue. The abstracts in each issue are arranged in a useful classification scheme. Examples of major subject divisions are: history and theory of sociology, social psychology, mass phenomena, the family and socialization, social differentiation, political interactions, and radical sociology. These general headings are subdivided into more restricted categories such as: bureaucratic structures, social movements, social stratification, adolescence and youth, and sociology of occupations and professions. This periodical has greatly expanded its coverage in the last fifteen years and publishes six to seven thousand abstracts yearly from about 200 U.S. and foreign serials. Journals in related fields are partially abstracted for articles of relevance to sociologists.

World Agricultural Economics and Rural Sociology Abstracts

International in scope since 1959, this journal, published monthly by the Commonwealth Agricultural Bureau, London, England, includes short signed abstracts of books and periodical articles on topics in the areas of agriculture, economics, and rural sociology.

Topics included under rural sociology are demography, rural-urban contrasts and relationships, rural communities, attitudes and opinions, associations, and standards and conditions of living and working.

Women's Studies Abstracts

Books and articles pertaining to women are listed and summarized in this quarterly research tool under a variety of subject headings, some of which are: education and socialization, sex roles, employment, sexuality, family, health, and society and government. A special feature is the listing of the tables of contents of feminist journals and special women's issues of other journals. Book reviews and special bibliographies are also included. Each issue has a subject and author index (cumulated annually) and a list of the many U.S. and foreign periodicals which are scanned.

The following abstracting services are useful for locating relevant unpublished material.

Dissertation Abstracts International

Formerly *Dissertation Abstracts, DAI* is a monthly compilation of abstracts of doctoral dissertations submitted to University Microfilms by more than 250 cooperating institutions in the United States and Canada. "International" was added to the title in 1969 to reflect the inclusion on a regular basis of abstracts of dissertations accepted by European universities, and abstracts are consequently written in the language in which the complete work is written. The abstracts are divided into two major categories: Volume A—Humanities and Social Science, and Volume B—Sciences. Further breakdowns are by field, e.g., sociology, criminology, communism, etc. The descriptive abstracts include summaries of purpose, methods, and results of the individual studies. A retrospective index for volumes 1-29 was published in 1970, which makes *DAI* an excellent source for bibliographic reference. Volume 4 covers psychology, sociology, and political science, and volume 9 is an author index. A key-word index system of information retrieval is employed using the words comprising the titles of dissertations as the descriptors for a subject index. As a result, the same dissertation may appear under more than one heading depending on the number of key words in its title.

Masters Abstracts

This service, published quarterly by Xerox, University Microfilms, Ann Arbor, Michigan, represents a catalog of selected masters theses on microfilm and provides brief printed abstracts in journal form, indexed by subject and author. Complete reproductions of theses are also available. Selected masters theses from universities are included. Keep in mind that many university libraries keep on file copies of senior honors theses, masters theses, and doctorate dissertations written for their institutions.

INDEXES

Indexes to periodical literature list the author, title, and topic of published articles under classified headings and subheadings which may be cross-referenced. They appear on a periodical basis, thus narrowing the time lag between the original appearance of an article and its inclusion in a bibliographic source. Since they are not periodical in nature, bibliographies and guides to literature are less able to cope with the problem of currency. In addition to general guides to periodical literature, such as the *Readers' Guide to Periodical Literature,* there are innumerable specialized indexes which concentrate on certain areas of a subject and may overlap coverage of material and periodicals. Although one advantage of a good index is its comprehensiveness with regard to the journals covered, no index, even those within a single discipline, covers all periodicals relevant to its subject orientation. Furthermore, indexes are limited in two areas. First, they do not provide annotation, as do abstracts, making it difficult for the researcher to assess the relative importance of each entry for his or her purposes. Secondly, a new publication may not be included for some time in the coverage of the indexing journals.

GENERALIZED INDEXES

Current Contents: Social and Behavioral Sciences

This index (formerly *Current Contents in the Behavioral, Social, and Management Sciences*) is a weekly listing of the tables of contents of journals in such fields as anthropology, ethnic studies, history, ger-

ontology, drugs, education, psychology, sociology, and urban studies. Each issue has an author index and address directory which will
enable you to write to an author for a reprint of a listed article. The
publisher, Institute for Scientific Information in Philadelphia, Pennsylvania, offers a twenty-four-hour reprint service for the articles
listed in *Current Contents.* The address and telephone number for
this service is printed in each issue.

Public Affairs Information Service Bulletin (PAIS)

This index, chartered by the Education Department of the State
University of New York, has been published weekly since 1915 by
the R. S. Wilson Co. It is primarily a subject index to materials
(American and international) published in the English language
dealing with economics, social conditions, politics, public administration, etc., in the form of books, periodicals, pamphlets, government publications, reports of public and private agencies,
yearbooks, and other useful sources. Some sociological journals not
covered in the *Social Sciences Index* are included in *PAIS;* however,
the American Sociological Association journals are not included
(see *Sociological Abstracts* for these). The selection emphasis is on
statistical and factual information. The subject entries give full bibliographic information and there are cumulations five times a year.

Readers' Guide to Periodical Literature

This well-known guide, published semimonthly September to June
and monthly in July and August by H. W. Wilson Co., currently
indexes approximately 130 U.S. periodicals, primarily of general
and nontechnical content. Selections represent all important topic
areas in the arts, sciences, and humanities, and are classified under
specific subject headings with subheadings and cross-references. Title and author listings are also given. General news and commentary magazines, such as *Time, Newsweek, The New Republic, The
Nation,* and *Ramparts* are indexed in the *Readers' Guide,* along with
more specific periodicals like *Society* and the *Annals of the American
Academy of Political and Social Science.*

Social Sciences Index

This quarterly publication of the H. W. Wilson Co. was formerly
part of the *Social Sciences and Humanities Index.* A need for specialization and the incorporation of a larger number of journals

necessitated a division of the parent index. (The other half became the *Humanities Index*.) Included are anthropology, area studies, economics, environmental science, geography, law and criminology, medical science, political science, psychology, public administration, sociology, and other related subjects. This interdisciplinary research aid is a subject and author index to approximately 263 periodicals (77 old titles and 186 new) including a number of international journals. Many journals treated in Chapter 4 are indexed in this important resource.

Social Sciences Citation Index (SSCI)

This important indexing service, which has been in existence since 1970, allows you to locate references in three ways from three separate but related indexes that appear together each year in three installments (January-April, May-August, September-December), the last of which is an annual cumulation. The three indexes are a citation index (here the search starts with the name of an author or organization known to have published material on your topic and gives you listings of other authors who have cited these articles), a subject index based on significant words in the titles of articles, and a source index with complete bibliographic information on all listings. Depending on the kind of searching you want to do—cited author searches, cited reference searches, key word searches, author searches—one of the three indexes will be the most effective place to begin. Information gleaned from the initial search (title words, authors, citations) can then be used to get more information from the other indexes. Since this service indexes over one thousand social science journals completely and also selectively indexes articles relevant to the social sciences from other journals, coverage of the field is quite extensive.

FOREIGN INDEXES

British Humanities Index

Formerly *Subject Index to Periodicals, 1915-1962*, this is published quarterly in two parts with an annual cumulation by the Library Association of London. This publication is a subject index to over 300 British periodicals relating to the arts, politics, social science, area studies, contemporary history, and philosophy. Relevant journals indexed include: *Human Relations, Journal of Jewish Studies, British Journal of Sociology, New Left Review, New Society,* and *Sociological Review.*

Internationale Bibliographie der Zeitschriftenliteratur aus allen Gebieten des Wissens

This international bibliography of periodical literature, published semiannually since 1964–1965 by Felix Dietrich Verlag, Osnabrück, West Germany, covers all fields of knowledge. The text and titles are in English, French, and German, and arranged by subject with an author index. This current index to general periodicals, the largest indexing service in Western Europe, is international in scope and analyzes the contents of about eighty-three hundred periodicals from all parts of the world.

INDEXES OF BOOK REVIEWS

Book Review Digest

Published monthly since 1905 with annual and semiannual cumulations by the H. W. Wilson Co., *Book Review Digest* indexes selected book reviews in approximately seventy-five American and English periodicals. The periodicals indexed are primarily general in character; however, fifteen major social science journals are also included in the list of sources. Entries are classified by author with subject and title indexes; brief excerpts accompany each referenced entry.

Book Review Index

This journal was published monthly since 1965 but was suspended from 1969 to 1971. Printing resumed with three issues and an annual cumulation in 1972; retrospective issues covering 1969–1971 were published in 1974–1975. Beginning in 1973, bimonthly and annual issues were continued by the Gale Research Co. of Detroit, Michigan. This is an index to book reviews which appear in over 200 American, British, and Canadian periodicals of general, specialized, and scholarly content. Reviews appearing in such newspapers as the *Guardian, New York Times, London Times Literary Supplement*, and the *Christian Science Monitor* are also listed, as well as those appearing in the *New York Review of Books*. This is an extremely useful tool for tracking down reviews by sociologists or social scientists on new or key works in the discipline; these reviews may assist you in placing sociological works within the context of current and historical trends and schools of thought. Remember that most of the scholarly journals in Chapter 4 contain book reviews.

SPECIALIZED INDEXES

Alternative Press Index

Since 1969 this quarterly publication has indexed "publications which amplify the cry for social change and social justice." Research on local power structures, industries, political figures, and social conditions is indexed under a detailed subject heading list originally developed by members of the Social Responsibilities Round Table of Librarians in New York. Standard reference information is given for each entry. This is an especially good source for topics in the areas of contemporary social movements, social change, and political sociology. The index includes the names and addresses of the alternative periodicals covered; some of these are described in Chapter 4 of this handbook. The Alternative Press Centre in Baltimore, Maryland, publishes the index. One should be aware of the time lag in the coverage when using this aid.

Biography Index

This publication, published quarterly with four-year cumulative volumes since 1937 by the H. W. Wilson Co., indexes long biographies.

Business Periodicals Index

Appearing monthly since 1958 with quarterly, semiannual, and annual cumulations, and published by the H. W. Wilson Co., this publication is a subject index to about 170 periodicals in the fields of accounting, advertising, banking and finance, general business, insurance, labor and management, specific industries and trades, personnel, public administration, and similar concerns.

Education Index

As the title indicates, this index, published monthly since 1929 by the H. W. Wilson Co., is a guide to educational material. It includes topics relevant to all levels of the educational structure, and educational research in such fields as social studies, comparative and international education, applied science and technology, psychology, mental health, etc. This author-subject index indexes primarily periodicals, although it also may include yearbooks, bulletins, monographs, proceedings of conventions, and material printed by the United States government. References to such topics as universities and student problems, school systems and the teaching of sociology (the social sciences) can be found in this source.

Essay and General Literature Index

This publication, prepared under the auspices of the American Economic Association, Homewood, Illinois, Richard D. Irving, Inc., since 1961, covers journal articles since 1886. Its companion, *Index of Economic Articles in Collective Volumes*, began publication in 1968.

Indicus Medicus

This publication contains information of medical topics from all relevant scholarly literature. There is a listing by topic, by the author's last name, and alphabetically by title. This is a useful reference source because there are so many sociological factors and aspects to health and illness encompassed by the field of medical sociology. Many relevant articles appear in psychiatric or public health journals, and *Indicus Medicus* indexes many of these periodicals. If you cannot locate sufficient information in the index, you should ask the librarian if you might use the "Medlars" retrieval system, a computerized system through which the librarian can give you a bibliography on any topic drawn from the medical literature covered therein.

Journal of Economic Literature

Incorporating the *Journal of Economic Abstracts*, this publication has appeared since 1963, sponsored cooperatively by the contributing journals under the auspices of the American Economic Associations.

Le Monde, Index Analytique

Published since 1967 by *Le Monde* in Paris, with annual volumes covering each year since 1965, this index is an especially good source for coverage of the military and political aspects of the Indochina conflict.

Population Index

This index is published by the office of Population Research, Woodrow Wilson School of Public and International Affairs, Princeton University, for the Population Association of America, Inc. The following major resources are utilized in addition to those of the Office of Population Research: New York Public Library, the United Nations Headquarters Library, current acquisitions of the Princeton University Library, and the library of the New York Academy of Medicine. *Sociological Abstracts* and *Indicus Medicus* are included in the list of bibliographic sources appearing in the cumulative index. Issues of this index include information on bibliographies, new periodicals, and official statistical publications, as well as indexing for material available on such fields as marriage, divorce, and the family; trends in population size; internal migration; fertility; regional population studies; demographic and economic interrelations.

Standard Periodical Directory

Prepared by Oxbridge Publishing Co., New York, this index deals with specialized trade journals and newsletters including labor union publications and religious periodicals.

Vertical File Index

Published monthly (September–July) since 1932 by the H. W. Wilson Co., and previously entitled *Vertical File Service Catalog* (until 1954) this index lists currently available pamphlets, booklets, leaflets, and mimeographed materials arranged alphabetically by subject with titles, paging, publishers and publication dates, descriptive notes, and prices or conditions under which they may be obtained. Free pamphlets and foreign publications are also included. This can be a helpful reference to material, often of a miscellaneous nature, which is not listed elsewhere.

NEWSPAPER INDEXES

Newspapers are invaluable sources of data—historical as well as contemporary. The problem of accessibility to the staggering yearly accumulation of articles has led several newspapers to provide indexing services.

Index to the Times

This publication appeared quarterly from 1906 to 1956 and bimonthly thereafter, and is prepared in London by the Times Newspapers, Ltd.

New York Times Index

This index is published semimonthly, with an annual cumulation (currently appears about eight months after the end of the year) by the New York Times Co., since 1851. It summarizes and classifies news and editorial matter in an alphabetical arrangement by subject, person, and organization. Detailed entries are arranged chronologically under the alphabetical headings and are accompanied by a reference to the news story in which it appeared by giving the date, page, and column of the paper. Frequently the indexed references contain enough information to cancel the need to look up the original item. The comprehensiveness of the newspaper and the thoroughness of the index make this a valuable research resource.

Wall Street Journal Index

The *Wall Street Journal Index,* published monthly since 1958 in New York by Dow Jones and Co., Inc., appears in two sections: corporate news and general news. Annual cumulations are provided. The journal reports on economic trends and developments, individual firms and businessmen, and political matters affecting business. The index refers to the New York edition of the paper.

BIBLIOGRAPHIC AIDS

For a comprehensive listing of published works and complete bibliographical information on published material, refer to the following sources.

Books in Print

This publication has appeared annually since 1948, and is published by the R. R. Bowker Co., New York. It indexes *Publishers' Trade List Annual* by author, title, and series, giving the publisher and price of the book and covering only the publishers included in *Publishers' Trade List Annual.* From 1967 to 1973 it had been issued in two volumes: an author index and a titles index. Since 1973, it has changed to three volumes: an author index, a titles index, and a subject index. There is now an additional index issued six months after the yearly volume which lists new titles and updated information.

Cumulative Book Index

Published monthly, with annual and semiannual cumulations, by the H. W. Wilson Co. since 1928, this index lists books in the English language by author and title. Coverage is current and reasonably comprehensive. Publishers supply the information.

Library of Congress Publications

The Library of Congress in Washington, D.C., publishes two bibliographies. *Library of Congress Catalog, Books: Subjects, A Cumulative List of Works Represented by Library of Congress Cards* is a subject listing published quarterly with annual cumulations. *The National Union Catalog* is "a cumulative author list representing Library of Congress printed cards and titles reported by other American libraries." It is published monthly with quarterly, annual, and quinquennial cumulations. Because both of the above rely on reports of library cataloging departments, there is consequently a lag between the appearance of a book and its listing in one of the catalogs. This is not a problem for those sources which depend on publishers' reports.

Paperbound Books in Print

Published in New York by the R. R. Bowker Co. since 1955, this formerly monthly index is now released in March and November, listing author, title, and subject of new titles in paperback, and titles still in print.

Publishers' Trade List Annual

Published in New York by *Publishers' Weekly* since 1873, this is an annual compilation of publishers' catalogs which provides a list of most of the books currently in print in the United States. However, not all publishers are included.

Subject Guide to Books in Print

Published in New York by the Bowker Co. since 1957, this is an annual subject index to *Publishers' Trade List Annual* which indexes titles according to the subject established by the Library of Congress. Since 1968 it is published in two volumes.

For a comprehensive list of books published in Great Britain, the British Museum publishes a *General Catalogue of Printed Books* (London: The Trustees of the British Museum). Books copyrighted in Great Britain are listed in the *British Bibliography Annual Volume* (London: The Council of the British National Bibliography, Ltd.), which appears monthly with quarterly and annual cumulations. *The English Catalogue of Books* (Sauderstead, Surrey: The Publishers; Circular, Ltd.) is an annual compilation of publishers' reports. Comparable volumes are to be found in France, The Netherlands, Germany, Italy, etc. These can be useful in broadening one's scope of study.

MICROFILM REPRODUCTIONS

Guide to Microforms in Print

This catalog has been prepared in Washington, D.C., by Microcard Editions since 1961.

National Register of Microfilm Masters

This catalog has been prepared by the Library of Congress in Washington, D.C., since 1965 with the cooperation of the American Library Association and the Association of American Research Libraries.

Subject Guide to Microforms in Print

This source has been prepared in Washington, D.C., by Microcard Editions, since 1962.

The above references are lists of books, journals, and other materials available on microfilm and other microforms from American publishers. Back issues of newspapers are stored on microfilm and are generally available on interlibrary loan to libraries that do not possess their own copies.

Newspapers on Microfilm

The Library of Congress publishes this list that announces both the availability and locations of newspaper collections that are stored on microfilm.

PERIODICALS DIRECTORIES

N. W. Ayer and Son's Directory of Newspapers and Periodicals

This directory, published in Philadelphia by the N. W. Ayer and Son, Inc., since 1880, serves as a guide to American towns and cities, their principal industries, publications, and means of transportation.

Standard Periodical Directory

This directory is published by the Oxbridge Publishing Company. Coverage extends to periodicals in the United States and Canada. Like Ulrich's, the classification is by subject. However, unlike Ulrich's, this guide does not indicate indexing sources for the periodicals. This source does include house organ publications not listed in Ulrich's.

Ulrich's International Periodicals Directory

This directory, published in two volumes by R. R. Bowker Co. every two years, is classified by topics. A classified list of periodicals, as well as an index to new periodicals, is provided along with abstracting and indexing services. A title and subject index lists all titles and subjects with cross references. Coverage is international but selective.

Union of International Associations Directory of Periodicals Published by International Organizations

This directory of general, geographical indexes is published by Palais d'Egmont, Bruxelles, Belgium, with the assistance of UNESCO and first appeared in 1953; the second edition was in 1959. Two types of publications are listed: (a) periodicals published by supernational and intergovernmental institutions and (b) periodicals published by international nongovernmental organizations. English or French is used according to the language used by the organization supplying the information. Arrangement is by subject classification.

BIBLIOGRAPHIES OF BIBLIOGRAPHIES

The following research tools are master lists of bibliographies from various sources. In other words, these reference guides will tell you where to find good bibliographies on various subjects.

Bibliographic Index

This cumulative bibliography of bibliographies is a semiannual publication of the H. W. Wilson Co. with the cooperation of the Library of Congress and the New York Public Library. It has been prepared since 1938 with annual and three-, four-, or five-year cumulations. The bibliography examines approximately sixteen hundred periodicals, both English and foreign language, for bibliographic material; also indexed by subject are bibliographies published as parts of books, books, pamphlets, and articles. While coverage is sufficient for some topics, for others it serves as an introduction to subjects which should be researched in specialized subject matter indexes.

A World Bibliography of Bibliographies and of Bibliographical Catalogues, Calendars, Abstracts, Digests, Indexes and the Like

This bibliography is prepared by Theodore Besterman and the fourth edition is revised and greatly enlarged, appearing in five volumes.

BIBLIOGRAPHIES OF BOOKS AND ARTICLES

ABS Guide to Recent Publications in the Social and Behavioral Sciences

The first edition of this bibliography appeared in 1965, and the fourth supplement in 1969. It is an annotated selective list of books, pamphlets and unbound items, and some foreign language books and articles published from late 1967 to 1968, all of which first appeared in *New Studies: A Guide to Recent Publications in the Social and Behavioral Sciences*. ABS guide series is kept current bimonthly in a regular section of the American Behavioral Scientist periodical and as the separate ABS publication *New Studies*. Arrangement is alphabetical by author with an index classified by topics and methods in the social and behavioral sciences.

International Bibliography of the Social Sciences, Sociology

This bibliography has been published since 1952 by Tavistock Publications Ltd., London. It is sponsored by UNESCO and prepared by the International Committee on Social Science Documentation. The sociology volume is one of four and is compiled annually by the committee. The other three volumes are economics, political science, and social and cultural anthropology. The purpose of the volumes is to "supply each social science discipline with the basic bibliographic instruments essential to it." There are no annotations, and the entries are listed under a detailed classification scheme with author and subject indexes included to facilitate use. The three to five thousand listings are drawn from books, periodicals, and reports and official publications of governments, without limitation as to language or country of origin; only scientific publications are included. The five major divisions of subject matter are: (A) History and Organization of Social Studies; (B) Theories and Methodology of Sociology; (C) Social Structure; (D) Social Control and Communication; (E) Social Change; (F) Social Problems and Policy. Demography and social psychology are not included. There is a time lag of about two years and volumes 1-4 (1951-1954) appeared as issues of *Current Sociology*. Selectivity and infrequency of publication limits the comprehensiveness of this documentation service, although it is certainly a valuable international source.

London Bibliography of the Social Sciences

The first four volumes, published in 1931-1932 by the British Library of Political and Economic Science, London School of Economics and Political Science in London, catalogued the holdings of nine London libraries and collections, including books, pamphlets, and documents in several languages. Subsequent volumes, 5-14, published between 1934 and 1967, have expanded the list and kept it up to date. This is the most extensive bibliography covering all of the social sciences. The improved sixth supplement (London: Mausell Information/Pub. Ltd.) was published in 1970, and includes works which appeared in print less than a year ago. Volume 21 provides full subject indexes, including a complete list of subject headings used. The bibliography is strong in economics, political science, and sociology, and also contains some references in history, anthropology, and education.

Social Science Information

This professional journal is published by Mouton under the auspices of the International Social Science Council with the assistance of UNESCO and the VIth Section of l'École Pratique des Hautes

Études (Paris) six times per year. It abstracts periodical articles in the fields of sociology, economics, and politics, and in addition to publishing scholarly articles on research of development, data sources, and other topics, this journal provides several inventory and bibliographic services. "The Sociology of the Social Sciences: An International Bibliography," which appeared in the February 1970 issue, represents the first installment of a bibliography to be published biannually. "Selected references to material dealing with the social, economic, and political organization of the social sciences in various countries have been annotated and organized into an analytical framework." Other services have included: (1) "Studies Concerning Concepts in the Social Sciences" (December 1969), listing the principal studies devoted to the current concepts in the social sciences arranged by concept headings (e.g., "action," "anomie," "violence"), and (2) "New Periodicals in the Social Sciences," the tenth supplementary list, bringing the previous world lists up to date with titles, countries, and a cumulative index for 1969. A new feature beginning February 1970 entitled "Selected Translations" lists English translations of selections originally published in French. This will continue as a special section of *Social Science Information* until it is established as a new journal. Similar ventures are being considered for other languages.

BIBLIOGRAPHIES OF BOOKS AND ARTICLES (SPECIALIZED)

Communism in the United States

This bibliography was compiled and edited by Joel Seidman and published by the Cornell University Press, Ithaca, New York, in 1969. Useful annotated descriptions and listing of good historical material (articles and pamphlets) make this a valuable source. Listings are alphabetical by author with a subject index, and the material is restricted to writings of and about the American Communist Party, beginning with the formation of American Communist parties in 1919. Some items are included relating to its predecessor, the left wing of the Socialist Party.

Current Sociocultural Change Literature

This bibliography is an annotated classification of selected interdisciplinary sources prepared by Edward Knop and Kathryn Aparicio and published in 1967 by the Center for the Study of Cultural and Social Change, Department of Sociology and Anthropology, University of North Dakota, Grand Forks, North Dakota. This is a fairly comprehensive listing of articles and books on topics relating to sociocultural change, with coverage extending from 1950 on. Introductions and essays are provided by the authors, as well as one-sentence descriptions of the listings. Coverage includes the following dimensions of change: cultural and institutional, structural, demographic, ecological, and ideological-psychological, in a number of settings (advanced urban industrial settings, transitional urban industrial, advanced agricultural settings, and folk-agrarian settings). Topics include social control, assimilation, acculturation, innovation and diffusion, planned changes (grass roots community developments, administrative-change programs), methods for studying change, theories of change, social disorganization and responses to sociocultural lag, and marginality and alienation.

A Guide to Social Science Resources in Women's Studies

This annotated guide, compiled by Oakes and Sheldon, is organized according to academic disciplines with appropriate subdivisions. It covers anthropology, economics, history—both U.S. and European—psychology, sociology, and contemporary feminist thought. Sociology is divided into the following subdivisions: general, women and society, marriage and motherhood, sex roles and socialization. It also contains sections on bibliographies, journals, other resources, and author and subject indexes.

A Guide to Working-Class History

Faler, Green et al. have written a guide to resources about the history of working people in North America, including a section on Canada.

International Bibliography of Research in Marriage and the Family

Distributed by the University of Minnesota Press for the Minnesota Family Study Center and the Institute of Life Insurance, the introduction states that, "The bibliography should make it less difficult for the interested person to surmount interdisciplinary boundaries and gain a broader perspective on existing knowledge of the family." The compilers, Joan Aldous and Reuben Hill, have prepared 12,850 references from journals and books, monographs, pamphlets, bulletins, and sections of books are indexed by Key-Word-in-Context based on titles. A subject index, complete reference list, author list, and periodicals list are also provided. Empirical data, descriptions of the family in historical eras, case histories, and some theoretically oriented items (where empirical evidence is limited to illustration) are included in the bibliography. The original bibliography covered the years 1900–1964. A second volume was published in 1974 which included the years 1965–1972. In 1974, a new journal, *Inventory of Marriage and Family Literature*, was introduced to continue Joan Aldous' and Reuben Hill's work. The first volume covered 1973–1974 and continues on an annual basis.

Nationalism and National Development

Prepared by Karl W. Deutsch and Richard L. Merritt, this interdisciplinary bibliography was published by the MIT Press, Cambridge, Massachusetts, in 1970. It contains over six thousand references, with author and Key-Word-in-Context indexes, on topics relating to nationalism, including the sociological aspects (general, sociology of conflict and war, elites, and social stratification); the economic, social anthropological, social psychological, and political aspects; processes of national differentiation and assimilation; colonialism, imperialism, and decolonization; nationalism outside the Western world, etc.

The Nature of Conflict, Studies on the Sociological Aspects of International Tensions, Tensions and Technology Series

This bibliography, prepared by the International Sociological Association in collaboration with Jessie Bernard, T. H. Pear, Raymond Aron, and Robert C. Angell, was published in 1957 by UNESCO in

Paris. It represents an up-to-date survey and evaluation of research by sociologists and social psychologists into the nature, conditions, and implications of human conflict, and particularly conflict between nations. The first part consists of five chapters: (1) The Sociological Study of Conflict by Jessie Bernard; (2) The Psychological Study of Tensions and Conflict by T. H. Pear; (3) Conflict and War from the Viewpoint of Historical Sociology by Raymond Aron; (4) Discovering Paths to Peace by R. C. Angell; and (5) Planning Future Research. The second part consists of an annotated bibliography topically subdivided along the following lines: (1) Sociology and psychosociology of intergroup conflicts: tensions, stereotypes, prejudices, strategy, and communication; (2) International Relations; (3) Racial Conflicts: colonialism; and (4) Industrial Agrarian Conflicts: class problems. The approach is international in scope.

The Negro in America

This excellent sourcebook of information and references, compiled by Mary L. Fisher, prepared by Elizabeth W. Miller, and published in 1970 by the Harvard University Press, Cambridge, Massachusetts, seeks to make accessible "significant writings," and to "intensify the problems and to mark the urgency of their solutions." The second edition, revised and enlarged, has references to English language materials published in the United States, primarily since 1954, drawn together with older sources which are of seminal value or are illustrative of historical background, attitudes, and trends. The content encompasses clinical, empirical, prescriptive, polemical, scholarly, and journalistic works. The scope of the second edition has been expanded to give more coverage to black history and social institutions and to economic, political, and social conditions. Topics include demography, employment, economic status and problems, urban problems, education, intergroup relations, protest theory and practice, black nationalism, and black power. Some annotations are provided; however, the chief value of this source lies in its comprehensiveness and clear organization.

The Negro in the United States

This selected bibliography, prepared by Dorothy B. Porter and published in 1970 by the Library of Congress, Washington, D.C., is a compilation of bibliographies, guides, indexes, encyclopedias, dictionaries, biographies, and annuals dealing with various topics—social conditions, crime and delinquency, family, organizations, politics, race relations, riots, and black history. The main body is composed of Library of Congress holdings on blacks selected on the basis of frequency of request for particular works in large libraries, presence in collections on blacks, or inclusion in numerous bibliographies and reading lists from colleges and universities. Selective topics covered in addition to those mentioned above are discriminatory practices, efforts to obtain political and economic freedom, educational and cultural history of blacks, urban blacks, and religious life.

Occupational Literature

Edition by Gertrude Forrester and published in 1958 by the H. W. Wilson Co., this publication provides an annotated bibliography of books and pamphlets arranged alphabetically by occupation. This source has been updated to 1971.

Political Elites: A Select Computerized Bibliography

This systematic bibliography was published by the MIT Press, Cambridge, Massachusetts, in 1968, and prepared by Carl Beck and J. Thomas McKechnie. It includes nonformal as well as formal elite studies, and attempts to give a fairly representative reflection of the ideological diversity and theoretical and conceptual issues evoked in the study of political elites. The aim is to provide an extensive, representative, but not exhaustive, account of the literature, books, and journals. Citations are listed in three parts. Section I is a Key-Word-Out-of-Context title listing in which an article or book appears as many times as it contains key words; Section I also provides reference codes to complete citation listings enumerated in Section II. Section III is a list of authors. Each study is further classified according to its relevance to one or more of seven general topics of elite analysis: general elite theory, definition of elites, composition of elite perceptions and norms, and methodology of elites. (See also Beck, Carl, James M. Malloy, and Wm. R. Campbell, *A Survey of Elite Studies* [Special Operations Research Office, American University, 1965] which examines the paradigms used in the categorization and explanation of political elites. This source provides a sample inventory of general statements on elite theories, definitions of elites, and propositions about the behavior and structure of particular elite groups in various types of political systems.)

A Selected Bibliography on Values, Ethics, and Esthetics in the Behavioral Sciences and Philosophy: 1920–1958

Prepared by Ethel M. Albert and Clyde Kluckholn, this bibliography was published in 1959 by The Free Press, Glencoe, Illinois.

Social Stratification: A Research Bibliography

As pointed out in the introduction by the authors, Norval D. Glenn, Jon P. Alston, and David Weiner, this field is expanding rapidly and becoming more important and dominant in sociology. This creates a situation in which it is difficult to keep up with the literature. This bibliography, published by The Glendessary Press, Inc., Berkeley, California, in 1970, serves as a beginning, and although a very extensive one, it does not cover the field entirely. Only publications in English are included (with some translations). No doctoral dissertations, master's theses, unpublished papers of professional meetings, or book reviews are listed. No census reports are listed except for monographs and a few of the "Current Population Reports" issued by the U.S. Bureau of the Census. With regard to journals, primarily U.S. and British sociological journals were reviewed for applicable items. No mass circulation magazines were searched, with a few exceptions. Also, no systematic search was undertaken for the period before 1940 or after April 1968, although a few items falling outside of these bounds are included.

The book is divided into two sections: Social stratifications, and social mobility and correlates of stratification. These in turn are broken down into more detailed categories. There are no annotations or attempts to judge the quality of the publications, and no academic publications were excluded on grounds of quality. The authors do provide brief introductions to each section and an author index is included. In Section I additional bibliographies on particular topics in the field are cited.

Survey Research on Comparative Social Change:
A Bibliography

This bibliography was published by the MIT Press, Cambridge, Massachusetts, in 1968, and compiled by Frederick W. Frey with Peter Stephenson and Katherine Archer Smith, and with the assistance of the staff of Human Factors in Modernization Project, Center for International Studies, Massachusetts Institute of Technology. This is a fairly comprehensive bibliography of cross-national survey research and of survey research in developing societies. Sixteen hundred individual annotations are listed, and only English language periodicals are researched through 1967. Some major topics headings include: comparison of groups; family, group, and interpersonal relations; demography and women as a group; communications, education, political institutions, economic behavior and institutions; and attitudes and behavior.

Women's History Research Center

The *WHRC* is a small tax-exempt foundation which

maintained the *International Women's History Archive,* by and about the current women's movement, and a *Topical Research Library* of two thousand files, which document the position of women: past and present, in all walks of life, in many countries and ethnic groups, in history, in women's organizations, in events, and in roles. The *Archive* and the *Library* constituted the *Women's History Library,* which had been created by hundreds of women and organizations over the past six years, and was used by activists and scholars from all over the U.S. and other countries.

(Quoted from the October 1974 newsletter)

The library's collections are now held by Northwestern University in Evanston, Illinois, and the University of Wyoming, Laramie. Microfilms of materials drawn from these collections on women's publications, law, and health and mental health have been ordered by an extensive list of colleges and universities across the country. Publications available from *WHRC* by mail include: *Directory of Women's Periodicals; Women's Studies Courses; Bibliographies on Women;* listings on rape, prostitution, films, art, and *Synopsis of*

Women in World History. For further information write to the Women's History Research Center, Inc., 2325 Oak Street, Berkeley, California 94708.

Women's Liberation and Revolution: A Bibliography

The second edition of this valuable research tool, compiled by Sheila Rowbotham, was published in 1973 in Bristol, England, by Falling Wall Press. Comprehensive listings cover feminism and revolutionary politics, the family, culture, equal rights, consciousness, national liberation movements, women and colonialism, and women in history.

The Women's Movement in the Seventies
An International English-Language Bibliography

This bibliography was prepared by Albert Kirichmar and published by Scarecrow Press, Metuchen, New Jersey. It is a fairly comprehensive listing of eighty-six hundred dissertations, books, pamphlets, research reports, periodical articles, and government documents on topics relating to change, attempted change and continuing problems facing women. The major drawback of this work is that sources were limited to those published between 1970 and 1976, thereby eliminating prominent authors in the subject areas. However, author and subject indexes are invaluable and bibliographies and reference sources provide information beyond the confines of this book. Citations are arranged first by geographical area then subject, which includes: economics, education, law, politics, history, religion, philosophy, sociology, anthropology, physical science, psychology, and literature. Although references within the sociological area are narrow and shallow, this book is a good beginning for further sources.

Women's Work Is . . . "Resources on Working Women"

This excellent bibliography and resource guide provides descriptive information and summaries of material on working women drawn from a wide variety of sources, including books, journal articles, labor union periodicals, newspapers, government and U.N. reports, and films. The material is organized into chapters dealing with the facts and figures of women's employment, health and safety issues, day care, women's double shift of paid and family work, working women's history, the concerns of women internationally, resources for organizing women, the rise of the pink collar worker, and working women as a concern of the church. The summaries are clear, well-written, and informative; poetry, graphics, and bold type subheadings enliven the format and make the material more accessible. This guide, edited by Bobbi Wells Hargleroad, is published by the Institute on the Church in Urban-Industrial Society and intended for use as a resource by church, women's, and labor groups. If this booklet is unavailable at the library it may be ordered directly from the Institute at 5700 South Woodlawn Avenue, Chicago, Illinois 60637.

Women in America: A Guide to Books

Barbara Haber's fully annotated narrative bibliography of books dealing with women covers the years 1963-1975. Its purpose is to highlight authentic female experiences. The books are organized by topic. Topics covered include abortion, black and native American women, education, health, feminism, history, law and politics, life styles, literature, marriage and related issues, prostitution, psychology, rape, sex roles, sexuality, and work. Neither reference books nor drama and poetry are included in this valuable new resource.

Women in American Labor History, 1825-1935

This is a very interesting annotated compilation of articles, books, pamphlets, government publications, and monographs on women at work and in the labor movement. Sections cover specific industries, trade unions and problems related to organizing, working conditions, strikes and lockouts, protective legislation, worker education, labor leaders, and women's organizations supportive of labor. Two useful features are Appendix A: Archival Collections in the U.S. Relating to Women and Labor and Appendix B: Publications of the U.S. Women's Bureau Through 1935. In addition to general books and journal articles, the editors (Martha Jane Soltow, Carolyn Forche, and Murray Massre) have also surveyed the periodicals, publications, and convention proceedings of a number of labor unions and other organizations of relevance to working women such as the American Federation of Labor, the Knights of Labor, the Amalgamated Clothing Workers, the International Ladies Garment Workers, and the National Women's Trade Union League. This bibliography was produced and published by the School of Industrial and Labor Relations and the Libraries of Michigan State University at East Lansing, Michigan, in 1972.

Women in the United States: An Historical Contribution

This annotated narrative bibliography of issues and resources on the history of women in the United States can be purchased by sending one dollar to The New England Free Press, 60 Union Square, Somerville, Massachusetts 02143. It is compiled by historians Ann Gordon, Mari Jo Buhle and Nancy Schrom Dye, all well-known scholars.

A Working Bibliography on the Negro in the United States

This work, compiled by Dorothy B. Porter and published by Xerox, University Microfilms, 1969, contains a good section on reference tools. A few significant periodical references are included in the bibliographic section. In addition, a list of current periodicals relevant to black studies is provided. There is a somewhat different selection of paperbacks than that noted in the 1970 volume by this author (*The Negro in the United States;* Washington; Library of Congress); these are comprised primarily of English language monographs. This volume is somewhat more relevant and easier to follow.

BIBLIOGRAPHIES OF BOOKS AND ARTICLES (AREA STUDIES)

American Universities Field Staff, A Select Bibliography: Asia, Africa, E. Europe, and Latin America

This bibliography was published in New York by the American Universities Field Staff, Inc., in 1960, with supplements from 1961 to 1971. It lists some sixty-eight hundred books and journals, with some annotations and a biennial supplement, for the areas indicated.

An Annotated Bibliography of Directed Social Changes

This bibliography, prepared by Donn Vorhis Hart and published in Syracuse, New York, at Syracuse University, Maxwell Graduate School of Citizenship and Public Affairs, Center for Overseas Operations in 1961, contains 405 items with emphasis on anthropological literature.

Bibliography of Social Science Periodicals and Monograph Series

This series of bibliographies has been prepared by the Foreign Manpower Research Office, Bureau of the Census, U.S. Department of Commerce in Washington, D.C., U.S. Government Printing Office, 1961–1965. Each publication covers one country for the entire postwar period. The selection of countries includes primarily those of the communist world (Yugoslavia, Bulgaria, Russia, etc.), as well as other countries using less familiar languages.

Foreign Area Studies and the College Library

This helpful introductory reference guide to area studies is edited by Morehouse Ward and was published in New York by the State Education Department, University of the State of New York, Foreign Area Materials Center, Occasional Publication no. 1, 1965. It lists bibliographies, reference services, acquisitions programs, and other activities.

Hispanic Foundation of the Library of Congress, Handbook of Latin American Studies

This scholarly bibliography in the behavioral and humanistic sciences has been published annually since 1936 in Washington, D.C., by the Library of Congress, Hispanic Foundation.

SECONDARY SOURCES

Handbooks, resource guides to the literature, encyclopedias, and dictionaries are useful secondary sources in which material is selected, reviewed, and evaluated; these secondary sources are excellent means for reviewing the issues and research in a particular area of interest. One problem inherent in these reviews is the lack of currency. Handbooks, for example, are usually at least a year or two behind the most recent research when they are published and tend to become quickly dated. In the case of sociological material of classical importance and the historical development of the discipline, this problem is reduced.

HANDBOOKS

Annual Review of Sociology (Also Psychology, Anthropology)

This yearly review, begun in 1974, contains approximately twenty-five chapters which discuss current research and theoretical developments covering a wide array of sociological topics. Some of these have included: "The Organization of Health Service," "The Construction of Reality," "Marx's Conception of Class," and "Models of Network Structure." The *Reviews of Anthropology and Psychology* cover the same ground for their respective disciplines.

Handbook for Social Research in Urban Areas

Edited by Philip M. Hauser and published by UNESCO in Paris in 1965 as part of the Technology and Society Series, this handbook has chapters written by international contributors on urban research. The chapters are organized into two major sections. The first, dealing with social research data and procedure, is concerned primarily with a discussion of the areal units for urban analysis, sources of data for social research in urban areas, use of field and case studies, and the usefulness of various types of research approaches. Part Two includes discussions of the different types of studies in specific areas of urban social research: general studies of urbanization, demographic studies, and studies of social organization, social and personal disorganization, urban plant and administration, and migration and acculturation.

Handbook of Contemporary Urban Life

This collection of essays edited by David Street and published in 1978 by Jossey-Bass of San Francisco represents the first collective attempt in recent decades to renew the Chicago School of Urban Sociology. The various authors focus on causes and consequences of living in cities and, although most of the papers are speculative, they possess extensive citations. The vast majority of the papers deal only with U.S. urbanization (only one by Brian Roberts ventures outside the U.S.) and, more specifically, most focus on well-known central cities in older metropolitan areas. This approach can be either a strength or a weakness, depending on your area of interest. Four major issues are covered by this collection: are urban and rural differentiations declining, is differentiation within the metropolis increasing, persistence of local sentiments in mass society, and the relationship of various societal institutions to urbanization.

Handbook of Medical Sociology

This handbook, edited by Howard E. Freeman, Sol Levine, and Leo G. Reeder, was published in 1963 by Prentice-Hall, Inc., New York. Following an introduction and two general sections dealing with contributions to the sociology of medicine and the evolution of social medicine, it is divided into four sections: (1) Sociology of Medicine; (2) Practitioners, Patients, and Medical Settings; (3) Sociology of Medical Care; and (4) Strategy, Method, and Status of Medical Sociology. Each of the separate chapters contains a list of references and, in addition, Chapter 20, "Social Research in Health and Medicine: a Bibliography," by Ozzie G. Simmons, provides extensive listings of relevant material arranged in accordance with the organization of the book.

Handbook of Small Group Research

Coverage in this handbook by A. Paul Hare, published by The Free Press, New York, 1962, includes (1) group process and structure (norms and social control; interpersonal choice; roles; decision process; social interaction); (2) six variables that affect the interaction process: personality, social characteristics, group size, task communication network, and leadership; and (3) performance characteristics. An appendix treats research methods and the technique of factor analysis, and a subject index is provided which includes the abstract numbers for many articles included in *Psychological Abstracts* and *Sociological Abstracts*. Pages 416-496 comprise an extensive bibliography section.

Handbook of Social Psychology

This revised and enlarged second edition of the 1954 *Handbook*, edited by Gardiner Linzey and E. Aronson, published in five volumes by Addison-Wesley, Reading, Massachusetts, in 1968-1969, covers the entire range of social psychology and provides a review of the research, theory, and information in the field. Volume 1 delineates the historical origins of social psychology and presents the systematic positions which have been developed in the field: Freudian theory, role theory, stimulus-response theory, etc. Each theory is discussed by one of its major proponents. The remaining four volumes contain the following material: (2) research methods: such as interviewing, attitude measurement, and data analysis; (3) the individual in a social context: such topics as person perception, psychology of language (psycholinguistics), etc.; (4) group psychology and phenomena of interaction; and (5) applied social psychology. Extensive references are given for each chapter. Author and subject indexes are provided.

Handbook of Work, Organization, and Society

Edited by Robert Dubin and published in 1976 by Rand McNally, Chicago, this handbook will be valuable to anyone with an interest in the sociology of work, occupations, or organizations. However, there are major topics which are not covered and, thus, it cannot serve as an overview of the traditional fields of industrial, occupational, or organizational sociology. The editor attempts to cover three themes: (1) orientation toward the future, (2) analysis of value systems different from Western capitalism, and (3) understanding aspects of work behavior that have seldom been considered. The following subjects are covered: work and leisure, work and the individual, working behavior, work organizations, executives and managers, work and society, cross-cultural perspectives, and the postindustrial culture. The strength of this handbook lies in its excellent individual chapters.

Rand McNally Sociology Series

Handbook of Marriage and the Family, edited by Harold T. Christensen and published in 1964, reports theoretical and methodological orientations and substantive findings, as well as applications and normative considerations for research on the family. The family is treated as a social institution and as a small group association, in terms of its internal workings. The introduction points out that such topics as child development, the youth cult, women's roles, demographic analysis, sexual behavior, and household economics, are intentionally ignored or treated as subsidiary in relation to the main focus. It is important to note that while this source can be useful as a comprehensive coverage of the main current of sociological research on the family, the student should also be aware of the growing body of literature on the sociology of women and sex roles which is often critical of the implications, assumptions, and applications of traditional family research.

Handbook of Modern Sociology, edited by Robert E. L. Faris and published by Rand McNally and Co., Chicago, Illinois, in 1964, summarizes all major research areas of modern sociology, interrelating material and indicating trends in the contemporary development of the discipline. Material covered includes theory, methodology, development of sociological thought, mathematical models and computer simulation, family, kinship, marriage, social movements (with a particularly useful bibliography), race relations, the small group, population, social differentiation, and collective behavior. Numerous references are provided for each topic. This differs from a general textbook in that there has been an attempt to include "frontier" research and an indication of new directions rather than merely a presentation of established concepts and principles.

In *Handbook of Organizations*, contributions from authorities in the field are organized by the editor, James G. March, to report and to summarize sociological knowledge about human organizations. Published in 1965, this handbook presents methodologies, references, concepts, ideas, applications, and theoretical and substantive analyses. Literature on specific institutions such as schools, prisons, business organizations, the military, political parties, and public bureaucracies is reviewed. Additional coverage includes decision-making, communications, management, theory, field methods, small groups and large organizations, and social structure and organizations. Each article includes a lengthy bibliography.

Review of Child Development Research

Edited by Martin L. Hoffman and Lois Hoffman, published by the Russell Sage Foundation, New York, 1964, and prepared under the auspices of the Society for Research in Child Development, these two volumes collate and interpret research in child development, covering such topics as the effects of the mass media, the development of moral character and moral ideology, and the consequences of different kinds of parental discipline.

Review of Educational Research

A source of narrative bibliography can be found in this journal, published five times a year since 1931 by the American Education Research Association, National Education Association. In a manner similar to *Education Abstracts*, each issue is devoted to a specific area in educational research. The essays are written by specialists in the field and are evaluations as well as reviews of the literature; bibliographies accompany each article. The research literature is usually reviewed in three-year cycles; however, some topics may appear more frequently than others. Each issue has a subject index which cumulates annually.

UNESCO: Narrative Surveys

UNESCO has provided several sources of narrative surveys: *Current Sociology, The International Social Science Journal,* and *Education Abstracts.* These surveys are generally valuable, providing good coverage of existing literature, usually conforming to high standards, and aiming at a "reasonable" degree of objectivity.

GUIDES TO THE LITERATURE

A Guide to Appalachian Studies

This is a special issue (Autumn 1977) of the *Appalachian Journal,* "A Regional Studies Review," which is published at Appalachian State University in Boone, North Carolina. Scholars in the fields of anthropology, history, folklore, sociology, political science, urban studies, and religion, among others, reviewed and assessed the literature on Appalachia in their respective disciplines. The authors of the review essays discuss the major themes, interpretations, and theoretical debates in the literature and suggest key questions for future research. Their suggestions provide a good source of ideas for term paper topics as well. Several useful appendices add to the comprehensiveness of the guide; these include a bibliography of Appalachian studies, a guide to general educational resources in the region, a guide to current periodicals, a selected bibliography of unpublished theses and dissertations, and a directory of organizations and individuals working in or writing about the region.

Latin American Review of Books (vols. 1 and 2)

These very useful research tools are published by Ramparts Press and edited by Colin Harding (1 and 2) and Christopher Roper (1). Review 1 includes comprehensive review essays of books on international relations, land reform, church and education, guerrillas, Brazil, Argentina, Central America and the Caribbean, the Andean countries, and publishing in the field of Latin American studies. Review 2 includes articles not tied to newly published books and long review articles on United Popular experience in Chile, urbanization in Latin America, recent Argentine politics, future of the Brazilian economy, etc. These are excellent sources for bibliographic references and a guide to current analyses and debates in Latin American related research.

The Literature of the Social Sciences

The approach of this introductory survey and guide published by the London Library Association in 1960 in London is more bibliographical and international in outlook than Hoselitz (next item). It is a less detailed source and provides a useful basic starting point for a review of literature in the social sciences.

A Reader's Guide to the Social Sciences, revised edition

This series of narrative surveys, edited by Bert F. Hoselitz and published in New York by The Free Press in 1970, includes coverage of sociology, history, geography, political science, economics, anthropology, and psychology by specialists in the respective fields. The section on sociology, written by Peter Blau and Joan Moore, discusses the development of sociology, outlines the substantial intellectual areas, and reviews the influential contemporary sociological literature in selected areas.

Sociology in the U.S.A.: A Trend Report

Edited by Hans L. Zetterberg and prepared and published by Documentation in the Social Sciences, UNESCO, in Paris, 1956, this guide covers the period of 1945-1955. Reviews and surveys of the literature, charting major studies, research activities, and general issues, tendencies, and preoccupations in various areas, have been commissioned from specialists who were thought to be in close touch with developments in the field and whose accounts would constitute authoritative guides to the progress of the discipline. "A Guide to American Sociology," by Zetterberg, opens the book; an extensive bibliography (pages 131-156) closes it. Chapters deal with methodology, social institutions and groups (political sociology, sociology of law, education, knowledge, the family, small groups), vertical and geographical stratifications (rural and urban sociology of stratification), and some social problems (crime, ethnic relations, mental health).

Sources of Information in the Social Sciences, A Guide to the Literature, second edition (1973)

This guide to the literature was prepared by Carl M. White and associates and published by the American Library Association. A general chapter on the literature and references of the social sciences is followed by individual chapters written by specialists on the fields of history, economics and business administration, sociology, anthropology, psychology, education, geography, and political science. Each subject is treated in two parts: (1) a bibliographic review of the developments and literature in the field, listing the most significant empirical and theoretical studies on various topics in the field; and (2) an annotated bibliography of reference materials—bibliography and sources—pertinent to each subject. The general review of sociology covers the following areas: social theory, methods, and substantive topics such as the family, and political sociology, deviance, organizations, and stratification. The annotated list of sociological sources ranges from reviews and bibliographies to books of statistical tables and directories of unpublished information.

Women's History Sources

A geographical listing of repositories with materials pertinent to the study of women. Edited by Andrea Hinding and published by Bowker, it promises to be an essential guide to historical societies, collections, and archives across the country highlighting materials pertinent to the study of women.

REFERENCE AND RESEARCH GUIDES

European Periodical Literature in the Social Sciences and the Humanities

The purpose of this handbook, prepared by Paul E. Vesenyi and published by Scarecrow Press, Inc., Metuchen, New Jersey, in 1969, is to assist the researcher in locating periodical articles published in Europe. Indexes, abstracts, dictionaries, union lists, and miscellaneous bibliographies are utilized.

Guide to Reference Books

This guide, written by C. M. Winchell and published by American Library Association in Chicago, Illinois, in 1967, reports on reference books in American libraries, and was first published in 1902 and kept up to date through periodic supplements. It is the most comprehensive book of its type in print. The first supplement, including material published in 1965-1966, was edited by Eugene P. Sheehy in 1968. In the eight and ninth editions, eight thousand reference books are catalogued in five major categories: general works, the humanities, the social sciences, historical and area studies, and pure and applied sciences. Selected reference books are listed and evaluated with an indication of comparative value of the books. Each field is introduced with a description of the types of reference tools available and special group features. The section on sociology is not comprehensive, dealing mainly with reference material concerned with social conditions and social welfare, criminology, and racial groups. Coverage of general references and bibliographies is good.

Guide to Reference Material, vol. III, Social and Historical Sciences

This is a somewhat smaller British counterpart of the Winchell, edited by A. J. Walford and published by Library Association in London, 1959, 1963, 1968 supplements. Sixty percent of the items listed were published in Great Britain, but the annotation is especially meaningful for those reference works in foreign languages where Winchell seems to be weak. In addition to a general section, coverage of the social sciences and humanities includes such fields as sociology and social work, statistics, cultural anthropology, education, psychology, and political science. There is a useful section dealing with sources of biographical information.

Research Resources

This comprehensive, interdisciplinary reference tool is compiled by J. B. Mason and published by American Bibliographic Center, Clio Press in Santa Barbara, California, 1968. It provides worldwide annotated coverage of hundreds of research aids, including books and periodicals. Materials in the general social sciences are reviewed: Chapter 3 covers indexes and abstracts in the social sciences, one section of which is devoted to sociology. In addition, guides to bibliographic reference works and U.S. government publications are listed. This quite extensive and useful guide can assist you through the maze of research material in the library, a goal of the handbook as well. It provides annotated lists of reference materials on numerous topics, including sociology, and is cross-referenced with Winchell, White, and Walford where applicable.

Sources of Business Information

This excellent overall source for research on corporations and the business world was compiled by E. T. Conan, Jr., and published in 1949 by Prentice-Hall, Inc., Englewood Cliffs, New Jersey, with revised editions in 1964 and 1970, University of California Press, Berkeley and Los Angeles. It lists bibliographies, manuals, textbooks, periodicals, etc., primarily American.

RADICAL AND ALTERNATIVE RESEARCH GUIDES

A number of social change organizations and research agencies have published valuable manuals for investigating special topics such as community organization and development, the corporate economic structure, and the social bases of the tax system, real estate and property. For example, in 1970 the North American Congress on Latin America (see Chapter 4) prepared the NACLA Research Methodology Guide. Although the material in this guide is somewhat dated, it still remains a useful reference and bibliographic aid for research on power structure and elites. Comprehensive summaries of sources for generating material on various topics have been compiled and reviewed.

Additional sources of information on alternative research can be found in:

Hill and Shapiro, "Training the Radical Researcher: A Course on Bibliographic Methods for Document Research"

This article which appeared in the Winter 1978 issue of *The Insurgent Sociologist* (see Chapter 4) developed out of a seminar conducted by a sociologist and a librarian at the University of Oregon. The aim of this course, like that of this book, was to provide students with greater knowledge facility in using reference tools and thereby decrease their sense of intimidation, and eliminate the feeling of being overwhelmed by the library. We found this article useful for updating some of the material in Chapters 5 and 6 of this handbook; some supplementary sections are relevant to radical or alternative research: alternative research manuals, organizing manuals, biographical sources, and directories of corporations and executives.

NACLA Research Methodology Guide

This extremely useful reference guide and bibliography for research on power structures is published by North American Congress on Latin America, Inc., and available at P.O. Box 57, Cathedral Station, New York, New York 10025, and P.O. Box 226, Berkeley, California 94701, for $1.00 plus postage. Comprehensive summaries of sources for generating material on various topics have been compiled and reviewed. The topics include: personalities and elites (with a good section on biographical sources of data); political parties; corporations; the media industry; labor organizations; the military-industrial complex and the universities; the police; the church; the health industry; imperialism and the Third World—researching underdeveloped countries. All kinds of research tools are listed, including books, periodicals, government documents, bibliographies, directories, indexes, yearbooks, etc.

NACLA has also published several studies on Latin America, the university-military complex, the Columbia University power structure, the Hanna industrial complex in the Midwest. They also publish a monthly NACLA Newsletter; feature articles are accompanied by reprints and translations of important articles, book reviews, and significant research documents.

Raising Hell, a Citizen's Guide to the Fine Art of Investigation

This pamphlet was written by Dan Noyes of the Center for Investigative Reporting and published by *Mother Jones* magazine. It was designed to facilitate the effective exercise of the public's right to know; it is based on the premise that citizens must know how to investigate the facts in order to have an impact on decisions which affect their lives. The information in this booklet is also useful to students who want to investigate social issues of local or national importance which are not adequately treated or referenced in the traditional social science sources. In the tradition of muckracking, the guide introduces the student to the location and use of the mass of library and public records which provide facts about business and government affairs. In addition to sections on investigating individuals, corporations, government, property, and public records, a general list of resources has been assembled in the "Investigative Checklist" and the "Investigative Library."

ENCYCLOPEDIAS

Encyclopedia of Educational Research

This encyclopedia was a project of the American Educational Research Association and has been published in its third edition by Macmillan and Co., New York, in 1960. Coverage includes critical evaluations, synthesis, and interpretation in four areas: human development; the relationship of the church, state, and the economy to education; educational history; and identification of the major educational functions and tasks. The lengthy articles are signed and dated and provide extensive bibliographies.

Encyclopedia of Philosophy

This encyclopedia, edited by Paul Edwards and published by Macmillan and Co., New York, in 1967, appears in eight volumes and covers the discipline of philosophy as well as the relationships between philosophy and other disciplines. Articles are written at the lay and professional level and include coverage of the most influential philosophers and the history of philosophical thought.

Encyclopedia of the Social Sciences

This encyclopedia was edited by E. R. A. Seligman and Alvin Johnson and published in fifteen volumes in 1930-1935. ESS treats the science of sociology in the light of the thirties as IESS reflects the sixties.

International Encyclopedia of the Social Sciences

Edited by D. L. Sills, this seventeen-volume set including index is published by Macmillan and Co., New York, 1968. It is a comprehensive work intended to provide general reviews of the knowledge in various disciplines including psychology, political science, anthropology, statistics, economics, social thought, history, law, geography, psychiatry, and sociology, for educated laymen, students, and social scientists in allied fields. Contributions for the topical and biographical articles are drawn from major scholars in all fields of the social sciences.The articles are moderately long but generally concise and comprehensible due to the five-thousand-word limitation. Extensive cross-references are provided, as well as excellent bibliographies covering both the historical development of the subject and work currently being done in the area. This is a very good source for "official" bibliographies; the encyclopedia is useful to students and researchers as an introduction and review of what is already known about a topic. The IESS was designed basically to reflect the state of the social sciences in the sixties.

General encyclopedias covering a broad range of topics include the *Encyclopaedia Britannica* and the *Encyclopedia Americana.* The reference desks of many libraries contain encyclopedias published in other countries and in languages other than English.

DICTIONARIES

Several dictionaries have been published which can be useful in understanding the derivation and usage of specialized and popular sociological terms and concepts which appear often in the literature.

A Dictionary of Social Science

Written by John T. Zadrozny and published by Public Affairs Press in 1959, this source includes easily understood definitions of the more important terms used in sociology, political science, economics, population studies, psychology, physical anthropology, prehistory, and jurisprudence. Written for the social scientists and laymen, it includes colloquial words and some foreign terms. Many of the terms included are from the popular rather than technical vocabularies of the various disciplines.

A Dictionary of Sociology

Edited by Mitchelle G. Duncan and published by Aldine Publishing Co., in 1968, this dictionary defines terms from social psychology, social and cultural anthropology, and political science, as well as sociology, for those just beginning the study of sociology.

A Dictionary of the Social Sciences

Edited by Julius Gould and William Kolb and compiled under the auspices of UNESCO, and published by The Free Press in New York in 1964, this dictionary defines, in essays signed by contributing specialists, widely used key concepts in the fields of sociology, social psychology, economics, political science, and anthropology. The terms tend to be general rather than specific: highly technical terms are omitted. The articles vary in length from several paragraphs to several pages. Etymology and usage by various schools are stressed, and all major definitions of a term are given, common usages as well as accepted scientific usages; illustrative quotations from the literature are sometimes included. Bibliographies are not included. This is the first of several dictionaries in the social sciences, each in a different language, which have been planned by UNESCO.

A Modern Dictionary of Sociology

This dictionary, written by George A. Theodorson and Achilles G. Theodorson and published by the Thomas Y. Crowell Co., in 1969, has definitions ranging from several lines to several hundred words and covering all of the important concepts in sociology, including many related terms from such fields as psychology, cultural anthropology, philosophy, statistics, and a smaller number from economics and political science. Cross-references and short discussions of some definitions are provided; where possible, the original source of the term is given.

Chapter
Six

---

governmental and
nongovernmental sources
of data

GOVERNMENTAL SOURCES OF DATA

Very extensive and diverse sources of data exist in the forms of
governmental reports, investigations, surveys, and other types of
research. The United States government is one of the largest publishing organizations in the world; abundant resources and access to
information not widely available to others enable government agencies to produce data on subjects ranging from labor statistics to
congressional committee hearings on the powerlessness of migrant
field workers. Governmental sources of data are especially important for two reasons: (1) While a private organization or researcher
can only request information, the government can require the submission of data by individuals or corporate bodies; and (2) in many
instances, only the government can afford to collect, analyze, and

publish statistics with the necessary frequency and comprehensiveness (this is especially true of census and labor statistics).

Although some of the most interesting and vital government documents are frequently classified and restricted, a great deal of material is available to the public on request. The key obstacle in searching out this material is ignorance about the kinds of data available and the procedures involved in locating and obtaining government reports. However, the first of the "Ten Theses on Power Structure Research," published by the North American Congress on Latin America does verify the existence of such data:

The very complexity of modern technological society compels the U.S. power structure to produce a continuous flow of accurate data on every aspect of human endeavor. It is safe to assume, therefore, that the information needed for an investigation of any segment of U.S. society is available somewhere, in some form.

Governmental sources can be mined for pertinent information if you familiarize yourself with the basic techniques involved in finding out what exists and how to get it.

Government publications are widely available, both in libraries and through free distribution or low-cost purchase. Effective use of government documents depends on familiarity with: (1) The organization of government publications in libraries; (2) the special indexes, catalogs, bibliographies, and price lists which enumerate available government documents; and (3) the particular agencies which produce information relevant to sociological research.

GOVERNMENT DOCUMENTS AND THE LIBRARY

The most useful collections of U.S. federal government documents are found in "depository libraries," designated by the Superintendent of Documents. All state libraries and libraries of land-grant colleges and universities are named federal depositories. These libraries regularly receive free of cost any document published in a previously selected series or category. Depending on its status as a "complete depository" or a "selective depository," a library will receive either virtually every item printed at the Government Printing Office or a selection of titles. The *Monthly Catalog of U.S. Gov-*

ernment Publications, discussed below, indicates which documents are available to libraries, by the placement of a large black dot near the title of the item; these documents are also listed in a continually revised *Classification List of Government Publications for Selection by Depository Libraries*. Many states and regional areas are served by newly developed "regional depositories" which have been charged with the task of collecting and maintaining the most complete possible collection of current and old federal documents. Items from these collections are available to researchers at libraries in the region on interlibrary loan. Libraries which do not participate in the depository program may have arrangements to receive documents from various executive agencies. While there is a depository system for United Nations publications and a few states are experimenting with automatic distribution of their documents to libraries, only a few large libraries participate in these programs. Libraries which must purchase or specifically request desired material will necessarily have much smaller and more highly selected collections.

Once you have determined the extent and nature of the collection of government documents in the library or libraries to which you have access, you will want to find out how the collection is organized and stored. There are several possible cataloging arrangements for government documents:

1. They may be classified, cataloged, and shelved like other library materials (according to the Dewey Decimal System or the Library of Congress System). In this case, use the card catalog to locate items by issuing agencies and titles. Sometimes government publications are classified and cataloged like other library materials but kept in a special file or section of shelves. In this case "Gov. Doc." or a similar code will be added to the call number.

2. The documents may be arranged on the shelves alphabetically by issuing body in a separate collection with a separate catalog.

3. Items may be arranged according to the Superintendent of Documents classification system in a separate collection with a separate catalog. Some libraries use a combination of the above techniques for different portions of their collection of government publications, depending on the type and the frequency of use.

The Superintendent of Documents classification numbers serve as sales numbers and are cited in all catalogs and lists issued by the

Government Printing Office. In libraries which utilize this cataloging system, you can consult printed bibliographies such as the *Monthly Catalog* for shelving locations, instead of the normal card catalog. This system groups information in four indexes: title, author, subject, and series/report. Each passage gives a short subject summary, frequency of publication, availability, beginning dates, and any cross-classification information.

A classified list of government authors according to the Superintendent of Documents System can be found in *Annotated Bibliography of Bibliographies on Selected Government Publications and Supplementary Guides to the Superintendent of Documents Classification System* (fourth supplement by Alexander C. Body, Western Michigan University, 1970, pp. 109-116), and in Volume 1 of the 1971 edition of *Guide to U.S. Government Publications,* which also includes an annotated listing of all governmental agencies. Be sure to note each symbol in the classification number as each represents an important item of information necessary for location of the document. A source for guidance in locating and understanding U.S. government documents is *Government Publications and Their Use,* by Laurence F. Schmeckebier and Roy B. Eastin (second edition, revised, Brookings Institution, 1961). Remember too that a documents or reference librarian may be able to help you use this kind of material in a way best suited to your particular needs.

Three general rules about government document citations should be kept in mind:

1. Authors are government agencies, not individuals. Individual authors represent government departments which assume responsibility for the contents of publications.

2. The corporate author of a government document may be an agency or one of its subdivisions. For example, the National Institute of Mental Health is a subdivision of the Public Health Service, which in turn is a subdivision of the Department of Health, Education, and Welfare. In most cases NIMH would be considered the author of a report issued from that office. However, since you might not know where the chief responsibility rests in a specific case, you should always note the complete citation, including the names of any committee, bureau, office, or subsection mentioned.

3. Most government documents are issued in numbered or annual series, each series having a title such as "bulletin," "circular," "monograph," "leaflet," or "report." The library will indicate in its card catalog or record of holdings which items in the series it has available (e.g., "monographs 6, 10, 32, 69 . . ."). When you copy citations to government documents, be sure to include the series title and number (or year) if this information is given.

INDEXES, CATALOGS, AND BIBLIOGRAPHIES OF GOVERNMENT PUBLICATIONS

The single most useful tool for locating pertinent U.S. government documents is the *Monthly Catalog of U.S. Government Publications* (U.S. Superintendent of Documents, 1895 to date: before 1940 entitled *Monthly Catalog of U.S. Government Documents*). This index is the most comprehensive list of publications issued by the departments and agencies of the U.S. government, and it includes the executive, legislative, and judicial branches. Only administrative and confidential (or restricted) publications are omitted. Each monthly catalog provides a listing of all new publications received during the previous month of issue and is ready for distribution at the end of the current month. In addition, the catalog provides a preview list of major publications not yet off the press. Indexes are compiled annually (appearing in the December issue), and for five and ten year periods. Items are listed under the alphabetically arranged names of the issuing bureaus, agencies, and departments. A table at the beginning of each issue gives a complete list of the corporate authors with the beginning item number for each agency's publications for that month (the numbering system is continuous from January to December). Also, a detailed subject-author index gives the item number for each document. Other information about each document includes: the issuing agency, title, series title, series number, paging, date, price, Superintendent of Documents number, and the availability of the item (e.g., for sale, distributed to depository libraries, for official use only, available from the issuing agency).

A supplementary general index for U.S. government material is the *Catalog of the Public Documents of Congress and of all Departments of the U.S. for the Period March 4, 1893-December 31, 1940* (U.S. Superintendent of Documents, 1896-1945, 25 volumes). Commonly called the *Documents Catalog,* this basic index is used more frequently than the *Monthly Catalog* for the period it covers. The arrangement of publications within each two-year volume is by subject and issuing agency, with numerous cross references. Other indexes available in the library cover historical accumulations of government documents prior to 1893.

Documents issued by the various states can be located most quickly in the *Monthly Checklist of State Publications,* published since 1910 by the Library of Congress. This index lists alphabetically by state and agency those items received by the Library of Congress. Complete bibliographic information is given but there are no annotations. Two special features are a monthly list of the publications of interstate and regional agencies, and a semiannual list of state periodicals. The *Checklist* is not a complete catalog of state documents; however, it is current and does include many important publications. Some states are now listing or indexing their own documents. A librarian may be able to provide you with more information about this.

Another reference tool is the *Guide to U.S. Government Publications* by John L. Androit (1978; ed. McLean, Va., by *Documents Index*) which serves as an up-to-date and comprehensive annotated guide to the important series and periodicals currently being published by the various U.S. government agencies. It also has a complete listing of the Superintendent of Documents classification numbers since the turn of the century to the present. This publication appears biannually in a set of four volumes. Bibliographic information includes the Superintendent of Documents classification number, beginning dates, frequency of publication, availability, and depository item number. Arrangement is by call number, but each volume contains a title index in the back.

A new indexing resource is now available which provides the quickest and most complete access to congressional documents. The *Congressional Information Service Index to the Publications of the U.S. Congress* (volume 1, number 1, January 1970, Congressional Information Service) is published monthly with quarterly and yearly cumulations. This abstracting and indexing service purports to be the master index to the contents of congressional publications. Each issue is divided into two parts: the summary section lists and describes the publications of the House, Senate, and Joint committees; the index section includes indexes according to subjects, authors (corporate or individual), affiliations of authors and witnesses, subjects discussed by individual witnesses, numbers of bills, reports and documents, names of committee chairmen, and popular names of laws, reports, bills, etc. Bibliographic information and availability are indicated. The annual cumulative volume gives the complete bibliographic information including the Superintendent of Documents classification number, the Library of Congress card number, and the Government Printing Office *Monthly Catalog* entry number. Check the library for other indexes covering the period prior to January 1970.

The Congressional Information Service has brought out another new indexing resource which is a comprehensive guide and index to the statistical publications of the U.S. government. *American Statistics Index* has six major functions: identify the statistical data published by all branches and agencies of the federal government, catalog the publications providing full bibliographic information, announce new publications as they appear, describe the contents of these publications fully, index this information in full subject detail, and micropublish all publications. This index is published monthly with annual supplements. Each edition is issued in two sections: an abstracts section that contains full descriptions of the content and format of each publication, organized by ASI accession number; and an index section that contains comprehensive subject, name, title, and report number indexes. Although this index first appeared in 1974, there is a retrospective edition which covers 1960 to 1974.

All of the documents on a particular subject which are available for sale at the Government Printing Office are listed in numbered sales catalogs called *Subject Bibliographies*. *Subject Bibliography Indexes* are issued monthly and are distributed free to libraries and individuals. Individual reports are arranged by subject and supply researchers with the necessary number to locate it.

Bibliographies of Individual Agencies

Bibliographies and indexes of individual agencies may also prove useful as they are sometimes more thoroughly indexed or annotated than more general guides. A few examples of specialized research aids follow.

U.S. Bureau of the Census. *Catalog of U.S. Census Publications, 1790-1945* (1950, title has varied slightly). Since 1945 this catalog has been issued on a current basis each quarter and cumulated to the annual volume. Monthly supplements add to the regular monthly and quarterly reports, enabling users to be informed frequently on the appearance of new publications. This source is an indispensable tool for research involving census statistics. Part 1 lists and describes the general publications of the Bureau for the final volumes of the major censuses. Excellent subject and geographic indexes are provided. Also included are useful histories of various series and types of statistics as well as annual lists of statistical publications by other agencies which the Bureau of the Census helped to prepare. Part 2 contains a catalog of data files and special tabulations available from the Bureau on census material (see section on data banks in this chapter).

U.S. Department of Commerce, basic volume. *United States Department of Commerce Publications Catalog and Index* **(1972, with annual supplements).** Titles of the department are arranged by division and series with some annotations and a subject index. Information is given on how to obtain the documents, which include population statistics of the Bureau of the Census, a division of the department. For information prior to 1972, consult: *A Catalog and Index of Selected Publications of the Department and Its Predecessor Agencies up to October 1950* (1790-1950).

Department of Labor. *Publications of the U.S. Department of Labor* **(1961-June 1966; 1962-June 1967; 1963-June 1968; 1965-June 1970; January 1970-December 1975).** This subject list of publications of the Department of Labor is intended as a simplified guide for people interested in labor problems. The publications are available in many public libraries and government depository libraries. Since this source is not intended as a library guide, the customary precision of library subject listings is not followed. A useful feature is a list of pertinent periodicals by subject. Information given in chart form on the reports and publications of the department includes the year, price, bureau, type of publication, and the number; the titles are arranged by major subjects such as occupations, equal employment, women workers, etc. No annotations or descriptions are provided.

U.S. Bureau of Labor Statistics. *Publications of the Bureau of Labor Statistics* **(January-June 1977).** This is a semiannual annotated bibliography of the Bureau of Labor Statistics publications. Publications, with a brief description, are listed by subject and bulletin or report number. It also includes a separate listing of publications of each of the ten regional offices. Retrospective reports for July 1975 to December 1976 are available on microfiche.

U.S. Commission on Civil Rights. *Catalog of Publications* **(annual).** This catalog includes descriptive listings of reports, hearings, conference publications (in and out of print), on civil rights issues in the areas of education, housing, voting, law enforcement, jobs, etc.

Statistical Bibliographies

Andriot, John L. *Guide to U.S. Government Statistics* **(3rd, 1961, Arlington, Va., Documents Index).** This is an annotated bibliography of federal government publications which contain statistical information; publications of the judiciary, executive, and legislative branches and independent agencies of the U.S. government are listed by department and issuing bureau with a description of the publication, type of statistics, and the frequency of publication. The detailed coded subject index also indicates the type of statistics found in each source.

Bureau of the Budget. *Statistical Services of the U.S. Government* **(prepared by the Office of Statistical Standards, Executive Office of the President/Bureau of the Budget; revised edition 1968).** This is an extremely useful basic reference document on statistical programs of the U.S. government. Part 1 describes the statistical system of the federal government and methods of collection, tabulation, and presentation of data. Part 2 consists of brief descriptions of the principal economic and social statistical series collected by government agencies. For each of about 50 subjects—including population, health, education, social services, manpower, employment and labor, etc.—this reference work indicates which agencies are concerned and what kinds of data are collected and are available. Also included is an annotated list of the major statistical publications of federal agencies and the responsibilities of these agencies.

U.S. Department of Commerce, Bureau of the Census. *Directory of Federal Statistics for Local Areas: A Guide to Sources* **(1976).** This volume is a useful bibliographic aid in the search for data on metropolitan areas, counties, cities, or other geographic divisions below the state level. Information concerning the availability of statistics from 1960 to date is given for specific topics in the areas of income, wealth, health, housing, labor, population, communications, earnings, etc. Frequency and source of the figures are also noted, with complete citations in the appendix and a subject index at the end of the volume.

U.S. Department of Commerce. *Statistical Abstracts of the U.S.* An appendix entitled "Guide to Sources of Statistics," appears in each annual volume.

Note: See below the specialized bibliographies of government documents from various departments and agencies (Bureau of the Census, Bureau of Labor Statistics, etc.).

Wasserman, Paul, and Eleanor Allen and Charlotte Georgi, editors. *Statistical Sources; A Subject Guide to Data on Industrial, Business, Social, Educational, Financial, and Other Topics for the U.S. and Selected Foreign Countries* **(Gale Research Co., Detroit, Mich., 4th, 1974, p. 13).** This guide has been designed to provide a selected and annotated description of key statistical sources drawn from U.S. and foreign governmental and nongovernmental publications such as almanacs, periodicals, annuals and yearbooks, and census volumes. The principal statistical sources for each country are identified and an annotated bibliography of the major statistical compilations is appended. Social as well as economic statistics are covered. The emphasis is, however, on American materials.

GENERAL SUMMARY VOLUMES
OF GOVERNMENT STATISTICS

Social Indicators **(1976).** This publication, prepared by Denis F. Johnston, is published by the Bureau of the Census. Although this index has selected indicators of social problems, it does not organize them around any issues. Its many charts and tables contain a wide variety of statistics for American society and social change, but they don't provide enough detail to help with program operations, and there is too little sophistication to deal with realistic program evaluations. Despite its problems, this index is a great source of data and if one is creative enough to see beyond the numbers, it can provide a vast supply of information. A useful companion is *The Annals* (January 1978) edited by Conrad Taeuber. Mr. Taeuber has brought together sixteen articles which comment, interpret, and criticize, utilizing the data of *SI* (1976). Together, these two volumes are the most comprehensive review of recent social trends.

U.S. Bureau of the Census. *Statistical Abstracts of the U.S.* **(annual, 91st edition, 1970, U.S. Department of Commerce, Bureau of the Census).** This national data book and guide to sources has been published annually since 1878 and is the standard summary of the most important federal government statistics on the social, political, economic, and cultural organization of the United States, including such topics as vital statistics, population, immigration, education, law enforcement, science, communications, education, etc. This is a convenient volume for statistical reference and is generally the best place to begin a search for state or national statistics. Each section is prefaced with an introductory essay designed to explicate the tables which follow. This work is also intended to serve as a guide to other statistical publications and sources. Each table in the book is annotated as to source, indicating what agency or agencies were responsible for the data. Often the reader can find more detailed statistics by going to the publications of these agencies, some of which are indicated in this chapter. The appendix includes an excellent bibliography of statistical sources and a useful guide to state statistical abstracts. Supplements to this publication are the following volumes:

U.S. Bureau of the Census. *Historical Statistics of the U.S.; Colonial Times to 1970* **(1976, U.S. Department of Commerce, Bureau of the Census).** While *Statistical Abstracts of the U.S.* does include some retrospective statistics for from ten to twenty years, this supplementary volume should be consulted for full historical information. This periodically revised and updated supplement offers more than six thousand statistical time series on data dating back as far as 1789 in some instances. Also included are definitions of terms, a descriptive text, specific source notes, and a quite detailed alphabetical subject index.

U.S. Bureau of the Census. *County and City Data Book* **(1962, 1972, 1977).** This other companion volume to *Statistical Abstracts of the U.S.* is published at five-year intervals and offers statistics on a local and regional basis; the compilation provides basic statistics for unincorporated places, cities, counties, standard metropolitan areas, and urbanized areas, with the amount of information given for a city dependent on its size. Information has been extracted from the major censuses and other sources on such topics as population characteristics, business, industry, government, housing, and vital statistics.

U.S. Bureau of the Census. *Pocket Data Book* **(issued biennially since 1967; Statistical Information Division, U.S. Bureau of the Census).** This useful book contains statistical tables for population, immigration, government, labor, law enforcement, health, education, welfare, income, finance, etc. As indicated by the title, this is a convenient summary volume of important government statistics covering the current social, economic, and political life of the nation.

The following is a partial selective listing, by government agency, of governmental statistical sources of data, which may be useful in sociological research.

U.S. Department of Commerce
Economic Development Administration
(research on depressed areas)
Office of Business Economics

U.S. Department of Commerce. *Overseas Business Reports* **(irregular, a series of nearly 200 reports per year).** Written principally as background information for businessmen, these reports are also distributed for student and public use. Each report, on the economy of a particular nation or region, contains a bibliography.

Census Bureau (censuses on population, housing, government, business, etc.)

U.S. Bureau of the Census. *Census of Population* **(decennial, 1790 to date).** The complete census contains many volumes of tabulations providing detailed breakdowns and significant correlations for social and economic factors such as employment, income, housing, occupation, race, education, mobility, and urban-rural residence. In the interval between the decennial taking of the census, the Bureau publishes *Current Population Reports,* which contains population estimates and studies of the factors noted above based on statistical samples.

U.S. Bureau of the Census. *International Population Reports* **(irregular).** These are brief reports, giving population estimates and projections for various countries.

U.S. Bureau of the Census. *International Population Statistics Reports* **(irregular).** These are statistical research studies on population, manpower, and the labor force in particular countries, compiled from scattered, usually foreign language sources.

U.S. Bureau of the Census. The following annual current population reports of population characteristics are prepared by the Bureau of the Census:

Households & Families, **by type**

Household & Family Characteristics

Marital Status and Living Arrangements

Geographic Mobility: March 1975-March 1978. (including distribution by age, sex, race, residence, number of children, employment status, income, receipt of public assistance and poverty status).

U.S. Bureau of the Census. *Census Monographs* **(irregular).** Projected as a series of seven volumes providing in-depth analysis of 1960 census data, these monographs are similar to a commercially published series based on the 1950 census. The first monograph in the series is titled "Trends in Income Distribution in the U.S." by Herman P. Miller (1966). Other areas of concern are education, race, the family, "rural America," and the "metropolitan community."

U.S. Bureau of the Census. *Census of Governments* **(decennial 1850-1890; 1904; 1913; decennial 1922-1942; quinquennial from 1957).** This census emphasizes public finance and public employment at the state and local level. State figures and nationwide statistics according to the level of government are provided for previous periods in *Historical Statistics on Government Finances and Employment* (appearing as volume 6, no. 4 of the 1962 census). Currency is maintained by several series of bulletins, chiefly *Governmental Finances (GF)* and *Government Employment (GE).*

U.S. Bureau of the Census. *Current Population Reports. Consumer Income* **(series P-60, annual).** *Income in (year) of Families in the U.S. and Income in (year) of Persons in the U.S.* **(Published prior to 1967 in *Income of Families and Persons in the U.S.*).** These are statistical bulletins concerned with the income of individuals and families, average income, and consumer income trends.

U.S. Bureau of the Census. *Consumer Buying Indicators* **(series P-65, quarterly).** This source publishes estimates of intent to purchase automobiles, housing, and major household equipment.

U.S. Bureau of the Census. *Family, Money, Income 1947-1971* **(Technical paper no. 35).** This is a summarization for twenty-five years of statistics.

U.S. Bureau of the Census. *A Student's Workbook on the 1970 Census.* This publication acquaints new users of the *1970 Census of Population and Housing* with the basic information needed to successfully assess and use this data base. Major topics covered include the publication program, census geographic concepts, subject data content, and reference sources. Practice exercises are included.

U.S. Congress

Hearings, reports, documents from House, Senate, and Joint committees, inclusive of judiciary, education, labor, public welfare, foreign affairs, etc., and special committees.

Joint Economic Committee. *Economic Report of the President: Hearings* **(annual).** These are multivolume hearings, with many supporting documents, containing statements by leading economists, including members of the Council of Economic Advisers and representatives of government, business, and labor organizations. Each year at the close of the hearings the Committee issues the *Joint Economic Report on the Economic Report of the President, with Minority and Additional Views,* a Senate or House report of over 100 pages, presenting point-by-point comments and recommendations.

Senate Labor and Public Welfare Committee. *Selected Readings in Employment and Manpower* **(1964-66, 9 volumes, 88th and 89th Congresses).** An extensive compilation of special studies by government agencies, testimony before the committee, and reprinted articles, this work deals with employment and manpower; many of the sections contain tables and charts.

House, Education and Labor Committee. *Poverty in the U.S.* **(1964, 88th Congress, 2nd session).** This informal handbook was prepared with the assistance of seventeen government agencies and is largely based on special tabulations by the Bureau of the Census. A bibliography and an appendix of tables and charts are included.

U.S. Office of Business Economics. *Growth Patterns in Employment by County* **(1965, 8 volumes).** Employment changes in eight regions of the country are analyzed and presented in a form which enables economic development planners to compare regions, states, and counties.

U.S. Commerce Department. *Money, Income, and Poverty Status of Families and Persons in the United States.* This publication is released by geographic section and year. It reports estimates for families and unrelated individuals by money income and poverty status for a given year and region. Divisions are given for states within the region.

U.S. Office of Business Economics. *Personal Income by States since 1929; a Supplement to the Survey of Current Business* (1956). This publication contains per capita income information through 1949 and total income through 1953, brought up to date in the August issues of the *Survey.*

Office of Business Economics. *Survey of Current Business* (monthly) and *Business Statistics* (biennial). This publication discusses significant economic indicators for business use—employment and population, finance, domestic trade, international transactions of the U.S., etc. *Business Statistics* includes historical statistics (1929 to date) as well as explanatory notes on the sources and methods used in compiling the data.

Office of the President. *Economic Indicators* (monthly, President's Council of Economic Advisors, Wash., D.C.). This publication presents the basic statistical series produced by federal agencies on prices, employment and wages, production and business activity, purchasing power, credit, money, and federal finance, and the total output of the economy. The chief value of this source is the summary review of national business conditions. The midyear *Economic Review* and the *Annual Economic Review,* prepared by the same body, cumulate and amplify the material in *Economic Indicators.*

U.S. Department of Health, Education, and Welfare

Education Office, Head Start, and Child Development Bureau, Health Services and Mental Health Administration, Public Health Service, National Office on Vital Statistics (statistics on births, deaths, health and morbidity, marriage and divorce), National Institutes of Health, National Institute of Mental Health, Social Security Administration (research on family and medical economics, statistics on employment, taxable earnings, international social security), Social and Rehabilitation Service, Aging Administration, National Center for Social Statistics, and the Community Services Administration.

U.S. Department of HEW. *Trends* **(annual).** Health conditions, educational problems, consumer interests, social security, welfare, population and vital statistics are among the topics covered in this compendium of charts and graphs. National projections as well as historical data for a period of several decades are presented. This volume is published as an annual supplement and companion to the monthly *Indicators.* National trends as well as state data and rankings in health, education, and welfare are reported.

U.S. Department of HEW, Office of Education. *Digest of Educational Statistics* **(annual).** This is a collection of statistical material concerned with education at all levels and covering such subjects as educational level attainment, enrollments, finances, graduates, international education, libraries, research and development, and federal programs in the field of education. In some cases time series are included to provide historical background. A companion volume, *Projections of Educational Statistics to (year),* is published each year and contains articles as well as statistics.

HEW Office of Education. *American Education* **(vol. 1, 1965 to date, 10 times a year).** Superseding *School Life and Higher Education*, this publication covers preschool to adult education, new research and demonstration projects, major education legislation, school and college bond data, grants, loans, contracts, and fellowships.

HEW Educational Resources Information Center (ERIC) of the Office of Education. *Research in Education* **(monthly and annual).** See Chapter 5, "Guides to Research and Resource Materials."

HEW Office of Education. *Studies in Comparative Education, Education in (country)* **(irregular).** Background summary information on the country, its people, historical development, government and administration, and economic factors is provided for each study. Various aspects of the educational systems of a country, from preprimary to postgraduate work, are covered. Bibliographies are included.

HEW Office of Education. *Studies in Comparative Education.* **Bibliography: [year] publications (annual, since 1958).** Prepared as a cooperative project of the staff of the International Educational Relations Branch of the Division of International Education, this volume is designed to present an extensive and useful listing of timely materials concerned with education in other countries (U.S. materials are excluded). Listings of a general comparative nature, materials on individual countries in different geographic areas, and publications devoted to specific areas of countries are all included. Some other bibliographies of current use in comparative education are also listed.

HEW Office of Education. *Statistics of Education in the U.S.* **(annual).** This series basically continues the former *Biennial Survey of Education,* published from 1917-18 through 1957-58. Each publication in this annual series covers a particular area of educational statistics for a school year (e.g., 1958-59: Public Secondary Schools); the areas covered may differ from year to year. The final number summarizes the material in the previous numbers of the series as well as statistical material from sources outside the Office of Education.

HEW Office of Education. *New Dimensions in Higher Education* **(irregular). Prepared by Clearinghouse of Studies on Higher Education, Division of Higher Education.** This is a presentation of research findings and experiences on particular problems in the various fields of education which are of concern to colleges and universities. The reader is also directed to useful sources of additional information.

HEW National Institutes of Health. *Patients in Mental Institutions* **(Office of Biometry, Survey and Reports Section, National Institute of Mental Health. Annual, since 1938).** This publication provides data on the numbers and characteristics of hospitalized mental patients, the movement of patient population, and certain administrative data for public mental hospitals and institutions. Data is taken from the Annual Census of Patients of Mental Institutions, conducted by NIMH.

HEW Social and Rehabilitation Service. *Welfare in Review* **(bimonthly).** This work makes available research reports and statistics prepared in the Welfare Administration on public assistance programs, child health and welfare, juvenile delinquency, aging, and Cuban refugee resettlement. A subject and author index appears in the December issue, and early each year an annual statistical supplement is prepared.

HEW Children's Bureau. *Child Welfare Statistics* **(annual).** This publication includes data on children receiving child welfare services from state and local public welfare agencies, personnel in public child welfare agencies, selected expenditures for public child welfare services, and adoptions in the United States.

HEW Children's Bureau. *Research Relating to Children* **(irregular).** A clearinghouse for research on child life, this work presents the studies in progress concerning research programs, intelligence, behavior and personality, education, health services, and social services of and for children.

HEW Children's Bureau. *Juvenile Court Statistics* **(annual).** This work includes data on delinquency cases, traffic cases, dependency and neglect cases, and special proceedings handled officially by juvenile courts.

Vital Statistics of the U.S. (HEW, Public Health Service, National Office on Vital Statistics, annual). This division collects statistics on birth, death, marriage, and divorce rates for the nation, states, and some local areas. There is some discrepancy between the dates discussed and the appearance of the volumes; however, the *Monthly Vital Statistics Report* and its annual summary edition publish provisional statistics.

U.S. Department of HEW, Social Security Administration. *Social Security Bulletin* **(monthly).** This periodical contains articles pertaining to the various social security programs as well as the current social security operating statistics. An annual statistical supplement to the *Bulletin* is also published.

U.S. Department of Housing and Urban Development
U.S. Department of Labor

Women's Bureau, International Labor Affairs, Bureau of Labor Statistics (statistics on earnings, employment, labor force, occupations, unemployment, cost of living, working conditions), Employment Security Bureau (statistics on labor market, manpower, employment).

U.S. Department of Labor. *Manpower Report of the President and a Report on Manpower Requirements, Resources, Utilization, and Training* **(annual).** This is a comprehensive report on unemployment problems, manpower needs, labor mobility, government programs, and other areas of concern regarding labor and manpower. Tables and graphs accompany the text throughout, while one-third of the volume takes the form of a statistical appendix.

U.S. Department of Labor, Bureau of Labor Statistics. *Employment and Earnings of the Monthly Labor Force* **(monthly).**

U.S. Department of Labor, Bureau of Labor Statistics, *Monthly Labor Review.* These periodicals also contain summaries of recent developments in collective bargaining and other articles of interest to students of labor.

Bureau of Labor Statistics. *Handbook of Labor Statistics* **(irregular).** This work presents in one volume the major series produced by the Bureau of Labor Statistics and related series from other governmental agencies and foreign sources. A general presentation of the tables begins with the earliest date from which continuous, reliable, and consistent series can be given. Data for the last two years is given monthly in a majority of the tables and annually prior to that.

Bureau of Labor Statistics. *Employment and Earnings Statistics for States and Areas* **(Bulletin 1370, annual).** These large, comprehensive volumes (over 700 pages) report the average hours and earnings and employment by industry of the nonfarm work force in the years since 1939. This source also contains summary and analytical tables comparing employment and earning trends by region, state, and major area, providing good background information for economic and social studies.

Bureau of Labor Statistics. *Employment and Earnings Statistics for the United States* **(Bulletin 1312, annual).** This volume contains national employment statistics for the years since 1909 (depending on availability) and serves as a companion volume to the above-mentioned work. Current data appear in the Bureau's monthly periodical *Employment and Earnings and Monthly Report on the Labor Force.*

Employment and Earnings and Monthly Report on the Labor Force includes data on employment and earnings and on the labor force. Some topics covered are the number of payroll workers in nonfarm establishments, employment status of noninstitutional population (by age, sex, color, previous occupation), and duration of unemployment. Prior to February 1966, the *Monthly Report on the Labor Force* was issued as a separate publication.

Bureau of Labor Statistics. *Directory of National and International Labor Unions in the U.S.* **(annual).** This is a small reference work in two parts, containing a directory and a discussion, with tables, of union membership and structure in the United States. Additional statistics on union membership appear in the appendix.

Bureau of Labor Statistics. *Analysis of Work Stoppages* **(annual).** This work supplies information on strike activity as measured by the number of workers involved and the total worker-days of inactivity. Other data includes major stoppages, issues involved, industries and unions affected, geographic patterns, size and duration of stoppages, method of termination, and disposition of issues.

Bureau of Labor Statistics. *Labor Developments Abroad* **(monthly).** This publication presents research information on recent labor developments in foreign countries, with articles on such topics as the general labor situation, trends in labor welfare, and new labor laws. Statistical tables on manpower, wages and prices, and comparative statistics on such subjects as wages and work stoppages in foreign industrial countries are also included.

Bureau of Labor Statistics. *Monthly Labor Review.* This is the official journal of the Department and Bureau, carrying articles on labor economics and industrial relations, summaries of studies and reports, and technical notes. The Current Labor Statistics section covers all current BLS statistical series on employment, labor turnovers, earnings and hours, work stoppages, productivity, and prices.

Statistical data on regions are issued as field agency publications released from Washington and from various regional offices of the BLS (e.g., New England Employment Monthly, New England Regional Office).

U.S. Department of Labor, Women's Bureau. *Handbook on Women Workers* **(biennial; from 1948–52 entitled** *Handbook of Facts on Women Workers).* This publication presents basic information on women's employment and occupations, the age and marital status of women workers, women's earnings and income, educational status, state laws affecting the employment and civil and political status of women, and organizations of interest to women.

Other publications of this Bureau include:

Legal Status of Women in the U.S. **(irregular).** Here there is a separate report for each state; these publications cover contracts and property, marriage and divorce, parents and children, and political rights of women.

Digest of State Legislation of Special Interest to Women Workers **(annual).** This publication enumerates state legislation enacted during the year on minimum wage, equal pay, hours, discrimination in employment, etc.

Family and Property Law [State] (date) **(irregular).** This publication discusses the laws regarding property rights of women, earnings, contracts, liability and family support, joint property, inheritance rights, marriage and divorce, age of majority, guardianship and political rights, by state.

Women's Bureau. *Women Workers in [State] (year)* **(irregular).** Separate releases for each state consist of a series of statistical tables on employment, age distribution, marital status, education, major occupational groups, industry groups, earnings and income.

Women's Bureau. *Summary of State Labor Laws for Women* **(irregular).** Separate releases by state cover legislation establishing standards for the employment of women.

Interdepartmental Committees such as those on Children and Youth, the Coordination of Federal Urban Area Assistance Programs, and the Status of Women, which issue annual reports, should also be noted.

U.S. Treasury Department

U.S. Internal Revenue Service. *Statistics of Income: Business Tax Returns; Corporation Income Tax Returns; Fiduciary, Gift, and Estate Tax Returns; and Individual Income Tax Returns* **(annual).** These statistics, covering the entire United States, represent important sources of current data for national income and wealth estimates; some historical tables are also included. Each part is issued in preliminary and final editions with occasional supplementary reports. A supplemental report, *Personal Wealth Estimated from Estate Tax Returns Filed During Calendar Year* (irregular) focuses on the age, sex, and marital status of top wealthholders ($60,000 or more) as well as the size and composition of their wealth.

U.S. National Commission on Technology, Automation, and Economic Progress. *Technology and the American Economy* **(Report in 7 volumes, 1966).** This important study consists of the report volume, five supplementary volumes containing background material prepared for the Commission, and a final volume of statements submitted by individuals and organizations. The titles of the appendix volumes are: "The Outlook for Technological Change and Employment" (vol. 1); "The Employment Impact of Technological Change" (vol. 2); "Adjusting to Change" (vol. 3); "Educational Implications of Technological Change" (vol. 4); "Applying Technology to Unmet Needs" (vol. 5); and "Statements Relating to the Impact of Technological Change" (vol. 6).

U.S. National Science Foundation
(Statistics on Governmental Research and
Scientific Manpower)

NSF. *Basic Research, Applied Research, and Development in Industry, 1977* (Survey of Science Resources Series, 1965). This report provides data on federal and industrial outlays for research and development in 1977, the number, location, and size of companies involved, the character of the research and development work, employment of scientists and engineers, and funding related to net sales and total employment. A valuable feature of the publication is the time series data showing trends from the mid-1950s.

U.S. NSF. *American Science Manpower* (biennial). This primarily statistical report of the National Register of Scientific and Technical Personnel provides data on the education, experience, salaries, geographic location, nature of employment, foreign language and area knowledge, and scientific technical subfields of U.S. scientists. Also covered are programs sponsored by the U.S. government and characteristics of women scientists.

U.S. NSF. *Federal Funds for Research, Development, and Other Scientific Activities* (annual, early volumes entitled *Federal Funds for Science).* This work provides information on amounts spent for research, agencies performing research, the character of the work, and the fields of science in which research is conducted. Each volume reviews a three-year period; the content is basically statistical with some interpretive text and graphs.

U.S. Department of State

U.S. State Department, U.S. International Development Agency. *Science, Technology, and Development* (1962–3, 12 volumes). These papers, prepared by experts from universities, foundations, business, and government in the United States for the U.N. Conference on the Application of Science and Technology for the Benefit of Less Developed Areas, treat such topics as natural resources, industrial development, health, communications, human resources, urbanization, international cooperation, and development policies and planning. Statistics, bibliographies, maps, and photographs are included.

U.S. State Department. *American Foreign Policy, Current Documents* **(annual).** This publication is a compilation of major published official papers, selected to indicate the scope, goals, and implementation of U.S. foreign policy, including topics such as overall policy, the U.N. and international law, developments in particular regions and countries, disarmament, trade, foreign assistance, international political developments, educational and cultural exchange programs, and the activities of the State Department. For information prior to 1956 consult:

A Decade of American Foreign Policy: Basic Documents, 1941-49 **(Senate Document 123, 81st Congress, 1950).**

American Foreign Policy, 1950-55: Basic Documents **(2 vols., 1957).**

UNITED NATIONS PUBLICATIONS

International organizations such as the European Economic Community, the Organization of American States, and the Organization for Economic Cooperation and Development also publish numerous documents. The United Nations is the most productive source of data for areas of international concern such as demography, economic stability and employment, economic assistance, health, education, and labor. U.N. publications are assigned U.N. document numbers and, in the case of those available for sale, sales numbers. Bibliographies usually cite both of these numbers. When you copy references to U.N. documents, be sure to include these numbers, as they may make it easier for you to locate the publications later. These numbers should also be cited when you use or footnote a U.N. document. The classification numbering system is similar to the Superintendent of Documents classification system in that a combination of letters and numbers is used to indicate the issuing agencies and series: the first alphabetical component represents the issuing body (for example, E: Economic and Social Council; UNESCO: U.N. Educational, Scientific, and Cultural Organization; IDA: International Development Association; ILO: International Labor Organization). The sales number consists of the year of publication shortened to the last two digits, a Roman numeral (or a numeral plus a letter) for a subject category, and an Arabic numeral designating the title (1st, 2nd, etc.) in that category for the year.

Perhaps the best introduction to the use and understanding of U.N. documents is *A Guide to the Use of U.N. Documents* (Brenda Brimmer, Linwood R. Wall, Waldo Chamberlin, and Thomas Hovet, Jr.: Dobbs Ferry, N.Y.: Oceana Publications, Inc., 1962), which includes reference to the specialized U.N. agencies and special U.N. bodies. This helpful guide provides an extensive description of the documents classification system, suggestions about methods of research, and lists of various U.N. publications both general and specific. *Everyman's United Nations* (U.N. Office of Public Information, 8th edition, 1968) gives a convenient introduction to the structure and work of the United Nations and its commissions and related agencies. Information on the basic series symbols of main organs and subsidiary organs of the U.N. is given in the *List of U.N. Document Series Symbols* (U.N. 1978). The alphabetical-numerical arrangement of the list is supplemented by an alphabetical index giving titles and broad subjects. Beginning and closing dates or notation of a continuing series is provided. Additions and corrections to the list are included every year in the *U.N. Documents Index Cumulative Index.* In addition, the best guide or organizational manual on the structure of the U.N. system of assistance is entitled *Assistance for Economic and Social Development Available from the U.N. System* (U.N. 1969, $1.50, U.N. Sales Section, New York, N.Y. 10017, sales number E.69.I.23). Key sources of information on U.N. assistance operations are summarized in this useful guide which can save you much frustration when dealing with the maze of U.N. documentation.

The U.N. publishes the following reference catalogs and bulletins which are essential for identifying and locating its documents:

U.N. Documents Index (U.N. Dag Hammarskjöld Library, 1950 to date). The *Documents Index* appears monthly with two separate annual cumulations: the *Cumulative Checklist* and the *Cumulative Index.* The documents—treating such topics as demography, criminology, international relations, environment, labor, social development, industrial and economic development, and human rights— are arranged according to the document number classification system based on agency and series. Bibliographic information for each entry includes the full title, date, number of pages, and the price or availability of the document. There may also be brief descriptions for some articles. Other features include: an index listing subjects, authors, and a few titles and a list of U.N. periodicals (see the *Cumulative Checklist*).

Since 1965, *Current Issues: Selected Bibliographies on Subjects of Concern to the U.N.* has been prepared semimonthly. Publications of the U.N. and those of its specialized agencies not covered in the *Documents Index* are listed without indexes.

The *Monthly Sales Bulletin* lists all new publications with details of the major titles; *Current Publications,* a supplement to the *Monthly Sales Bulletin,* lists selected documents grouped by subject matter or regional interest.

A guide to U.N. periodicals, yearbooks, surveys, bulletins, and reviews is provided by *Periodicals and Recurrent Publications.*

All U.N. publications issued since the founding of the organization are listed in *U.N. Publications 1945–1966, A Reference Catalogue* (U.N., New York, 1967). Classification is according to subject and geographic region. Annual supplementary editions keep this guide current. In addition, UNESCO publishes a bimonthly list of documents and publications which is cumulated annually.

The socioeconomic publications of the U.N. available for sale to the public are listed by sales number category in *U.N. Publications; Catalogue* (U.N., 1966). The basic volume is a 1963 catalog with supplements for the succeeding three years. The subject and regional groupings facilitate location of relevant material.

Major U.N. Statistical Publications
(abridged, representative listing)

United Nations. *U.N. Statistical Yearbook* **(annual, Statistical Office, Department of Economic and Social Affairs).** This is a primary source for international statistics on population, manpower, production, consumption, wages and prices, mass communication, health, vital statistics, housing, education, and so forth. Volumes have appeared annually since 1948 with material arranged by subject and indexed by country. Footnotes indicate where discrepancies in comparing data from different countries may exist. This source serves as a convenient compilation and summary of more detailed data presented in other U.N.-sponsored yearbooks. Statistics are updated on a monthly basis in *The Monthly Bulletin of Statistics.*

The Monthly Bulletin of Statistics: Monthly statistics on population, manpower, wages, etc. (seventy subjects) are compiled for over 200 countries and territories. Special tables illustrating important economic developments, as well as regular presentations of quarterly data for significant world and regional aggregates, are added features.

United Nations. *Demographic Yearbook* **(annual, Statistical Office, Department of Economic and Social Affairs).** Since 1948 a selected aspect of demographic data is focused on in each annual volume: Marriage and Divorce, 1968; Natality, 1965; Population Census Statistics, 1962-4; Mortality, 1961, etc. The cycle of topics is repeated and updated at irregular intervals. Data is provided on regions, countries, and in some cases, cities, and this data is the best source for international population statistics. Currency is maintained in the quarterly *Population and Vital Statistics Reports.*

Population and Vital Statistics Reports: Results of the latest population estimates and up-to-date vital statistics (such as birth, death, and infant mortality rates) are presented on a quarterly basis for each country of the world. Population aggregates for the world and each continent are compiled annually.

International Labour Office. *Yearbook of Labor Statistics* **(United Nations, ILO, Geneva, annual, 14th issue, 1971).** Principal labor statistics for more than 170 countries or territories are presented in tabular form grouped under such subjects as population, wages, labor, productivity, employment and unemployment, family living studies, industrial productivity indexes, and industrial disputes. The data is drawn from information sent to the ILO by national statistical services or from official publications. Whenever possible the data covers the ten years 1960-69; for some tables, data represents one month or one period near mid-1970. A useful bibliography of published sources is included in the appendix.

United Nations, Economic Commission. This organization publishes several annual detailed economic surveys: *Economic Survey of Africa since 1950,* succeeded by the statistical sections of the *Economic Bulletin for Africa; Economic Survey of Asia and the Far East; Economic Survey of Europe; Economic Survey of Latin America.* These publications offer an overall survey of the current situation and trends in both individual countries and regional areas. Special features, dealing with such topics as trade or economic planning in various countries or areas, are published in or with the annual volumes.

U.N. Bureau of Economic Affairs. *World Economic Survey* **(annual).** This volume is divided into two parts. Part 1 treats a particular problem such as industrialization, trade and development, or inflation. Part 2, entitled "Current Economic Developments," consists of separate sections on industrial countries, primary exporting countries, and centrally planned economies. Statistical tables accompany the text throughout.

U.N. Statistical Office, Department of Economic and Social Affairs. *Yearbook of National Accounts Statistics.* Published annually since 1956, this source provides statistics on national and domestic production, national income, capital formation, consumption expenditures, governmental revenue and expenditures, etc., for individual countries.

U.N. Statistical Office, Department of Economic and Social Affairs. *Compendium of Social Statistics* **(1963).** This is a compilation of statistical indicators for the international comparison of population, vital statistics, health, nutrition, housing, labor, social security, income, etc., during the 1950s. Tables are broken down by individual country and other characteristics such as urban-rural location, age, or sex.

U.N. Educational, Scientific, and Cultural Organization (UNESCO). *Statistical Yearbook* **(annual, French and English).** This yearbook reports current statistics on population, education, the press, radio, television, and other areas of international educational, cultural, and scientific organization, summarizing data from various UNESCO handbooks.

UNESCO, Department of Mass Communications, World Communications. *Press, Radio, T.V., Film* **(irregular, 4th edition, 1964).** This is a country-by-country assessment of communications facilities.

UNESCO *World Survey of Education* **(irregular).** Four existing volumes to date have been devoted to educational organizations and statistics (1955), primary education (1958), secondary education (1961), and higher education (1966).

In addition to these sources, the U.N. has also published a *Studies in Methods* series (Series F, No. 5, Rev. 1), titled *Handbook of Population Census Methods,* which is a very useful reference tool.

Three volumes deal with: (1) general aspects of population census; (2) economic characteristics of populations; and (3) demographic and social characteristics of populations. These volumes are a revision of previous manuals (I-II, 1958; III, 1959) prepared by the Statistical Office of the U.N.

STATISTICAL PUBLICATIONS OF FOREIGN GOVERNMENTS

Foreign governments also publish extensive statistical data. A current handbook of social, political, and cultural statistics is issued by almost every country. These vary a great deal in depth and quality, but many are published in English. Examples are *Canada Yearbook* (Canada Dominion Bureau of Statistics), *Annual Abstract of Statistics* (Great Britain Central Statistical Office), *Annuaire Statistique de la France* (Ministére de l'Économie et des Finances, Institut National de la Statistique et des Études Économiques), *Statistical Pocket Book of Hungary* (Budapest: Hungarian Central Statistical Office).

Some countries have published compilations of historical statistics as well. Check your library for availability of foreign yearbooks and handbooks. The following bibliographic aids will also assist you in locating foreign sources of statistical information: census material, abstracts, yearbooks, handbooks, etc.

Library of Congress. *An Annotated Bibliography of the General Statistical Bulletins of Major Political Subdivisions of the World* (Phyllis G. Carter, 1954).

***Statistical Yearbooks, An Annotated Bibliography of General Statistical Yearbooks of Major Political Subdivisions of the World* (Phyllis G. Carter, 1953).**
These publications enumerate statistical handbooks for countries, counties, and territories. They are outdated but excellent compilations of foreign statistical sources, especially useful for historical research.

Ball, Joyce, editor. *Foreign Statistical Documents: A Bibliography of General and International Trade and Agricultural Statistics, Including Holdings of the Stanford University Libraries* (Stanford, Cal.: Stanford University, The Hoover Institution on War, Revolu-

tion, and Peace, 1967). This work is an extremely useful listing of foreign statistical sources.

Harvey, John H. *Sources of Statistics* (Hamdeon, Conn.: Archon Books, 1969). This is a small but valuable listing of the main statistical publications of the United Kingdom (Britain) and some of the more important sources for the U.S. and for various international agencies.

Meyriat, Jean (ed.). *A Study of Current Bibliographies of National Official Publications* (compiled by the International Committee for Social Sciences Documentation. UNESCO Bibliographical Handbook no. 7, Paris: UNESCO, 1958). Entries are in French and English.

Wasserman, Paul, et al. *Statistics Sources* (4th edition, Gale Research Co., Detroit, 1974, p. 13).

Many foreign governments publish catalogs of their documents, e.g.: Canadian Government Publications, *A Monthly Catalog;* Great Britain, Her Majesty's Stationery Office, *Government Publications* (monthly), etc. Your library may maintain a collection of these and other such reference catalogs.

EVALUATION OF GOVERNMENTAL DATA

As we noted earlier, government agencies and international organizations are the major sources of statistical information. Even the nongovernmental studies using aggregate data, listed in the following section, draw heavily on government statistics. Although the figures are generally reliable, the sources should be evaluated carefully and limitations should be recognized.

Always check the currency of the data; sometimes the latest available statistics are not as recent as one might hope. In addition, changes in statistical methods or different departmental definitions of terms and categories, such as the definition of "income" or the constitution of the blue-collar or white-collar categories, may limit the comparability of tables published by different divisions. In using government statistics you should be clear on the definitions and categories used in each particular table. This is very important because the way a table is organized may influence the results significantly. A pamphlet published in 1969 by Victoria Bonnell and

Michael Reich, *Workers and the American Economy, Data on the Labor Force,* cites the following example: the Labor Department's category "production of nonsupervisory workers in the private non-agricultural economy" is deceptive because it omits public employees and nonproduction, nonsupervisory workers in mining, manufacturing, and construction.

The statistical measure—mean or median—should also be noted, as these can vary and thus affect the data.

In addition, methods of data collection may impose limitations on government statistics. For example, it is generally acknowledged that young, black males are underrepresented in the census of the population. One must question the assumption of the 1970 Census of the Population that the head of the household is a male. Also, because of the manner in which unemployment is measured, the unemployment rates are generally overly optimistic; here too, particular social groups are generally underrepresented.

These are just a few examples of the problems encountered in using governmental data. You should be aware that the publications of government agencies naturally strive to further the aims and objectives of these organizations by their selection and presentation of the "facts." You can become alerted to the possibility of this type of bias by becoming familiar with the work of the issuing body and by carefully checking prefaces, forewords, introductions, and footnotes. The more you become aware of exactly what the data represents, the slant of the presentation, and what is omitted, the more adept you will be at using these statistics in an illuminating manner.

NONGOVERNMENTAL SOURCES OF DATA

This section covers the following sources of information: volumes and collections of aggregated data, data banks, statistical yearbooks, and biographic data and directories.

General Reference Works

Dimensions of Nations: A Factor Analysis of 236 Social, Political and Economic Characteristics **(Rummel, Rudolph J., New Haven, Conn., and London: Yale University Press, 1970).** This work analyzes eighty-two countries through a large number of variables, including such "event" statistics of domestic violence as guerrilla warfare, riots, revolutions, general strikes, antigovernment demonstrations, and such foreign conflict variables as antiforeign demonstrations, wars, protests, sanctions imposed on other countries, and severance of diplomatic relations.

Indicators of Social Change, Concepts and Measurements **(edited by Eleanor B. Sheldon and Wilbert E. Moore, Russell Sage Foundation, N.Y., 1968).** Each chapter in this volume is written by a prominent sociologist specializing in a certain area—demography, economic growth, trends in the labor force and employment, knowledge and technology, changing politics of American life, family change, religious change, and such distributive features as consumption, leisure, health, and education. Aggregated features include social stratification and mobility and welfare and its measurement. Each chapter includes a review of the data, knowledge, and concepts in the field and a useful bibliography. The general orientation of this source leans toward a structural functionalist approach.

International Bibliography on Income and Wealth **(New Haven, Conn. Vol. 1, 1937-47).** Since 1948, this annotated quarterly report has been prepared by the International Association for Research in Income and Wealth and the National Institute of Economic and Social Research in London. The eighth volume of this annotated bibliography covers the four-year period from 1957 to 1960, inclusive. Like the previous volumes, this is a cooperative effort of national income scholars from nearly forty countries and numerous international organizations. Subjects covered in a comprehensive manner include the definition and measurement of national income and wealth, size and distribution of income, labor force estimates, social accounting, and economic analyses related to income or wealth, including international comparisons. This is an excellent source for locating data on countries outside the United States.

Population Redistribution and Economic Growth in the U.S. 1870-1950 **(Lee, Miller, Brainerd, and Easterlin, American Philosophical Society, 1957).** This three-volume work is a major nongovernmental source of quantitative information on population and population movements, redistribution of the labor force, and income by geographic region. The introduction by Simon Kuznets and Dorothy S. Thomas provides an excellent guide to the uses and limitations of the data. The volumes are divided as follows: Volume

I contains the methodological discussions and all of the reference tables; Volume II, by Kuznets, Miller, and Easterlin, "Analyses of Economic Change," examines the connection between population and labor force movements and economic growth; and Volume III, "Demographic Analyses and Interrelations," by Eldridge and Thomas, concentrates on the changes in population distribution since 1870. A very complete table of contents will assist you in finding the data you require.

The Population of the U.S. (Donald J. Bogue, The Free Press of Glencoe, Ill.). This dated but useful source presents figures for 1950-1960 on the following topics: size, growth, and distribution of the U.S. population, age, race, and sex composition, marriage and marital status, household and family status, fertility, educational attainment, internal migration and residential mobility, labor force, income and population, composition, occupational composition and trends, religion, housing, population in institutions, and future population projections.

World Handbook of Political and Social Indicators (Russett, Bruce M., and Hayward R. Alker, Jr., Karl W. Deutsch, and Harold D. Lasswell. New Haven, Conn., and London: Yale University Press, 1964). This collection and analysis of quantitative data contains enumerations of seventy-five variables for as many as 133 countries. Information is given on vital statistics, family and social relations, government and politics, human resources, wealth, education, health, and communications. Some processed data, such as David McClelland's indices of achievement motivation, are included (in this case, for forty-one countries), and indices showing the inequalities of the distribution of income in twenty countries are also presented. The analytic portion contains tables showing the correlations of the variables with each other, some types of multivariate analyses and their potential uses, and a discussion of the uses and limitations of aggregate statistics. The data from this source is maintained on punch cards with tape decks and code books by the Interuniversity Consortium for Political Research (Ann Arbor, Mich.) and the Yale Political Data Program (New Haven, Conn.).

World Population: An Analysis of Vital Data (Keyfits, Nathan and Wilhelm Flieger, Chicago and London: The University of Chicago Press, 1968). Official data on births, deaths, and population for as many countries and periods of time as possible is presented and used as a basis for other calculations such as life expectancy, age distributions, and rates of gross and net reproduction.

World Population and Production, Trends and Outlook **(W. S. Woytinsky and E. S. Woytinsky, The Twentieth Century Fund, New York, 1953).** This is a useful if somewhat dated statistical picture of the collective resources and economic performances of the nations of the world, including information on cities, consumption patterns, divorce rates, industry, human resources, and economic patterns. These two authors have also compiled another volume titled *World Commerce and Governments* (1955).

Human Relations Area Files

Aggregated data stemming from anthropological studies are presented in systematic form in the following sources.

These files contain ethnographic reports concerning peoples from all over the world; they are indexed in such a way as to make easily available all information on a particular aspect of culture. With a relatively minimum effort, you can write a cross-cultural paper on abortion, child training, power, old age, or any other comparable topic. For example, one of the coauthors used the files to investigate whether or not middle age and menopause were considered stressful in other cultures. She had access to the files at the University of Southern California in Los Angeles. There are other HRAF libraries throughout the country, such as those in Cambridge, Mass. (Harvard) and New Haven, Conn. (Yale). On this particular topic, information concerning available roles for women after menopause from thirty societies was gathered; these included the grandmother role, the economic role for women, the mother and mother-in-law roles, the magic and religious role, and the political role. Data was also collected on the residence patterns of the culture, the presence of a term for middle age, the status of women, and menopause. There was little information on psychiatric factors or on menopause (this information was provided only when there was a woman ethnographer). In spite of these *lacunae*, this investigation was a pleasant form of research, since the author did not have to waste much time in searching for books.

Anthropologists in general do not like the files. They suggest that one is likely to get a distorted picture of a culture pattern when it is not viewed in the context of the entire cultural background. This can be overcome to some extent by reading the entire xeroxed page the librarian will bring you rather than focusing entirely on the marked section relevant to a particular trait. Anthropologists do consider the files a good bibliographic source. However, do not use these files for an anthropology course without first checking with the professor. See also: Murdock, George Peter, *Ethnographic Atlas* (Pittsburgh, Penn.: University of Pittsburgh Press, 1967). Data for 862 cultures on forty-four variables such as class and caste, stratification, and community organization are included.

Data Banks

Unlike other information storage systems, such as the library, you can enter a data bank without a card and leave with one hundred thousand. Use of a data bank gives you an opportunity to look at the raw material of other studies, to reanalyze data in a new way or with different perspectives, and to make new comparisons in the light of recent developments. For example, legislation on abortion has changed drastically in the past decade; concomitantly, attitudes on abortion have changed, and the change has been reflected in the results of public opinion polls. It would be possible to trace the changes over time and to compare change in various population segments by writing to a data bank containing the necessary public opinion poll data. To continue with the example on abortion, in scanning the public opinion poll data you might find that it is primarily those under twenty-five years of age who are in favor of abortion. This fact might lead you to conclude that generational factors rather than a shift in position by individuals over time could account for the changes in public opinion on the issue of abortion.

One advantage in using archive material is that the student has access not only to published articles but also to material which has been collected but never written up for publication. For example, a great deal of census material will not appear in U.S. government publications from the Bureau of the Census. However, the complete set of census data can be found in a repository institution; a university or public library may buy the complete set of tapes for the decennial census.

Catalog of U.S. Census Publications, Part II, "Data Files and Special Tabulations."

The Bureau of the Census publishes only the most essential and most widely useful data in its reports of censuses and surveys, but a great deal more information is available to the public. The Bureau maintains data files in the form of punchcards and computer tape, which can be processed to provide almost unlimited subject cross-classifications and area tabulations. Some of these tape and punchcard files, which do not contain confidential individual records, may be purchased and used by the purchaser for making tabulations. All of them, under appropriate circumstances, can be used by the Bureau to prepare tabulations specified by customers. Special tabulations can also be prepared directly from files of filled-in questionnaires.

(Introduction)

Typically, data archives contain raw data; they will provide you with cards, magnetic tapes, a work deck, or the analysis itself. There are three user-oriented archive centers. The Roper Center for Public Opinion Research at Williams College contains the Roper and Gallup public opinion polls; this is also the largest existing file containing data from academic and commercial surveying institutes in a large number of countries. Survey data or other data produced by academic institutions is collected and stored by the Interuniversity Consortium for Political Research at Ann Arbor, Michigan; the International Data Library and Reference Service at Berkeley provides similar services. If your university belongs to any of these organizations you will be able to obtain surveys on cards or tape at little cost; otherwise costs will be somewhat higher. Information about the location of studies containing particular variables or attributes can be obtained from the Council of Social Science Data Archives, University of Pittsburgh, Pennsylvania. Since 1965, the CSSDA has coordinated the activities of data archives in the United States and Canada, providing relevant information on the availability of survey data in the U.S. and abroad. This organization has published a research guide entitled *Social Science Data Archives in the U.S.* (1967, CSSDA, 605 West 115th Street, New York, New York 10025) which lists social science data archives and depositories of data. The addresses, dates established, type of data, number of studies, procedures for use, library associations, equipment, future plans, and brochures and publications are provided.

Yearbooks

Numerous private, nongovernmental, and quasigovernmental organizations publish yearbooks, which are handy reference aids in research.

World Almanac and Book of Facts (The World Telegram and Sun **1868-1966; Newspaper Enterprise Association, Inc. for Doubleday, 1967-).** This source contains a greater and more complete variety of information than any other yearbook. Up-to-date facts and figures for a wide range of subjects—including statistics on society, industry, politics, finance, religion, and education for the countries of the world—are provided. Much rather obscure information is also included. Reliability is generally good and sources for many of the statistics are given. Since the listings are not alphabetical, the index in the front of the book must be used to locate relevant data.

American Yearbook **(publisher varies, New York, 1929-).** Narrative accounts of events and progress during the year for the United States and its territories, with articles on the internal affairs of the United States, are presented here. The arrangement is by large subject headings, but the book has a full table of contents and a detailed index. Most subject divisions include a list of periodical publications and a list of research institutes and sources where more information may be obtained.

Statesman's Yearbook: Statistical and Historical Annual of the States of the World **(since 1864, Macmillan and Co., Ltd., London, Melbourne, and Toronto, and St. Martin's Press, New York).** This yearbook includes up-to-date information about the governments of the world. For each country, statistical and descriptive material about the government's defenses, production, industries, commerce, agriculture, etc., is given. A list of suggested readings is provided at the end of the material on each country. Published in England, the yearbook discusses the British Empire first, then the United States, followed by the other countries. A full index is in the back. Topics covered include government, area, population, education, religion, justice, social welfare, and other useful statistical and historical data about the social, political, and economic activities and institutions of the nations of the world. Information about international organizations, as well as detailed reports of the individual states of the United States, is also presented.

The Europa Yearbook **(Europa Publications, Ltd., London; since 1926, and in the present bound form, 1959).** This two-volume survey and directory provides basic information on all countries, including details of constitution, government, political parties, legal systems, religions, media, recent history, universities, and sectors of the economy. Volume I includes a very detailed and useful description of all international organizations, featuring a descriptive breakdown of the United Nations by individual agencies. See also the more specialized regional volumes, concerning the Far East and Australia and the Middle East and North Africa, which include useful biographic sketches among other items.

International Yearbook and Statesmen's Who's Who **(London: Burke's Peerage Limited, since 1953).** This yearbook contains sections on international and intergovernmental organizations, the states of the world, and biographies of statesmen and individuals active in government, finance, industry, education, and other areas.

American Jewish Yearbook **(edited by Morris Fine, et al.).** This yearbook covers civic, political, communal, demographic, and international issues and events in Jewish life. It also contains a directory of agencies and organizations and necrologies. Publication is by the American Jewish Committee and the Jewish Publication Society of America. This source and other religious yearbooks can be important in providing demographic data by religion, a feature not included in the U.S. census of population.

Municipal Yearbook, **"The Authoritative Resumé of Urban Data and Developments" (annual since 1934, International City Management Association, Washington, D.C.).** Essays and tables are arranged to give an overview of recent urban developments in the following areas: city and community; science, technology, and the cities; public safety; city functions; public manpower; municipal finance; and small city data. Also included is an excellent section on sources of information and references. This organization maintains an Urban Data Service which supplies monthly statistical reports and survey data resources.

Book of the States **(Council of State Governments. Lexington, Kentucky, biennial, vol. 18, 1970–71).** This source hopes to provide authoritative information concerning the structures, working methods, financing, and functional activities of state governments. Information is presented in the form of narrative essays and statistical tables. Coverage of state services includes information on education, health, welfare, planning, housing and development, and labor and industrial relations. Since the volume is published every two years, emphasis is given to developments of the two years preceding publication. Coverage of the 1970-71 volume extends to late 1969.

Women's Rights Almanac. In 1974 the Elizabeth Cady Stanton Publishing Company began publishing this compendium of information on all aspects of women's rights, edited by Nancy Gager. Areas covered include politics, legal rights, employment, education, marriage and divorce, child care, women's organizations, and the international women's movement. Also included is a state-by-state directory with basic factual, statistical, and resource information. An appendix provides a bibliography of bibliographies on women.

Biographic Data

Sources of biographic data are necessary for systematic study of members of the elites—businessmen and financiers, political leaders, foundation trustees, lawyers, academicians and scholars, ethnic leaders, local elite members, etc. *Who's Who*-type references can be used to gather information about the social background of various elite members. Emergent data can be useful in showing changes in patterns of elite recruitment over time, comparative characteristics of elites in different countries, or similarities and/or differences between segments of elites within one country.

The most comprehensive review of biographic sources of data for U.S. power structure research is the section entitled "Personalities and Elites" in the *NACLA Research Methodology Guide* (see Chapter 5) compiled by G. Wm. Domhoff.

The single most valuable research tool for elite studies is *Who's Who in America: A Biographical Dictionary of Notable Living Men and Women* (Chicago, Ill.: A. N. Marquis Co.) published every two years. This work contains a great deal of information on most of the people it lists. "Who's Who" also exist for regions, states, and international areas (i.e., *Who's Who in the East; Who's Who in California; International Who's Who; Who's Who in Europe,* etc.) as well as for various professions *(Who's Who in Banking, Who's Who in American Politics, American Sociological Association Directory of Members,* etc.). The best and most recent guide to biographic information on specific topics is *Biographical Dictionaries: An Interna-*

tional Guide (1967, Gale Research Co., Detroit, Michigan). Another useful source is *Poor's Register of Corporations, Directories, and Executives* which lists alphabetically over 30,000 large and middle-sized companies in all industries and includes 260,000 brief individual biographies of individuals holding major positions in various corporations.

Notable American Women is a three-volume biographical dictionary which was prepared under the auspices of Radcliffe College and published by the Belknap Press of Harvard University Press. It covers prominent women from 1607 to 1950. The second edition, which is currently forthcoming (1979), will include women from 1951 through the 1970's, and contain a greater representation of Third World women.

EPILOGUE:
sociology at work in the community

In this handbook we have concentrated on familiarizing students with the basic tools of sociological research and writing. We hope that this information will make sociology coursework and projects more manageable and, therefore, more satisfying. In this concluding section, we feel it is important to look beyond the classroom and to consider the relevance of sociology to the individual and the community.

WORKING SOCIOLOGISTS

The work that sociologists do, and their choice of specialization, are shaped by changes in the overall occupational structure. Since most sociologists with advanced degrees teach, the greatest determinant of their job prospects is the state of the academic sector. Several factors are currently changing the outlook and structure of teaching opportunities for sociologists and other liberal arts professionals. One important trend is the drop in college enrollment, which is expected to continue over the course of this decade. While sociology has not experienced the extensive contraction that disciplines in the humanities such as history, English, and philosophy have already suffered, it is likely that uncertainty and job competition among social scientists will increase.

While teaching positions in colleges and universities are not likely to absorb the surplus of qualified sociologists, programs in adult and continuing education are expected to expand. This will open up teaching opportunities in a variety of new areas, such as labor education. For example, one of the authors (Linda Frankel) recently participated in an educational and cultural enrichment program of the Amalgamated Clothing and Textile Workers Union, funded by the National Endowment for the Humanities. She acted as a discussion leader and project coordinator, working with textile workers to explore the meaning of work, family, and community in the lives of working people.

Sociologists are also acquiring teaching positions in professional programs in such areas as law, medicine, public health, and business. Pauline Bart's position in the Department of Psychiatry in the School of Medicine of the University of Illinois is an example of this kind of crossover.

However, as teaching possibilities become more uncertain, sociologists must begin to seek ways to broaden their employment options. The American Sociological Association has encouraged and assisted in the exploration of alternatives to academic work. The ASA has placed greater emphasis on helping sociologists to strengthen their research, planning, and administrative skills, and to find new settings in which to exercise them—government, business, labor, and the health care system, for example, are being recognized and investigated as potential sources of employment for sociologists.

The ASA also recognizes that undergraduate sociology majors face difficult career decisions, whether they choose to continue in sociology, enter related professional or academic programs, or search for work upon completion of the B.A. degree. Therefore,

Doris Wilkinson, the Executive Associate for Careers, Minorities, and Women for the ASA, has developed a set of career resource materials to aid both undergraduate and graduate majors in determining their options. These materials, listed in "Career Resources" (ASA *Footnotes*, April 1980) are available free or at minimal cost from: Career Resources/Research Projects, American Sociological Association, 1722 N Street N.W., Washington, D.C. 20036. Included among these resource materials are two particularly useful bibliographies which list a wide range of information sources concerning how and where to look for a job:

"Career Bibliography II: More Resources for Sociology" by Doris Wilkinson. ASA *Footnotes*, December 1978.
"Career Resources for Women Sociologists" by Doris Wilkinson. SWS *Network*, January 1979.

Other items available from the ASA include:

Careers in Sociology, Washington, D.C.: ASA, 1977.
Majoring in Sociology: *A Guide for Students* by Doris Wilkinson. Washington, D.C.: ASA, 1980.
"Employment Projections, Job Seeking Tips for Undergraduate, Graduate Trainees," by Doris Wilkinson. ASA *Footnotes*, August 1978.
"Federal Employment for Sociologists?" by Doris Wilkinson. ASA *Footnotes*, March 1980.
"Women in the Profession: Data Sources for the Eighties," by Doris Wilkinson. Sociologists for Women in Society *Network*, January 1980.

Much of this material initially appeared in the ASA publication *Footnotes* or in the newsletter *Network* of SWS (Sociologists for Women in Society). Both of these newsletters are good sources for information on professional activities, conferences, publications, and employment and funding opportunities. Information about the SWS newsletter can be obtained from Janet Hunt, Editor, SWS *Network*, Department of Sociology, University of Maryland, College Park, Maryland 20742.

SOCIOLOGY AND THE WORKPLACE

Most students who are introduced to sociology in the classroom will not find jobs which directly tap this knowledge. However, sociology might provide them some insight into the structural features of a work setting such as an office, factory, or hospital; a sociological perspective could help ground personal dissatisfaction in the realities of a hierarchy of authority, for example, rather than in feelings of personal inadequacy. As Rosabeth Moss Kanter points out in *Men and Women of the Corporation* (N.Y.: Basic Books, 1979), many problems that women and minorities encounter in business and the professions stem from their visibility as tokens, and thus as targets of racism and sexism, rather than from any individual deficiencies.

Sociology can also sensitize students to the widespread tendency to "blame the victim." Since many sociology majors will find themselves acting in such roles as interviewers, counselors, social workers or probation officers in social welfare, correctional, or health care agencies, it will be important for them to have a better understanding of the social conditions and frustrations their clients face. Hopefully, some exposure to sociological perspectives will enable these workers to be more responsive to the needs of the people they serve.

SOCIOLOGY AND THE COMMUNITY

Sociological training can also be useful in jobs or research projects which serve the self-defined goals and needs of community groups. Insights into social problems, power relations, ethnic and workers' culture, for example, are valuable assets in projects aimed at increasing the capacity of community members to control and enrich their lives. Working for social change requires and develops an understanding of how the system works; this kind of process both tests and deepens sociological analysis.

The most comprehensive source of information about jobs for social change is the national newsletter *Community Jobs*, published by the Youth Project, 1704 R Street N.W., Washington, D.C. 20009. This monthly bulletin lists alternative career opportunities for organizers, counselors, interns, editors, canvassers, and the like in organizations working for social change. Many of these groups, in addition to organizing, also engage in advocacy research for which a sociological background would be useful. Advocacy research is designed to establish the causes and extensiveness of particular social problems and to critically evaluate the mechanisms which exist for redressing them. Many groups apply for public funding in the form of research and demonstration grants which must be oriented towards the study of a problem, rather than the provision of direct services. For example, The Center for the Prevention and Control of Rape of the National Institute of Mental Health is set up to conduct research on rape, rather than to provide direct services to women who have been raped. Skills in the development and writing of grant proposals—including presentation of the problem, literature review, and research design—can be an important contribution to advocacy research. A bibliography on selected grant resources, "Developing and Designing Research Proposals," is available from the ASA (Doris Wilkinson, SWS *Network,* April 1979).

Whether the study of sociology facilitates finding a job, coping with social institutions and bureaucracies, or participating in activities directed towards social change, a sociological perspective illuminates the connections between personal experiences and public issues, and is thus of value to both the individual and the community.

APPENDIX A
the dewey decimal
system of classification*

300—THE SOCIAL SCIENCES

301   Sociology—The science that deals comprehensively with social activities and institutions, as follows:

301.1	Social psychology
.2	Cultural processes
.3	Human ecology
.4	Institutions and groups
.5	Sociology of everyday activities and pre-occupations

*Note: The information reproduced above is based on Edition 17 of the Dewey Decimal System of Classification. Edition 19, which was published in 1979, has been revised considerably; therefore, consult your reference librarian to determine which edition is being used in that particular library to classify materials.

301.1	Social psychology
	Interaction between personality, attitudes, motivation of individuals and structure, dynamics, behavior of groups
301.15	Group behavior
301.151	Collective behavior
301.152	Stability
	Social control by coercion, persuasion, custom, taboo
301.1522	Group morale and loyalty
301.1523	Control of opinion, propaganda
	By public relations, publicity, indoctrination, rumor
301.153	For change (Social movements)
301.154	Opinion formation, public opinion
	Uses, measurement, effect of public opinion
301.155	Leadership
301.16	Mass communications processes
301.18	Behavior groups
301.181	The public at large
301.182	Crowds and mobs
301.183	Associations and meetings
	Formation, structure, workings
301.185	Cliques and gangs
301.186	Pressure groups
301.2	Cultural processes
	Conflict, compromise, assimilation, acculturation, cooperation, communication, others
301.24	Means and kinds
	Including effects of invention, discovery, war, technology, automation, mass communication
301.245	Kinds: Progress
301.246	Kinds: Regress
301.29	Historical and geographical treatment
301.3	Human ecology
	Adaptation to spatial and temporal environment

301.32   Population
                    Density, increase, decrease, movement,
                    characteristics, including migration within
                    a country
301.34   Community organization and development
                    Areal distribution, location, expansion,
                    pattern of growth (for planning social con-
                    ditions, see 309.2; kinds of communities,
                    301.35-301.37)
301.35-301.37.   Kinds of communities
301.35   Rural
301.36   Suburban and urban
301.37   State, provincial, national
301.4   Institutions and groups
                    Social characteristics and problems, im-
                    pact on society as a whole. For behavior
                    groups, see 301.18
301.402   Small groups
301.403   Large groups
301.404   Information organizations
301.405   Formal organizations
301.406   Institutionalism
301.41   The sexes. Man, Woman (feminism, superiority)
301.4121   Emancipation
301.4122   Careers
301.4126   In the home
301.413   Celibacy
301.414   Courtship
301.415   Sex life outside marriage
301.42   Marriage and family
301.421   Structure and functions of family
301.422   Nature and forms of marriage
                    Monogamy, polygamy, polyandry; inter-
                    racial, intercultural, interreligious mar-
                    riage; marriage between kin
301.423   Family and social change, including effects upon family
            of urbanization, mobility, technology, industrialization,
            war
301.426   Husband-wife relationship
                    Including planned parenthood

301.427	Intrafamily relationships
	Including mutual responsibilities (for husband-wife relationship, see 301.426)
301.428	Family disorganization, dissolution, adjustment
	Including death, separation
301.4284	Divorce
301.4285	Remarriage
301.43	Groups of specific ages
301.431	Minors
301.4314	Children (through age eleven)
301.4315	Adolescents (ages twelve to twenty)
301.434	Middle-aged
301.435	Aged (Social gerontology)
	Including retirement
301.44	Systems and criteria of social distinction and stratification
301.441	By economic status
	Wealth, property, income
	Including entrepreneur, self-employed, wage-earning status
301.442	By family and kinship
301.443	By location and duration of residence
301.444	By occupation
301.445	By amount of education
301.446	By religion
301.447	By race
301.448	By language
301.45	Nondominant groups
	Scope: prejudice, discrimination, segregation, desegregation, integration; refugees and displaced persons
301.451	Ethnic
	Indigenous and nonindigenous
301.452	Socioeconomic and religious

301.4521		Distinctive because of cultural practices
301.4522		Distinctive because of condition of servitude
301.4523		Distinctive because of low economic status
		(For groups distinctive because of condition of servitude, see 301.4522)
	301.4528–301.4529	Distinctive because of religious beliefs
301.4528		Christians
301.45281–		
301.45289		Specific denominations and sects
301.4529		Communicants of other religions
301.453		Of specific national origin
301.47		Groups of persons with physical and mental illnesses and handicaps
301.5		Sociology of everyday activities and preoccupations
		Social characteristics and problems, impact on society
301.52		Securing food
301.53		Securing clothing
301.54		Securing shelter
301.55		Working
301.56		Securing education
301.57		Enjoying leisure and recreation
301.58		Worshiping
309		Social situations and conditions
309(.09)		Historical and geographical treatment
309.1		Historical and geographical treatment
309.101–		
309.104		Historical periods
309.11–		
309.19		Geographical treatment
309.2	Planning	
		Development of programs to bring about desired change in conditions

309.22	International	
309.223		Technical assistance
309.2235			Peace Corps
309.22354–			By country
309.22359			of origin
309.23	National	
309.25	State, provincial, county	
309.26	City	

DEWEY DECIMAL CLASSIFICATION SCHEMES RELATED TO SOCIOLOGY

Education

370.19	Sociological aspects
	Philosophy, theories, principles
370.193	Educational sociology
370.1931	Community and school relations
370.1933	Role of the school in fostering society
370.193 32	Education for individual fulfillment
370.193 34	Education for social responsibility
370.193 4	Social problems affecting school organization
370.193 42	Integration
370.193 44	Segregation
370.193 46	Rural
370.193 48	Urban

Public Administration

| 355.001 | Bureaucracy |
| 355.022 | Sociology of military administration |

Welfare and Association

364.2	Causes of crime and delinquency
364.25	Social factors
364.254	Culture
364.255	Leisure, recreation
364.256	Social conflicts
364.26	Economic factors

365.3	Penal institutions
366–369	Associations (fraternal organizations, social clubs, military, patriotic, hereditary organizations)

Political Science

322	Relation of the state to organized groups
322.1	State and church
322.2	Labor movements and groups
322.3	Business and industry
322.4	Protest, pressure groups, reform movements
323	Relation of the state to individuals and groups
323.1	Nondominant groups
323.2	Revolutionary and subversive groups and individuals
323.3	Communities and social classes
323.4	Individuals
323.5	Political rights
323.6	Citizenship
324.3	Woman suffrage
329.006	Political organizations and institutions
329.02	Political parties
329.03	Pressure, interest groups
329.05	Public opinion (content, origin, political influence)

Economics

330.9	Economic situation and conditions
330.901–330.904	Historical periods
330.91–330.99	Geographical treatment
331	Labor
331.1	Industrial relations
331.2	Wages
331.3–331.6	Special classes of workers
331.3	Specific age groups
331.4	Women
331.5	Substandard wage earners
331.6	Other groups
331.7	Labor by occupation

331.8	Other topics
331.11	Labor force
331.12	Labor instability and stability
331.13	Unemployment and reemployment
331.15	Conciliation practices
331.18	Industrial relations in specific industries
331.19	Historical and geographical treatment of industrial relations
331.113	Discrimination in employment
331.114	Job qualifications
331.116	Employment bargaining
331.88	Labor organizations (Unions)
331.883	Company unions
331.886	Revolutionary unions
331.89	Disputes between labor and management
331.892- 331.893	Retaliatory measures by labor (strikes, walkouts, sabotage, boycotts, sit-down strikes, injunctions, political action
331.894	Retaliatory measures by management
331.898	Government intervention
332.1- 332.3	Financial institutions and their function
334-335	Methods of organization for distribution and consumption
334	Cooperative systems (consumer cooperatives)
335	Collectivist systems and schools (Marxian systems, state socialism, utopianism, anarchism, etc.)
338.6- 338.8	Systems and organization of production
338.6	Systems, types of industrial organization—cottage, small, large industries
338.7	Organization and structure of corporations, partnerships, etc.
338.8	Combinations-monopolies, trusts, holding companies
339	Distribution of capital goods and consumption of consumer goods; income and wealth

APPENDIX B
the library of congress
system of classification*

SOCIOLOGY

HM	General Works, Theory
HN	Social History and Conditions; Social Problems, Social Reform
HQ-HT	Social Groups
HQ	Family, Marriage, Woman
HS	Societies: Secret, Benevolent, etc., Clubs
HT	Communities, Classes, Races
HV	Social Pathology. Social and Public Welfare; Criminology
HX	Socialism, Communism, Anarchism

*Note: Students should be aware that the Library of Congress System of Classification is revised quarterly; therefore, some libraries may classify material according to an older or newer edition than that which is reproduced here.

General Works, Theory

HM:		Periodicals
	1	English
	3	French
	5	German
	7	Other
	9	Societies
		(Cf. H 10–19; HN 55, etc.)
	13	Congresses
	15	Collections
	17	Dictionaries
		History
	19	General
	22	By country, A–Z
		Under each:
		(1) General works
		(2) Biography, A–Z
	24	Philosophy. Theory. Method. Relations.
	25	Relation to social work
		(Cf. HN 29; HV 40)
	26	Relation to philosophy
		(Cf. B 63, Relation of philosophy to sociology)
	27	Relation to psychology
		(Cf. BF 57, Relation of psychology to sociology)
	30	Relation to ethics
		(Cf. BJ 51, Relation of ethics to sociology)
	(31)	Relation to religion, see BL 60
	(32)	Relation to education, see LC 189–191
HM	33	Relation to politics
		(Cf. JA 76, Relation of political science to sociology)
	34	Relation to law

	35	Relation to economics
		(Cf. HM 211, Economics elements, forces, laws)
	36	Relation to history and geography
		(Cf. HM 104, Historical sociology)
	37	Relation to anthropology
	38	Relation to science
	39	Relation to art and literature
		(Cf. PN 51, Relation of literature to sociology)
	41-43	Exhibitions. Museums.
	45-47	Study and teaching. Schools.
	51-68	General works. Treatises.
	73	General special.
	101	Civilization. Culture. Progress.
		(Cf. CB, History of civilization, JC 336, Social and evolutionary theories)
	104	Historical sociology
		(Cf. JC 179, R83-89, Rousseau's Du contract social)
	106	Evolution. Biological sociology.
	107	Anthropological sociology
	108	General special
	111	Degeneration
	116	Mutation (Progressive principle)
	121	Heredity (Conservative principle)
HM	126	Unity. Solidarity.
	131	Association. Mutuality. Social groups.
		(Cf. HM 201-221, Social elements, forces, laws)
	136	Individualism. Differentiation. Struggle.
		(Cf. JC 571, Individualism, Political theory)

141	The great man. Leadership. Prestige.
	(Cf. BF 412-431 Genius)
146	Equality
(149)	Social classes see HT

Social Elements, Forces, Laws

201	General works.
	Associative tendency, see HM 131
206	Environment. Regional sociology.
208	Physical elements, forces, laws.
211	Economic
	(Cf. HM 35, Relation of sociology to economics)
213	Intellectual
216	Moral
	Social justice, social ethics, etc.
219	Religious
221	Technological
	(Cf. CB 478, Technology and civilization. T 14, Philosophy of technology)

Social Psychology

	251	General
	255	Instinct in social psychology
	261	Public opinion
	263	Publicity. Propaganda.
	267	Tradition
HM	271	Authority and freedom
		(Prefer JC 571, Individual rights)
	276	Liberalism. Toleration.
	278	Passive resistance
		Crowds. Tumults. Revolutions.
	281	Theory
	283	History

| | 291 | Other special |
| | 299 | Miscellaneous special |

Social History and Conditions.
Social Problems. Social Reform.

HN:	3–5	General	
	8–27	History	
	29	Study and teaching	
		Special	
	30–39		The church and social problems
	40		Non-Christian sects
	41–48		Community centers. Social centers.
			(Cf. LC 221–235, Schools as social centers; HV 4175–4320, Social settlements; GV 51–158, Recreation centers)
	49		Other special
	51–940		By country

SOCIAL GROUPS

The Family. Marriage. Home. Woman.

HQ:	1–9	General	
	12–471	Sex relations	
	12–18		History
HQ	19–33		General works
	35–64		General special
	71–449		Abnormal sex relations
	71		General
	72		By country
	76		Homosexuality
	79		Sadism, etc.
	101–440		Prostitution
	450–471		Erotica

	503–1057	The Family. Marriage. Home. Child culture. Child study.	
	503–727	History	
	728–747	Treatises, etc.	
	750–799	Eugenics	
	763–767		Birth control. Abortion.
	769–780		Children. Care, Child study.
	781–785		Child life. Society among children.
	789–792		Children's rights. Children and the state. Protection of minors.
	796–799		Youth
	800	Celibacy	
	801	Courtship. Love letters.	
	802	Matrimonial bureaus	
	803	Trial marriage	
	804	Breach of promise	
	805	Desertion	
	806–808	Adultery	
	811–960	Divorce	
	961–967	Free love	
	981–996	Polygamy	
	998–999	Illegitimacy	
	1001–1048	The state and marriage	
	1051–1057	The church and marriage	
HQ	1060–1064	Aged. Gerontology (social aspects)	
	1101–2030	Woman. Feminism (Cf. GN, HD, HV, J, LC, HV, J, LC)	
	1101–1114		General
	1121–1154		History
	1161–1172		Occidental and oriental women
	1201–1233		Treatises
	1236–1380		Woman and the state

1381	Women and economics
1386	Woman (i.e., woman question) in literature
	Women in public services
	(JK–JQ, Women and the civil service)
1390	General works
1393	Woman and religion
1397	Woman in science and the arts
1399	Woman and civilization (JX 1965, Woman and peace movements)
	Woman in social reform, HN 49, W6
	Woman in industry, HD 6050–6220

Societies: Secret, Benevolent, etc., Clubs.

HS:	1–89	Societies (General)
	1–35	General
	51–55	Law
	61–89	By country
	101–330	Secret societies (General)
	351–929	Freemasons
HS	951–1179	Odd Fellows
		Other societies. By classes.
	1501–1510	Benevolent and "friendly" societies and mutual assessment fraternities
	1525–1560	Religious societies
	1601–2265	Race societies
	1601–1610	General
	1701–2190	By nationality
	2226–2265	By race
	2275	Occupation societies

2301-2460	Political and "patriotic" societies	
2501-3200	Clubs	
2501-2705		General
2721-3200		By country
3301-3365	Clubs and societies for other special classes (e.g., Boys' societies, girls' societies)	

Communities. Classes. Races.

HT:	51-500	Communities	
	51-65		General
	101-400		Urban groups. The City. Urban sociology.
	101-155		General
	161-325		Special topics
	161-165		Garden cities
	169		Territory
	201-221		Population
	231		Hygiene
	251-281		Mental and moral aspects
	321-325		Political and economic aspects
			By country, see HT 123-149
	351		Suburban cities and towns
	361-381		City and country
	401-500	Rural groups. Rural sociology.	
	401-423		General
HT	431		The country village and country town
	451-455		Population
	461-469		Mental and moral aspects
	471-485		Political and economic aspects
	601-1445	Classes	
	601-611		General
	621-635		Origin
	641-657		Classes arising from birth
	675-701		Classes arising from occupation
	680-690		Middle class
	713-725		Caste system

731	Freedmen	
751-815	Serfdom	
751-753		General
757-761		Origin and extinction
775		By period
781-815		By country
851-1445	Slavery	
851-893		General
901-905		Economic aspects
910-921		Religion and slavery
925-929		Race and slavery
941-950		Law of slavery
975-999		Slave trade
1025-1037		Abolition of slavery. Antislavery.
1048-1445		By country
1501-1600 Races		
1501-1525	General	
1531-1561	Special phases	
1575-1595	By race	
1581-1589		Negro

By country, see D, E, F, H, J

Social Pathology. Social and Public Welfare. Criminology.

HV:	1-696	General (Philanthropy. Charities. Poor relief.)
	1-38	General
HV	40-69	Charity organization
	70-83	State regulation of charities
	75-83	Law
	85-516	By country
	530-696	Special
	697-4959	Protection, assistance, and relief.
	697-1493	Special classes, by age
	697-700	Families. Mothers. Widows' pensions.
	701-1420	Children
	701-715	General
	721-739	Law and legislation

	741–803	By country
	835–1420	Special topics
	835–847	Foundlings
	851–861	Day nurseries Foster day care
	867	Baby farming
	873–887	Destitute, neglected, and abandoned children Aids and homes
	891–901	Feebleminded
	931–941	Fresh-air funds
	959–1420	Orphan asylums
	1421–1441	Young men and women
	1451–1493	Aged
HV	1551–3019	Defectives. Blind, deaf.
	3000–3019	Sick and infirm. Incurables, cripples, feebleminded, paupers, etc.
	3025–3174	By occupation
	3165–3173	Shop women, clerks, etc.
	3174	Other
	3176–3198	By race or ethnic group
	4010–4012	Immigrants
	4023–4470	Poor in cities. Slums.
	4023–4170	General
	4175–4320	Social settlements
	4330–4470	Salvation Army and the city poor

	4480-4630	Mendicancy. Vagabondism. Tramps.
	4905-4959	Antivivisection
	4961-4998	Degeneration
	5001-5840	Alcoholism. Intemperance. Temperance reform.
	5001-5072	General
	5074-5095	Alcoholism and the state. Regulation and control.
	5101-5121	Alcoholism and economics
	5125-5138	Alcoholism and education
	5141	Alcoholism and genius
	5145-5162	Alcoholism and the army
	5165-5169	Alcoholism and the navy
	5180-5184	Alcoholism and the Bible
	5185	Alcoholism and Judaism
	5186-5189	Alcoholism and the church
	5194-5197	Alcoholism and missions
	5198-5199	Alcoholism and native races
	5200	Alcoholism in colonies and the tropics
HV	5203-5247	Woman and temperance reform
	5251-5255	Pro-alcohol
	5258	Moderate drinking vs. total abstinence
	5261-5269	Public house reform and substitutes for the saloon
	5271	Light wines and temperance beverages
	5275-5283	Care and reclamation of inebriates
	5285-5720	By country
	5725-5840	Intemperance (other than alcohol)
	5725-5770	Tobacco habit
	5800-5840	Drug habits
	6001-9920	Criminology
	6001-6030	General
	6035-6197	Criminal anthropology

	6115-6190		Causes of crime. Criminal etiology.	
	6191-6197		Criminal ethnography. Race. Nationality.	
	6201-6249	Criminal classes		
			By country. See HV 6774-7220	
	6251-7220	Crimes and offenses		
	6251-6253		General	
	6254-6773		Special crimes	
	6774-7220		By country (including criminal classes)	
	7231-9920	Penology		
	7231-7431		General	
			By country, see HV 9441-9920	
	7551-8280	Police. Detectives. Constabulary.		
	7551-7923		General	
	7925-7929		Law. Regulation.	
	7935-8025		Administrative. Organization.	
	7938-7963			National
	7965-7985			State and county
HV	7988-8025			Municipal
	8031-8069		Police duties. Methods of protection.	
	8073-8078		Investigation of crimes	
	8081-8099		Private detectives. Detective bureaus.	
	8130-8280			By country
	8290		Watchmen	
	8301-9018	Prisons. Penitentiaries. Punishment and reform.		
	8301-8493		General	
	8661-8669		Treatises	
	8671-8686		Theory of punishment	
	8688-8691		Reparation to the injured	
	8692		The pardoning power	
	8693-8749		Forms of punishment (Modern)	
	8751-8931		Prison methods and practice	
	8935-8962		Penal colonies. Transportation.	
	8965-9018		Prison reform	
			By country, see HV 9441-9920	

9051-9430		Reformatories
9051-9230		The juvenile offender. Reform schools.
9261-9430		Reformation of adults
		By country, see HV 9441-9920
9441-9920	By country	

Socialism. Communism. Anarchism.

HX:	1-550	Socialism	
	1-8		Periodicals
	11		Societies. Associations.
	13		Congresses
	15		Collections
	17		Dictionaries. Encyclopedias.
	19		Study and teaching. Schools.
	21-63		History and biography.
HX			Special:
	51-54		Christian socialism
	56		Scientific socialism
	59-63		Communism: Left-wing socialism, bolshevism
	71-517		Theories. Systems. Criticism. By country.
	519		Socialism and cooperation
	521		Socialism and art
	523		Socialism and culture
	526		Socialism and education
	530		Socialism and the law
	531		Socialism and literature
	536		Socialism and religion
	541		Socialism and science
	544		Socialism and trade unions
	545		Socialism and war
	546		Socialism and woman. Socialism and the family.
	550		Socialism and particular social problems.

	626-795	Communism: Utopian socialism, communistic settlements.
	626-632	History
	651-780	Theories. Communities. By country.
	785	Communism and health
	791	Communism and education
	795	Communism and war
	806-811	Utopias
	821-970	Anarchism
	821	Periodicals
	826-828	History
	833	Treatises
	836-837	Law
HX	841-970	By country
	999	Illustrative materials

Education

	71-245	Social aspects of education
LC:	71-120	Education and the state
	73-97	Popular education.
	107-120	Public School Question. Secularization.
	129-139	Compulsory education
	142-145	School attendance
	149-160	Illiteracy
	171-182	Higher education and the state
	189-211	Educational sociology
	215-235	The community and the school
	223	Schools as community centers
	225	School and home
	1001-1091	Types of education
	1001-1021	Humanistic education. Liberal education.
	1043-1047	Vocational education

1051-1071	Professional education
1081	Industrial education
1090-1091	Political education
1390-5140	Education of special classes of persons
1401-2571	Women
2628-3750	Races, Indians, Negroes, Orientals, Immigrants
4929-4949	Upper-class education
4959-4979	Middle-class education
5001-5060	Working-class education

Economic Theory

HB:	301	Labor and wages
	601	Profit, Income
	701-751	Property, ownership
HB	771	Distribution
	801-845	Consumption
	849-875	Population
	881-3700	Demography, vital statistics

Economic History and Conditions. National Production.

| HC: | 30-59 | By period |
| | 95-710 | By country |

Economic History

HD:		Production
	19-21	General
	28-70	Organizations of production. Industrial management.
	71-76	The state and production
	82-89	Economic policy and planning
		Industry
	2321-2385	History and general works
	2421-2429	Trade associations
	2709-2930	Corporations; trusts

2951–3570	Industrial cooperation
3611–4730	The state and industrial organization
4801–8940	Labor
4906–5100	Wages
5306–5450	Labor disputes
5701–5850	Labor market; unemployment, labor supply
6050–6220	Woman labor
6228–6250	Child labor
6350–6940	Trade unions
6339	Labor and the intellectuals
6951–7080	Social conditions of labor

Index